CAREER JOURNEYS OF DIVERSE LEADERS IN HIGHER EDUCATION

This book provides a study of diverse leadership development through the extraordinary journeys of ten retired presidents and chancellors who have left an indelible impact on higher education.

Representing a rich multicultural background, each chapter tells a personal story of transformation and triumph, highlighting the various, non-traditional paths to senior leadership. Hailing from both private and public, two- and four-year institutions across the United States, these trailblazers showcase that excellence knows no bounds. Contributors reflect on the struggles and engagements with racialized ethnic realities and growing awareness of gender inequities. Discussion questions supply rich ground for meaningful engagement in book clubs, leadership classes, workshops, and institutes, prompting readers to plumb the depths of their own experiences in confronting justice, equity, and inclusion.

Filled with captivating narratives touching on the common threads of shared values and invaluable life lessons that weave through diverse experiences, this book is a testament to the power of inspiration and motivation for those considering or dismissing their aspirations to achieve leadership roles in higher education.

George Blumenthal is the Chancellor Emeritus at the University of California, Santa Cruz, USA, and a Member and Former Director of the Center for Studies in Higher Education at the University of California, Berkeley, USA.

Josefina Castillo Baltodano is the Founder and Executive Director of the Executive Leadership Academy at the University of California, Berkeley, USA, and Former President of Marian University, Wisconsin, USA.

Ding-Jo H. Currie is Distinguished Faculty and Director of the Leadership Institute for Tomorrow, California State University, Fullerton, USA; President, Lingnan Foundation, USA; and Former Chancellor of Coast Community College District, USA.

CAREER JOURNEYS OF DIVERSE LEADERS IN HIGHER EDUCATION

Climbing the Rough Side of the Mountain

*Edited by George Blumenthal and
Josefina Castillo Baltodano
with Contributing Editor Ding-Jo H. Currie*

NEW YORK AND LONDON

Designed cover image: Getty Images

First published 2024
by Routledge
605 Third Avenue, New York, NY 10158

and by Routledge
4 Park Square, Milton Park, Abingdon, Oxon, OX14 4RN

Routledge is an imprint of the Taylor & Francis Group, an informa business

© 2024 selection and editorial matter George Blumenthal, Josefina Castillo Baltodano, and Ding-Jo H. Currie; individual chapters, the contributors

The right of Josefina George Blumenthal, Josefina Castillo Baltodano, and Ding-Jo H. Currie to be identified as the authors of the editorial material, and of the authors for their individual chapters, has been asserted in accordance with sections 77 and 78 of the Copyright, Designs and Patents Act 1988.

All rights reserved. No part of this book may be reprinted or reproduced or utilized in any form or by any electronic, mechanical, or other means, now known or hereafter invented, including photocopying and recording, or in any information storage or retrieval system, without permission in writing from the publishers.

Trademark notice: Product or corporate names may be trademarks or registered trademarks, and are used only for identification and explanation without intent to infringe.

Library of Congress Cataloging-in-Publication Data
Names: Blumenthal, George R., editor. | Baltodano, Josefina Castillo, editor. | Currie, Ding-Jo H., editor.
Title: Career journeys of diverse leaders in higher education : climbing the rough side of the mountain / Edited by George Blumenthal and Josefina Castillo Baltodano with Contributing Editor Ding-Jo H. Currie.
Description: New York, NY : Routledge, 2024. | Includes bibliographical references and index. |
Identifiers: LCCN 2023055730 (print) | LCCN 2023055731 (ebook) | ISBN 9781032737652 (hardback) | ISBN 9781032669632 (paperback) | ISBN 9781003465812 (ebook)
Subjects: LCSH: Educational leadership. | Women in higher education--Social conditions. | Minorities in higher education--Social conditions. | Diversity in the workplace.
Classification: LCC LB2806 .C285 2024 (print) | LCC LB2806 (ebook) | DDC 371.2/011--dc23/eng/20240202
LC record available at https://lccn.loc.gov/2023055730
LC ebook record available at https://lccn.loc.gov/2023055731

ISBN: 978-1-032-73765-2 (hbk)
ISBN: 978-1-032-66963-2 (pbk)
ISBN: 978-1-003-46581-2 (ebk)

DOI: 10.4324/9781003465812

Typeset in Times New Roman
by MPS Limited, Dehradun

George Blumenthal, Ph.D
I would like to dedicate this work to my wife, Kelly Weisberg, and my children, Aaron and Sarah, who have always supported my work with extraordinary patience. I would also like to thank my many colleagues and mentors who made the rough side of the mountain a little less rough.

Josefina Castillo Baltodano, J.D.
Dedicates her chapter to her parents, Jose and Paula Castillo, her husband Carlos, her three daughters, Charisma, Alexa, and Diana, and her nine siblings, Paula, Velia, Jose, Michael, Gregorie, Richard, Olivia, and Norma, for their support and love. And finally to her beloved grandchildren, Charlotte, Luca, and Eva.

Ding-Jo H. Currie, Ph.D.
This chapter is dedicated to my grandson Alder Yunfeng Hsia, whose leadership will impact the future of our humanity toward unity in diversity.

Rupamanjari Ghosh, Ph.D.
Dedicates her chapter to her father, late Mr. Rabindra Ghosh, who planted the first spark, and to the faculty, staff, and students at Shiv Nadar University, Delhi-NCR, who made her work in the last 10 years worthwhile.

Alexander Gonzalez, Ph.D.
Dedicates his chapter to Gloria, his wife, partner, and inspiration. And to all the students, faculty, staff, and friends who shared in their higher education experience.

Janet L. Holmgren, Ph.D.
I dedicate my chapter to my daughters, Elizabeth and Ellen, who have made this journey with me, and to Josie Baltodano, whose vision and commitment made this project a reality.

Cassandra Manuelito-Kerkvliet, Ph.D.
I dedicate my chapter to the memories of Chiquito Manuelito and Choni Manuelito, sons of Chief Manuelito, both of whom died within a year of their October 10, 1882 arrival at Carlisle Indian Industrial School in Carlisle, Pennsylvania.

Horace Mitchell, Ph.D
My chapter is dedicated to Barbara Jean Barrett Mitchell, my high school sweetheart and my wife for more than 57 years. She has been by my side for every step of our shared journey.

Shirley Pippins, Ed.D.
I would like to dedicate my chapter to my parents, who made my journey possible, and to my children and grandchildren, who will stand on my shoulders. A special thanks goes to my daughter, Andrea, who edited my original manuscript.

Elñora Tena Webb, Ph.D.
I dedicate my chapter to leaders and learners: thank you for persevering, thriving, and achieving great good. Special gratitude to my family, especially my godchildren, nephews, and nieces – you are my inspiration. Deepest appreciation to my birth mother for being courageous. May we all remember our fortunes and inherent values.

CONTENTS

List of Contributors ix
Foreword xii
Preface xiv
Acknowledgments xvii
A Brief History of The Executive Leadership Academy xix

1 Seizing the Moment: How a First-Generation
 Astrophysics Student Made an Impact as the Leader
 of a Major Research University 1
 George Blumenthal

2 Hispanic Culture, Faith, and Leadership:
 A University President's Path from Philanthropy
 to Promoting Diversity and Inclusivity 28
 Josefina Castillo Baltodano

3 The Pathfinding Asian Woman President: Three
 Lessons for Leading an Inclusive College for
 the 21st Century 44
 Ding-Jo Currie

4 Creative Leadership in Institution Building: The Unconventional Journey of a Woman Quantum Physicist in India 70
Rupamanjari Ghosh

5 A Latino President's Retrospective: Diversity, Ethnicity, and Race in American Higher Education 91
Alexander Gonzalez

6 One Woman's Path to the Presidency of a Women's College 114
Janet L. Holmgren

7 An American Indian Woman Breaks Through Barriers to Reach Higher Education Leadership: My Climb to the Highest Rung 141
Cassandra Manuelito-Kerkvliet

8 From Segregation in Mississippi to University Leadership in California: Seizing Opportunities, Making a Difference, and Paying It Forward 151
Horace Mitchell

9 Divinely Ordered Steps to Leadership: Positioned for Purpose 178
Shirley Pippins

10 The Leadership Journey of the Black, Latina, and Native American College President: From Poverty to the Presidency 198
Elñora Webb

Afterword: Climbing the Rough Side of the Mountain *227*
Index *232*

CONTRIBUTORS

Josefina Castillo Baltodano, J.D., Founder and Executive Director, Executive Leadership Academy, University of California, Berkeley, USA, Former President, Marian University, USA. Josefina Castillo Baltodano, JD, has served as Founder and Executive Director of UC Berkeley's Executive Leadership Academy since 2011. Previously, she served as President of Marian University until 2009, where she transitioned it from a college to a university status. Baltodano has over 30 years in administration and teaching at UC Berkeley.

George Blumenthal, Ph.D., Chancellor Emeritus, University of California, Santa Cruz, USA, Former Director, Center for Studies in Higher Education, University of California, Berkeley, USA. George Blumenthal is an astrophysicist who served for 13 years as Chancellor of the University of California, Santa Cruz. During his career, he has also chaired the UC Academic Senate, directed the Berkeley Center for Studies in Higher Education, served on numerous nonprofit boards, and written two college-level astronomy textbooks.

Ding-Jo H. Currie, Ph.D., Distinguished Faculty and Director, Leadership Institute for Tomorrow, California State University, Fullerton, USA, Former Chancellor, Coast Community College District, USA. Ding-Jo's 40+ years in higher education, mainly in community colleges, include the honor in the American Association of Community College Leadership Hall of Fame and as Board Chair. A fervent champion for unity in diversity, she excels in DEI leadership development. As Lingnan Foundation president, she advances US-China higher education partnerships.

Rupamanjari Ghosh, Ph.D., Former Vice-Chancellor, Shiv Nadar University, Delhi-NCR, India. Professor Rupamanjari Ghosh served Shiv Nadar University Delhi-NCR in various founding roles, culminating as the Vice-Chancellor for two terms till January 2022. The University became an "Institution of Eminence" in India within a few years of its existence under her transformational leadership. She is a former Professor of Physics & Dean of the School of Physical Sciences at Jawaharlal Nehru University, New Delhi, India.

Alexander Gonzalez, Ph.D., President and Professor Emeritus, California State University, Sacramento, USA. Gonzalez spent over forty years at California State University as a faculty member, provost, and president of two campuses. A national leader in higher education, he served on numerous boards and commissions and helped establish critical pathways for future leaders; especially for women and people of color.

Janet L. Holmgren, Ph.D., President Emerita, Mills College, USA. Janet L. Holmgren is a Higher Educational leader who served as President of Mills College, Vice Provost of Princeton University, and in senior administrative roles at the University of Maryland and University Now. She has also chaired numerous HE boards, including the American Council on Education and the Carnegie Foundation.

Cassandra Manuelito-Kerkvliet, Ph.D., President Emerita, Antioch University Seattle, USA. Dr. Cassandra Manuelito-Kerkvliet became the first Native American woman to ascend to the presidency of a university outside the tribal college system and served seven years at Antioch University Seattle. Prior to this appointment, she served three years as the first woman president of Diné College, the first tribally-controlled community college located on eight campuses across the Navajo reservation.

Horace Mitchell, Ph.D., President Emeritus, California State University, Bakersfield, USA. Dr. Horace Mitchell became the fourth President of CSU Bakersfield in July 2004 after 36 years of experience in higher education. Under Dr. Mitchell's leadership, the university achieved national recognition for its efforts to extend the excellence and diversity of the faculty and academic programs, enhance the quality of the student experience, and strengthen community engagement.

Shirley Robinson Pippins, Ed.D., Senior Search Consultant and Executive Coach, Academic Search, Washington, DC, USA, Former President, Thomas Nelson Community College, USA. Dr. Shirley Robinson Pippins has decades of experience working in higher education. She has served as president of three colleges, a Senior Vice President of Programs and Services at the American Council on Education, a lead search consultant at Academic Search, and has held various leadership and coaching roles for educational not-for-profits.

Elñora Tena Webb, Ph.D., CEO and President, Signature Solutions Corporate Results, USA, President Emeritus, Laney College, USA. Elñora Tena Webb, PhD led as dean, vice president, executive vice chancellor, and distinguished as President Emeritus of Laney College. Her legacy as a strategist and partner with educational, policy, corporate, and civic leaders during four decades influenced 100,000 professionals who are contributors throughout and beyond the United States.

FOREWORD

The role of today's college president is more daunting than ever, with monumental challenges across the higher education landscape presenting a resilience test for campus leaders at all types of institutions. From grappling with the aftermath of the worst global pandemic in more than a century to responding to a profound moment of racial reckoning, unfolding against the backdrop of increasing polarization, partisanship, and the politicization of higher education, there is an urgent need for college and university leaders who can not only navigate complexity and overcome obstacles but who can reimagine and revolutionize higher education in ways that meet the equity mandate before us.

The presidential profiles contained in *Climbing on the Rough Side of the Mountain* detail the diverse experiences of transformational leaders from a wide range of institutions who provide models of excellence for the work ahead. Their compelling narratives, grounded in a shared opportunity to participate in and serve on the advisory board of the Executive Leadership Academy at the University of California, Berkeley, offer invaluable insights into how to champion equity, innovation, and excellence in higher education by demonstrating authentic leadership and moral courage during trying and uncertain times.

There are common themes woven throughout the stories of the authors – the importance of mentors and role models in their lives, the desire to make a difference in the world through service to others, an ability to find meaning, purpose, and joy throughout their careers, and the capacity to counter racial, gender, and ethnic stereotypes with a sense of optimism, compassion, and persistence arising from the foundational experiences of their upbringing.

As colleges and universities face the prospect of a lost generation of students, particularly African-American and Latinx males, due to COVID-19, the ensuing financial crisis, and growing skepticism around the value of college education, the equity-minded leadership showcased in these essays provides a roadmap for promoting student success, challenging racialized assumptions, and dismantling racist norms. Each of these leaders illustrates how campuses can ensure that they are places of welcome and belonging for all students by engaging in strategic risk-taking and innovation to counter the growing attacks on diversity, equity, and inclusion initiatives and by positioning their colleges and universities as anchor institutions in their communities, creating alliances with K through 12, business, industry, and individual citizens.

In the end, perhaps the most critical message conveyed by this collection is that if significant strides are to be made toward closing the equity gaps in student access and success in higher education, greater diversity in college and university leadership is imperative. Programs like the Executive Leadership Academy, aimed at identifying and preparing leaders from underrepresented groups for the presidency make outstanding contributions to diversifying the academy. Equally important is expanding the pipeline by fostering the capacity of future leaders to imagine themselves in these roles. By presenting the narratives of diverse presidents whose own non-traditional paths to leadership have impacted higher education in profound and lasting ways, this book serves that purpose in an unparalleled way.

Lynn Pasquerella
President, American Association of Colleges and Universities

PREFACE

Career Journeys of Diverse Leaders in Higher Education is a book about leadership, written by ten authors who have made transformational contributions as presidents or chancellors of a college or university: two Hispanic/Latinos, three Black/African-Americans, one (non-Indian) Asian, one American-Indian, one Indian, and two Whites. Many were the first in their family to graduate from college. All share a commitment to diversity, equity, and inclusion. All were selected to contribute to this book because they are current members of the faculty or the advisory board of the Executive Leadership Academy (ELA), sponsored by the Center for Studies in Higher Education, under the Goldman School of Public Policy at the University of California, Berkeley. They come from all types and levels of higher education, public and private – including an international author from a research university in India.

These narratives about becoming a leader revolve around distinctive individuals, each with different talents, backgrounds, and experiences. Yet taken together, they signify more than the sum of their parts. The pandemic years have ignited a deeper awareness and a new sense of urgency about the inequities that have long plagued American life, including education. *Career Journeys of Diverse Leaders in Higher Education* is written in this spirit and makes the case for institutional leadership that is more open to the talents of minorities and women, more focused on teaching multicultural competencies for a global world, and more dedicated to the still unfinished work of social justice.

It has roots in one of the oldest traditions of teaching – storytelling. There is a scholarly version of this tradition that grows out of such disciplines as literature, history, legal studies, and anthropology. According to James G. March, a distinguished scholar of organizational leadership, those who write in this vein are often concerned with cultural environments and prevailing social norms and how they shape, for better or worse, the lives of individuals and institutions. As its title suggests, the stories in this volume are concerned with just this kind of personal and professional struggle – the obstacles posed by racism and bias, one-dimensional views about who qualifies as a leader, the early educational neglect of minorities, the different, and the poor. Each story is a lesson in how these forces can be met and how leaders are made, not born.

Some present their path to leadership in a direct, how-I-did-it fashion, motivated by will and sheer determination. Others see their climb across the mountain as a calling or spiritual journey, and their style draws more on the language of metaphor and inner experience. Some face the additional task of reconciling the values they learned in another and more traditional culture with the individualistic, ambition-driven character of American society. For more people than one might expect, even the act of visualizing themselves as a leader can be a demanding psychological test.

Many tell how they found leadership in unexpected or untraditional ways, entering "through the side door" from a staff position to a presidency, for example. A common event in these accounts is a pivotal experience – an encounter with someone who turned out to be a mentor or a guide who recognized a capacity for leadership and helped along the way. In some cases, the defining moment was a critical setback or even a childhood disappointment. One author had such a moment when she was five years old and dressed up for a party at her kindergarten class. It happened to rain that morning, she fell into a puddle while waiting for the bus, and that was the end of her pretty dress and her party. This was the point, she writes, at which she told her mother "I will never be left behind again in my life." It was a lesson she never forgot.

Each of the ten leaders discusses specific achievements that made a lasting difference in the lives and fortunes of their institutions. But their stories are also rich in perspectives and advice about issues all academic leaders face, among them finding the right fit between leadership style and the organization you serve, the complexities of shared authority, and the search for balance between public and personal commitments. Some of the most important messages involve the qualities essential to good leadership – courage, confidence, authenticity, a willingness to take risks, and especially resilience.

Career Journeys of Diverse Leaders in Higher Education celebrates the beauty and rewards of teaching and learning in a multicultural and global environment. Above all, it is a series of stories intended to encourage and inspire.

George R. Blumenthal, Ph.D.
Former Director, Center for Studies in Higher Education, University of California, Berkeley
Chancellor Emeritus, University of California, Santa Cruz

Josefina Castillo Baltodano, J.D.
Founder & Executive Director, Executive Leadership Academy, University of California, Berkeley
Former President, Marian University

Patricia A. Pelfrey, Ph.D.
Senior Research Associate Emerita, Center for Studies in Higher Education, University of California, Berkeley

ACKNOWLEDGMENTS

We wish to convey our heartfelt thanks to all the authors who contributed their impactful stories and words of wisdom to this book. Additionally, we extend our deep appreciation to the editors for their dedicated efforts in shaping this publication. Special thanks goes out to Anthony Abuan for his invaluable recommendations and support in ensuring a harmonious alignment between the author titles and questions.

We extend our profound appreciation to President Lynn Pasquerella for her outstanding contribution to this book. As AAC&U President, her insightful foreword, rooted in decades of top leadership roles in higher education, captures our core mission. Dr. Pasquerella's generous review and foreword are highly valued.

Special thanks also go to Patricia Pelfrey, who contributed long experience with university presidents, insights drawn from her scholarly work on leadership, and careful editorial judgment in reviewing the original manuscript of the book. All enriched this project at a critical early stage in its development.

We also extend our gratitude to those who have consistently supported the Executive Leadership Academy and all of its initiatives.

Carol Christ – *Chancellor*, University of California, Berkeley

Lisa García Bedolla – *Interim Director*, Center for Studies in Higher Education, and *Vice Provost for Graduate Studies and Dean of the Graduate Division,* UC Berkeley

C. Judson King – *Former Director*, Center for Studies in Higher Education, UC Berkeley

Loui Olivas – *Founding President,* American Association of Hispanics in Higher Education

David Wilson – *Dean*, Goldman School of Public Policy, UC Berkeley

A BRIEF HISTORY OF THE EXECUTIVE LEADERSHIP ACADEMY

The Executive Leadership Academy (ELA) is a program sponsored by the Center for Studies in Higher Education (CSHE) at the University of California, Berkeley, under the Goldman School of Public Policy (GSPP). In 2010, Josefina Castillo Baltodano recognized the importance and value of diversity, and as a volunteer, she established a new executive leadership development program with a specific focus on increasing diversity in higher education. Dr. Baltodano's determination and enthusiasm led to the establishment of the Executive Leadership Academy in 2011. Judson C. King, who served as the Director of the Center for Studies in Higher Education at the time, shared and supported this vision. Understanding the significance of the program, Dr. King graciously offered space at the Center to facilitate its development.

During its initial years, the Executive Leadership Academy collaborated with the American Association of Hispanics in Higher Education, Inc. (AAHHE). Dr. Loui Olivas, the President of AAHHE at that time, worked closely with the ELA program. Additionally, the program has fostered collaborations with the American Council on Education (ACE) over the years. Distinguished senior leaders from ACE have served as esteemed faculty members for the program.

The inaugural session of the Executive Leadership Academy took place in San Antonio, Texas, for three days in early 2011. The program welcomed 28 fellows from various locations across the United States. The first program session featured 17 Founding Faculty members who volunteered their expertise. The ELA is a rigorous and focused training institute that equips future-oriented leaders in higher education to guide their institutions within an increasingly multicultural and global environment. The curriculum of the Academy is grounded in a comprehensive framework consisting of 26 executive leadership skills and 23 personality traits. Its purpose is to enable individuals from diverse backgrounds who aspire to positions such as deans, provosts, chancellors, and presidents to ascend the executive ladder.

Diversity and inclusivity are highly valued within the ELA program, and every effort is made to ensure a balanced representation across all aspects. As of 2023, our network of alumni consists of 574 individuals, with 25% identifying as Hispanic/Latino, 29% as White, 23% as Black/African-American, 12% as Asian/Pacific Islander, 2% as American-Indian/Alaska Native, and 9% as international participants. In 2017, the Executive Leadership Academy (ELA) hired Samantha A. Rushing, who later became the program's first full-time employee. Ms. Rushing, along with Dr. Baltodano and the program's Advisory Board, has played a crucial role in advancing and expanding the ELA. Their dedication ensures the exceptional quality and attention given to each program session, which holds great significance for both fellows and faculty.

Despite the challenges posed by the COVID-19 pandemic, the ELA program has demonstrated resilience and growth. To adapt to the unprecedented circumstances, the program began offering virtual programs in 2020. This flexible modality has been extended to the present, allowing for the necessary flexibility and versatility during these times.

The demand and enthusiasm for the ELA program continue to increase. In 2021, the Academy achieved a milestone by offering three programs in a single year for the first time. The initial two programs took place during the summer months in the United States, while the third program was held at Shiv Nadar University in Delhi, India, marking the program's inaugural international endeavor. Furthermore, in the year 2021, the Educational Leadership Academy (ELA) embarked on its inaugural fundraising initiative, namely the Indigenous Scholarship Fundraiser, as part of the UC Berkeley Giving Tuesday Campaign. The goal of integrating the ELA into this fundraiser was to secure financial resources that would facilitate full scholarships for promising Indigenous leaders to partake in our program. Thanks to the unwavering support and generosity of the ELA Community, the fundraiser surpassed its objectives in both 2021 and 2022, enabling us to award full scholarships to two deserving Indigenous leaders in each of the 2022 and 2023 ELA programs. The members of the Indigenous Scholarship Selection Committee include Samantha Rushing (Chair), Josefina Castillo Baltodano, Karen Biestman, Cassandra Manuelito-Kerkvliet, and Horace Mitchell.

Over the years, our Executive Leadership Academy (ELA) has been fortunate to have over 100 of the country's top leaders serve as faculty members. We take great care in selecting our faculty, ensuring that we have the most skilled individuals to teach the vital subjects covered in our curriculum. When offering our ELA program internationally, we maintain the same high standards for faculty while also considering the multicultural and global relevance of our teachings. In international programs, we include faculty members who are native to and possess extensive knowledge of the host country's higher education system. Additionally, we prioritize the involvement of senior administrators from the host country in designing our international program and its curricula. While working as a visiting scholar for the Center for Studies in Higher Education, Dr. Ram Sharma presented Dr. Baltodano with a proposal to expand the ELA program globally, particularly in India. Working closely with Baltodano, the program director, George Blumenthal, the Director of the Center for Studies in Higher Education at the time, initiated the ELA program at Shiv Nadar University, with the support of Partha Chatterjee, Professor and Head of the Department of Economics. Rupamajari Ghosh, Vice-Chancellor of Shiv Nadar University at the time, played a vital role in developing the curricula and implementing the program. Our faculty members are not only experts in their fields but are also deeply passionate about transforming higher education for the better. Many of our Founding Fellows and Founding Faculty have chosen to remain actively involved in the ELA program, serving on its Advisory Board since its establishment in 2014.

The Executive Leadership Academy Advisory Board is comprised of 15 servant leaders from both public and private universities across the country: Josefina C. Baltodano, George Blumenthal, Karen Biestman, Henry Brady, Johnnella Butler, Joseph Castro, Ding-Jo Currie, Alexander Gonzalez, C. Judson King, Dorothy Leland, Cassandra Manuelito-Kerkvliet, Sofia Ramos, Horace Mitchell, Elñora Webb, and Margaret Wilkerson. The members of the Advisory Board bring valuable expertise to the program, given their previous involvement. They effectively utilize their knowledge and the data provided by fellows' evaluations to provide practical recommendations for enhancing the Academy. These recommendations may include introducing new session topics, bringing in additional faculty members, exploring potential partnerships, and developing fundraising strategies. Additionally, the Advisory Board plays a crucial role in identifying, recruiting, and nominating prospective fellows for the program. Furthermore, many board members continue to offer guidance as mentors to the fellows even after their graduation.

With the support of the Advisory Board, the ELA offered five spaces in the July 2023 ELA program for selected Ukrainian leaders to participate with a tuition waiver. We invited applications from senior executive leaders (rectors/vice-rectors/deans) in the Ukraine and received more than 40 applications for the opportunity. Because of the overwhelming interest, we also established the Ukraine Professional Development Seminar intending to offer training and support to a larger number of Ukrainian higher education leaders who had expressed their interest.

With unanimous approval and support of the Advisory Board, the ELA was honored to extend an invitation to five distinguished Ukrainian leaders to join our premier July 2023 ELA program, with the added benefit of a tuition waiver. We extended invitations for applications exclusively to senior executive leaders in the Ukraine, including rectors, vice-rectors, and deans. The response exceeded our expectations, with over 40 highly qualified candidates expressing their interest in this unique opportunity. Given the overwhelming interest, we recognized the need to provide training and support to a larger number of Ukrainian higher education leaders who shared their enthusiasm. In response, we established the Ukraine Professional Development Seminar.

The ELA Ukraine seminar brought together a distinguished cohort of nearly 30 Ukrainian university leaders for an intensive one-day virtual professional development seminar. The event provided a platform for participants to network with prominent American higher education executives, enrich their leadership skills, and gain insights into the dynamic landscape of the US higher education system. This initiative was co-chaired by Igor Chirikov (Senior Researcher and SERU Consortium Director, CSHE) and Joseph Castro (Affiliated Faculty, CSHE & Advisory Board Member, ELA) with support from Samantha Rushing (Associate Director, ELA); who all served on the selection committee for the ELA program scholarships and Seminar program. Everyone who participated in the seminar (both staff and faculty) did so on a volunteer basis.

The Executive Director, Josefina Castillo Baltodano, expressed interest in creating a book that would elegantly present the remarkable abilities and knowledge possessed by our esteemed faculty and advisory board members. The book would also emphasize the unique and inspiring journeys that each of these individuals have embarked upon in their pursuit of leadership excellence. In 2022, the ELA (Executive Leadership Academy) began working on a project known as the Presidential Profile Book, titled "Career Journeys of Diverse Leaders in Higher Education: Climbing the Rough Side of the Mountain." This book compiles the stories of ten retired presidents and chancellors who have made a significant impact on higher education. These leaders are either board members or faculty members of the ELA program.

The focus of this book is to showcase the successes of these leaders, particularly concerning their efforts in promoting diversity, inclusion, and social justice. The group of educators featured in this book represents a diverse multicultural background, including private and public institutions from across the United States. Additionally, a private university in India is also highlighted. What sets ELA apart is its commitment to fostering multicultural leadership and advancement in higher education.

The purpose of this book is to emphasize the various non-traditional paths that these leaders took to achieve senior leadership positions and to inspire and motivate others who may be considering similar roles in higher education. The book explores common themes that weave through the narratives, highlighting shared values and the lessons learned from different experiences. It also underscores the significance of storytelling as a means to teach leadership. We are pleased to share that the text generated significant interest and has been acquired by Routledge for publication in 2024.

Samantha A. Rushing
Associate Director & Executive Assistant to the
Board Executive Leadership Academy
University of California, Berkeley

1

SEIZING THE MOMENT

How a First-Generation Astrophysics Student Made an Impact as the Leader of a Major Research University

George Blumenthal

Abstract

George Blumenthal's trajectory to his 13-year chancellorship at UC Santa Cruz is based on three principles: (1) requiring that his work have a real impact, a significant advance in some way, (2) treating people with respect and decency, expecting that to be fully reciprocated 99% of the time, and (3) seizing opportunities whenever they present themselves. An astrophysicist and administrator, he seized early opportunities for both scientific research and graduate school involvement in institutional activities beyond science that provided a foundation for his later engagement with and understanding of the complexities of and possible synergies among institutions, faculty governance, and administrative leadership. As a faculty member and later administrator, Blumenthal served as department chair and in faculty governance positions; worked with Santa Cruz's legendary provost, Herman Blake, in building Oakes College, the multicultural community at UCSC; and served in the UC Office of the President. His story provides numerous examples of how opportunities arise when a leader at various career levels addresses thorny issues from a basis of understanding institutions, expecting the realistic best of others, embracing compromise to overcome resistance, and knowing who you are and your potential amid institutional growth and change.

Introduction

As you will see in this narrative, several principles have been key to success throughout my career. One is a determination to have a real impact–to insist that my work provides a significant advance in some way. Another

DOI: 10.4324/9781003465812-1

principle is to treat people with respect and decency with the expectation that 99% of the time it will be fully reciprocated. In addition, I have found it essential to seize opportunities whenever they present themselves.

First-Generation Student

I grew up in Milwaukee, Wisconsin, in a middle-income family. My parents owned a small Venetian blind business, which they ran jointly. I was a latchkey kid while growing up. By the time I graduated from high school, I knew that I loved physics – I actually found it so easy even when others complained bitterly about how hard it was. I had thought about going into engineering when I got to college, but my high school physics teacher gave me some great advice. He suggested I study physics because, with that background, I could always switch to engineering. But the reverse would not be so easy.

So, after high school, I attended the University of Wisconsin-Milwaukee, an urban university. My parents couldn't afford to send me elsewhere, and as a first-generation college student, I had no idea that there were academic scholarships available to attend other colleges. But this choice was fortunate for me in the end. I was able to graduate with a major in physics in three years. Throughout most of my college career, I worked 20–25 hours a week, mostly for the Milwaukee Public Library system checking out and shelving books. The faculty at UWM helped me tremendously by offering special independent studies classes in advanced subjects that were not yet part of the curriculum.

One faculty member had a tremendous impact on me. During my final year, Robert Greenler in physics asked me if I'd like a job working for him. I gladly accepted and quit my job at the library. Bob was an experimental physicist who studied the surfaces of materials using infrared radiation. My job was to run a computer code that calculated the reflective properties of those surfaces. That job was really boring. But one day, Bob mentioned to me his interest in atmospheric phenomena and mentioned one in particular that I'd never heard of called a sun pillar. Under the right cloud conditions, a sun pillar is a bright pillar of light rising from the sun when the sun has just risen or is about to set. So I asked him what causes sun pillars, and he explained the phenomenon. But his explanation didn't make any sense to me, and I told him as much. So, he pulled out the standard book on atmospheric phenomena and showed me the standard explanation. Ultimately, I convinced him that the explanation had to be wrong. So, Bob asked me if I wanted to drop the surface work and spend my time figuring out sun pillars. I agreed instantly.

I worked on that question for the next six months and ultimately did figure out the correct explanation. When I discussed it with Greenler, he agreed and said to me "Guess what, George. Right now, you and I are the only people in the world who really understand this." I was inspired when I heard that, and I soon realized that I wanted to do research and create new knowledge in my career.

After graduating, I was off to graduate school at the University of California, San Diego. I had been fortunate enough to receive an extremely high score on the Graduate Record Exam in physics, which led to a National Science Foundation graduate fellowship to the school of my choice. UCSD had an outstanding physics program, and exchanging the freezing weather of Milwaukee for the balmy weather of Southern California was a good trade. So, at the ripe old age of 20, never having been west of the Mississippi River, I set off to San Diego.

I started graduate school in 1966 intending to study elementary particle physics because I really did want to work on some of the most fundamental questions in science. During my first year, I learned a great deal about the subject, but by the end of the year, I realized that it didn't really excite me. So, I figured that if I didn't want to study the tiniest structures in existence, why not study the biggest things in the universe, including the universe itself? I approached one of the astrophysics faculty members, Bob Gould, asking whether there was a project I might work on. That was one of the best decisions I ever made. I started doing calculations about how super high-energy particles in the universe, called cosmic rays, interact with matter and radiation. Bob and I later published that work in a highly prestigious journal, and it received a fair amount of attention.

During my third year of graduate school, while my advisor was off on sabbatical in Australia, I became heavily involved with issues beyond science. I was elected to be the student representative of the department, thereby beginning my long history of service to the university. By this time, my political views had evolved, and I became highly engaged with issues such as civil rights, abortion rights, and the war in Vietnam. I was in the last group of graduate students who were able to keep a deferment from the military draft throughout their graduate school years, so I saw firsthand the effects of the war on my fellow students.

So, I participated in hatching a plan to organize the first anti-war march through downtown San Diego, which in those days was an exceptionally politically conservative city with strong connections to the military. Organizing such a march was no small matter. I made trips to the police department to secure the necessary permits to allow a march to close streets to traffic. We had to do extensive training of monitors for the march to ensure that confrontations could be avoided to maintain it as a peaceful event. But eventually, we finished all of that work. Although on the morning of the march, local media falsely claimed that the march had been canceled, I proudly joined the first rank of this 5,000-person march for peace through San Diego, ending up in Balboa Park with speeches and celebration. For me, this was an accomplishment for which I take great pride.

The next year, after my advisor returned to campus, I put my nose to the grindstone and worked very hard to complete my dissertation. My thesis was on high-energy cosmic ray particles and the interactions that they undergo. In addition to my thesis, I also wrote an important paper on how magnetic fields arise in the large-scale universe. Ultimately, I received my Ph.D. and was off to a postdoc in Cambridge, Massachusetts with the X-ray astronomy group headed by future Nobel laureate, Ricardo Giacconi. They had just launched the first satellite devoted fully to X-ray astronomy, which was called UHURU.[1] It was an exciting year working with that group.

Faculty Years

My hiring as an assistant professor at the University of California, Santa Cruz, was rather unusual. I first learned of the position through Bob Gould, my thesis advisor, about a week before I was to leave for Cambridge. He persuaded me to fly up to the campus to give a talk on my research before I departed. It turned out to be a great experience, and I was pleased some weeks later when I received the offer of a faculty position. This was the last of five faculty positions that were funded at UCSC in astronomy by the National Science Foundation, with the promise that the campus would permanently fund the positions when the grant ended. As a consequence, I was one of the few faculty hired only by a department[2] rather than jointly with one of the residential colleges, but I was joining a premier department.

Not long after arriving at UCSC, I planned to meet a close friend for dinner in San Francisco. However, unbeknownst to me, he had planned a dinner including his girlfriend and one of her close friends named Kelly Weisberg, who was then finishing her Ph.D. at Brandeis University. Kelly and I began to see each other, and after a couple of years (including a six-week bicycle trip through Europe), we got married. Kelly soon completed her law degree at Berkeley, and she joined the faculty at Washington University in St. Louis, which meant that we spent our weekends flying across the country to see each other. Fortunately, within two years, Kelly joined the faculty at UC Hastings College of Law in San Francisco, which certainly helped us to settle down and raise a family. I feel so unbelievably fortunate since Kelly has supported all of my career choices, and she also taught me so much over the years that has contributed to my later successes.

Early in my faculty career, I wrote a number of well-received articles on cosmic X-ray sources, and I soon joined a colleague in researching what was going on in the centers of active galactic nuclei, which we now know contain massive black holes. That research was extremely interesting, and I ultimately received tenure based on that work around the time of my marriage. Soon thereafter, a chance encounter changed the course of my research.

Back during my graduate school years, I had been fascinated by the question of how galaxies formed. However, it was clear that something fundamental was missing from all theories of galaxy formation. For example, we observe that all galaxies have a mass between about a million and a quadrillion times the mass of our Sun. But no theory was able to explain that mass range. There were other problems as well, and once I began teaching, I enjoyed proving to my advanced undergraduate and graduate classes that galaxies could not exist! Clearly, there was something wrong with my argument, but I didn't know what it was.

One day, in the astronomy reading room, I encountered one of my contemporary colleagues, Sandy Faber, surrounded by huge stacks of journals. When I asked her what she was doing, she told me she had been asked to write a review article about the rotation of galaxies. At the time, some folks, such as astronomer Vera Rubin, were claiming that galaxy rotation data gave the surprising result that galaxies were filled with large quantities of invisible dark matter. I asked Sandy whether she believed this evidence for dark matter, and she said it couldn't possibly be true. A few days later, I ran into her again and asked how her review article was coming. She astonished me by saying that after critically examining the evidence, she was now convinced that dark matter does exist! She also said there was about ten times more dark matter in galaxies than there is visible material such as stars.

So, I decided to refocus the direction of my research toward understanding the role of dark matter in the formation of galaxies and other large-scale structures in the universe. Ultimately, my colleagues and I developed what is now known as cold dark matter theory, which is still today the standard model of how galaxies form. Soon after developing the theory, I created a graph of the kinds of masses and densities that galaxies should have based on the theory, and one day a colleague came to my office with data from Sandy Faber on the distribution of real galaxies. You can imagine the excitement we felt when we overlaid those two pieces of graph paper, and the two matched perfectly. Following up on that research occupied me for several years to come.

A few years later, I became involved in something I never imagined doing: writing an astronomy textbook. I was approached by a former student, then a faculty member at Arizona State University, about joining a team he was putting together of seven active researchers to write an introductory textbook. Somewhat to my surprise, W.W. Norton agreed to publish the book. Perhaps not surprisingly, with seven authors, the book, *21st Century Astronomy,* took far longer to complete than it would have had there been a single author. But it was reasonably successful.

The book has been sufficiently successful that it is now in its seventh edition. There is also a shorter one-semester book called *Understanding Our Universe,* which is now in its fourth edition. Despite the eminence of the initial group of authors, I was not pleased that we were all middle-aged white males. So, over the years, as authors dropped out, I have replaced them with a more diverse group. For the past few editions, I have been the only remaining author from the original seven, and my co-authors have been two outstanding women astronomers.

Despite the absence of urgency to do so, soon after I arrived at UCSC I decided to join one of the residential colleges as a fellow. It happened when I met Professor J. Herman Blake, the first Black faculty member at UCSC. Herman and a colleague were determined to start a new college which later was named Oakes[3] College. Herman's vision was to build a college that supported students from a wide range of ethnic and socioeconomic backgrounds, providing strong support for those students. He was also determined to build a rigorous science program because Herman believed that students from all backgrounds deserved to have opportunities in every field but also had an obligation to work hard to achieve their goals. I felt it was a most worthy enterprise.

It was really an exciting time to build a brand-new college in that way. I was one of the founding faculty members, and we soon had a cadre of very committed faculty. The vast majority of the faculty were, like me, quite junior, which was a mixed blessing. On the one hand, these young faculty had energy, drive, and commitment. But on the other hand, each of us knew that our tenure clocks were ticking, and we needed to establish strong research credentials. But it was fun working with such dedicated people, even though we often had long meetings trying to work on plans for the future. All of that effort was clearly worth it when we brought in our first class of Oakes students. By now, there are well over ten thousand graduates of Oakes College.

As a college provost, Herman had a particularly nice practice of periodically visiting faculty in their offices to hear about how things were going. Despite being rather shy and reticent in those days, I expressed some of my frustration to Herman about the stresses on junior faculty who are building the college and who report to two masters, their college and their department. I said there were just too many meetings, and sometimes meetings in the department and college even conflicted with one another. Herman thanked me for my frankness before he departed. The next day, he phoned me and told me he had been thinking about my comments, and he felt I had a perspective that needed to be heard. So, he asked me to join the college executive committee! And of course, I accepted. Serving on the executive committee for the next few years was an eye-opening educational experience for me. I learned first-hand about the range of issues that arise in running an academic enterprise. Little did I know that this was preparing me for what was to come.

Within my department, I was also destined to serve as the department chair, first while an associate professor, and later again when I was more senior. Although officially, the dean appoints department chairs, in my department we had a different tradition. The department would traditionally meet and hold an election, and the loser had to become chair. No one wanted to do the job because it took away from teaching and research, which is what all of us wanted to prioritize.

Fortunately, my first term as chair only lasted a couple of years. My main goal at the time was to convert the department from paper to electronic communication. I know it feels like so long ago, but email had just come into our world, and I wanted to change to this new mode of communication. But it wasn't easy. Surprisingly, not all members of the department even knew how to use email. Indeed, I spent several hours teaching one of my slightly more senior colleagues how to use email. Naturally, for the graduate and undergraduate students, this was no big deal. Ultimately, the transition was successful.

While it was an educational experience for me, I did find being chair to be quite a burden. The main difficulty at that time was the chaos within the dean's office. We had three different deans in two years, and I was frustrated by the difficulty of getting clear answers from that office. Because my research was so exciting at the time, I was happy to let the position go.

A decade later, I was elected *in absentia* as chair while I was completing a year-long sabbatical at Harvard. I ended up serving two three-year terms largely to deal with the issue described below. At the time, I had zero interest in a larger administrative role. In fact, twice I turned down offers to be an acting dean at the university. My children were still fairly young, and I wanted to spend time with them as they grew up. In addition, I didn't think I had either the skills or the drive to move very far up the administrative ladder. I wanted to do research and teaching.

The big issues facing the department at that time arose from the 7.1 magnitude Loma Prieta earthquake in 1989. By far, the most damage from that earthquake was to the Natural Sciences II building that housed astronomy and physics.[4] That building, which was very long and narrow, sustained extensive structural damage and would have collapsed had the earthquake lasted a few more seconds. Subsequently, as a stopgap measure, the university shored up the building with giant beams to keep it habitable. But it did need a permanent fix, which occurred only several years later, after I'd become chair.

The plan was to move astronomy and physics for two years into another building, Kerr Hall, which was slated to become the new administrative building of the campus, housing the chancellor. I was worried that my faculty would be unhappy about moving into what had been a social sciences building, with little laboratory space. So, a month or so before the move, with a colleague, Sandy Faber, I went over to inspect Kerr Hall. Sandy's reaction astonished me. She thought the building was fantastic for us and that we should never return to Natural Sciences II. Her reasoning was quite logical. While Natural Sciences II was a long thin building with narrow corridors and no space for interactions, Kerr Hall had wide halls with alcoves where people could have spontaneous conversations. And that type of interactive space was something my department really craved.

It turns out that Sandy's desire to remain permanently in Kerr Hall was indeed the overwhelming position of both the physics and astronomy departments, which I felt obliged to support. However, the chancellor's office had its eye on Kerr Hall, so this idea did not have much support within the administration. I ultimately spent nearly three years pushing for a better building for astronomy and physics. In the end, the new chancellor, M.R.C. Greenwood, made a rather Solomonic decision. She gave physics and astronomy a brand-new building, which allowed the administration to move into Kerr Hall. About a decade later, when it was announced I was appointed the acting chancellor of the campus, my friend Steve Thorsett, then the dean of sciences, reacted by saying, "Gosh, George. I guess you're willing to do anything to get back into Kerr Hall!"

Academic Senate and Regental Service

Within the UC system, the academic senate, whose membership is essentially the ladder rank faculty within the system, has primary authority over curricular matters, grading, degree requirements, and admissions criteria. It must also be consulted on academic personnel matters and budgetary issues within the university. There is only one UC Senate, which has ten branches on each of the various campuses.

As a brand-new faculty member, when I first entered my new office, I found a thick binder called *The UC Academic Senate Manual* sitting on my desk. I was so naïve that I thought I was obliged to read it from cover to cover. As a young faculty member, I thought I should volunteer for some senate committees, and doing so allowed me to meet faculty from other departments on the campus and throughout the system. It was another good learning experience.

Later, after my department chair duties were completed, I served on the campus Privilege and Tenure (P&T) committee and then became its chair for three years. The privilege and tenure committee investigates grievances by faculty and helps resolve them. It also conducts formal hearings if those cases are not resolved or if there is a faculty discipline matter brought to the committee against a faculty member accused of violating UC's Faculty Code of Conduct. Before I assumed the chairship, there had not been a P&T hearing in 15 years, so it was a shock that we had to hold two such hearings during my first year as chair. I won't discuss the substance of those cases, but I want to convey that I did find the Senate rules governing such hearings to be arcane, vague, convoluted, and difficult to understand. As a consequence of chairing the campus P&T committee, I served for a year on the systemwide University Committee on Privilege and Tenure UCPT) and then chaired that committee for two years. UCPT is a policy committee, which I truly enjoyed. I helped resolve a major dispute between the President of the University and the Academic Senate over what criteria would be used in a new policy on faculty incompetence. The President insisted on his criteria, so we insisted on as many procedural checks and balances as possible before a faculty member could be dismissed for incompetence.

Another key change I implemented involved getting legal advice for campus P&T hearing committees. No such advice had been previously available, but I helped establish a position with the University's Office of General Counsel that was assigned to providing such legal advice for campus committees. Of course, such a person had to be separated by a legal firewall from the rest of the general counsel's office. In any event, this program was a resounding success, and every campus P&T committee praised this program when we reviewed it a couple of years later.

Having seen how poorly the senate bylaws dealing with faculty grievances, discipline, and termination were written, I persuaded the committee to do a complete rewrite of the bylaws. We separated grievances, discipline, and termination into three separate bylaws to make it easier for hearing committees. For the first time, we established standards of proof[5] required for each category of hearing. We established timeframes by which hearings had to be concluded, and we wrote the rules to encourage early negotiated resolutions of disputes. This was a major effort, but we got it done, and I helped to shepherd it through the formal approval process of the Senate.

Having worked to modernize the Senate's P&T bylaws, I then persuaded the President's office and the Senate leadership to modify the UC Faculty Code of Conduct as well. The Code of Conduct included all of the rights and privileges of faculty members as well as their obligations. It also included the procedures to resolve cases and the disciplines that faculty might face for violating the Code of Conduct. A joint Senate-administrative task force was set up with me as chair to take on those issues. I won't go through all the changes we proposed, but there were many such changes including a reconceptualization of the disciplinary sanctions that would be available in case of violation of the Code. I had to do a great deal of outreach around the UC system to get everyone on board, but our changes were supported by the Senate and the President, and they were ultimately approved by the Board of Regents.

During this period, the UCSC division of the Senate was going through difficulties. The campus senate meetings were organized in a town hall format,[6] and several meetings had degenerated into nonproductive shouting matches, leading to some loss of confidence by the faculty in the senate. Shortly before the normal transition of senate leadership, I received a call in summer 2001 from the division's Committee on Committees telling me that the chair-designate had withdrawn from consideration and asking if I would agree to chair the division for two years. After discussing it with my wife, I agreed.

I was determined that the Senate would be a smoothly running body during my term. Before chairing my first senate meeting, I read *Robert's Rules of Order* cover to cover – twice. I was very tough at these meetings and insisted on strict adherence to the rules of order, and as a result, we got a lot done at these meetings. Many faculty congratulated me on our more smoothly running senate. During my term, I also reorganized the senate office which helped the committees to run more smoothly.

As a consequence of chairing the division, I was also a member of the systemwide Academic Assembly, the legislative body of the Senate, and of the Academic Council, the executive committee of the Senate. Dozens of interesting issues came before the Council each year, but I'll briefly mention three that I was personally involved with.

One of those concerns is the academic freedom policy. It arose because of a highly controversial course on Palestinian Poetry being taught at Berkeley. The description of this course encouraged those not agreeing with the instructor to avoid taking the class – this is inappropriate, and the Regents and the President were furious about it. At the President's urging, Robert Post, one of the leading experts on academic freedom in the country and then a Berkeley Law faculty member, drafted a new academic freedom policy for UC setting forth much more clearly the rights and obligations of faculty members. It was exciting to be a part of that discussion, and a year later, when I was chair of the senate, I initiated further discussion of student freedom of expression, which was later incorporated into UC policy. Many years after that, I jointly led a task group that extended the academic freedom policy to cover individuals based on the academic activities they are engaged in rather than just based on their titles.

The second issue concerned romantic or sexual relationships between students and faculty. At the time, no such policy existed in the Faculty Code of Conduct. A draft policy was being considered that would bar such relationships when there is also a student/teacher relationship or the likelihood of one in the future. This was somewhat controversial, and for a while, I was quite skeptical of the proposed policy. But I did my research, checking what other universities were doing and checking the model policy of the American Association of University Professors. None of them seemed very good to me, so I ultimately informed the Senate chair that I'd fully support her proposed policy. She responded by saying that was great, and she wanted me to take charge of getting this policy adopted by the Senate. Although there were controversies, we did get the policy approved by the Academic Assembly and eventually by the Board of Regents as an amendment to the Faculty Code of Conduct.

I also agreed to lead the effort to revise the entire set of bylaws of the Academic Senate. That process took two years, but I am proud of the fact that we brought those bylaws into the 21st century. These revisions also brought uniformity to the committee structure and some sense of consistency to the bylaws. Ultimately, these major changes were passed virtually unanimously. In the end, I feel that when I die and go to hell, they'll make me chair of the bylaws committee!

After two years chairing the UCSC division, I was encouraged to agree to another term, but instead, I decided to run for election as vice chair and chair of the systemwide senate. I was elected to a one-year term in each office. During both years, I also served as one of the two faculty representatives to the UC regents. All of this meant that I had to move my office to the UC Office of the President (UCOP) in Oakland, where my office was on the top floor, opposite to the President's office. I decided to commute daily from our home in Monte Sereno. At the urging of my wife, Kelly, I also made another decision. For all of my career, I wore shorts or jeans with running shoes every day. Kelly persuaded me to buy some jackets and ties to wear in this new role. I guess I didn't want to be branded as the weirdo from Santa Cruz, so I decided to conform to the rather conservative dress code at UCOP.

What an exciting and stimulating time it was! While I was vice chair, I benefitted enormously from the mentoring of the chair, Larry Pitts, who was a neurosurgeon from UCSF. During those two years, I met regularly with the President, the Provost, and several of the other senior vice presidents. I attended all regents' meetings and participated in their discussions, even during closed and regents-only sessions. As chair, I was a member of the President's cabinet. In addition, I sometimes joined meetings with the Governor and testified before legislative committees. And of course, I chaired the Academic Council and the Academic Assembly.

There were so many interesting issues we dealt with during that period. We successfully pushed for extended release time for faculty who were new parents. We enacted several measures that made it easier for community college students to transfer to UC. I'm particularly pleased that we were able to change the University's criteria for promotion and tenure to explicitly recognize not just faculty service to advance diversity but also excellence in teaching and research that advances diversity in society.

One of my goals was to establish a new division of the academic senate at the recently opened UC Merced campus. I felt that the campus was approaching a critical mass of faculty needed to successfully run a division, and most of the academic council agreed with me. What slowed the process was my stubborn insistence that the campus provide resources to hire staff to serve the division. So, I had protracted negotiations with their chancellor and provost, and after we reached an agreement, I brought the issue to the Academic Assembly, which approved it with little opposition. Thus, was born the UC Merced division.

One issue that impacted both my role in the Senate and on the regents concerned the Livermore and Los Alamos National Laboratories, which UC had operated for many decades since their establishment. Because of some serious management issues, the US Department of Energy decided to hold a competition for those vying to manage the labs, and the regents had to decide whether to compete. Factors in favor of competing included the management fees UC would collect, the potential collaborations between UC faculty and the labs, and the high-value public service UC would be providing. On the other hand, some felt that it was unethical for a university to be engaged in classified research on weapons of mass destruction and that the opportunity costs of running these labs were just too great. I felt that this was a decision of such importance to the university that putting aside my personal views, I wanted the entire UC faculty to weigh in on this issue. So, with the help of the Senate's national laboratory committee, I created an electronic poll on this issue to be sent to all UC faculty. The challenges of creating and conducting such a poll of 16.000 faculty on ten campuses were substantial, but in the end, about a third of all faculty responded. Somewhat to my surprise, a very substantial majority of faculty who responded supported competing for the labs. I was able to report this to the regents before their decision.

I became heavily involved in one other issue facing the regents, namely, the question of whether the regents should add two staff advisors to participate in regental discussions. Because the regents seemed very much divided on this issue, they formed a special committee to consider the staff advisor positions, and I was placed on this committee. I strongly favored giving staff a real voice while the regents are considering issues facing the university. But it was clear that the vote on this was going to be close.

So, I decided to propose a compromise. I proposed that the staff advisors sit on only two regent committees and that the staff advisor positions be established only provisionally with the regents reviewing the positions after two years. That mollified many of the critics. I argued to the staff leadership that this was like getting the camel's nose under the tent – there was no way the regents would cut this off after two years. Ultimately, the establishment of the staff advisor position passed the regents with only one dissenting vote, and two years later, that dissenter enthusiastically joined the other regents in voting unanimously to make the positions permanent. It has been a great success for UC, and as I predicted, the advisor's role has expanded significantly over the years. When I became a chancellor a year later, I began to meet with the two staff advisors before every regents meeting to brief them on all the issues coming to the regents. I kept that up throughout my thirteen years as chancellor.

The two years I spent in Oakland were exciting and rewarding. While working at UCOP, I did feel rather isolated from the UC academic enterprise, and to mitigate that, I organized a research seminar series at UCOP, which was rather successful. Later, I was gratified to receive, in my first year of eligibility, the Senate's biennial Oliver Johnson Award for outstanding service to the academic senate.

Chancellor of UC Santa Cruz

When my term as Senate chair ended, I returned to UCSC and resumed my work as a professor of astronomy & astrophysics. I remained involved with several systemwide committees I was on; I was appointed as one of the UCSC Academic Assembly representatives, and the campus Provost did involve me in some issues where my contacts at UCOP would prove helpful to the campus.

In June, while I was traveling with my daughter on the East Coast looking at colleges for her, I received a shocking call from the Campus Provost, Dave Kliger. Dave told me that the chancellor, Denice Denton, had committed suicide by jumping off the roof of a 42-story high-rise in San Francisco. He then further stunned me by telling me he was recommending that I be appointed as the acting chancellor to replace her.

When I returned to campus for Denice's memorial service, I started to hear more buzz about this from leaders at the Office of the President. So, I had to take it seriously. I did have serious doubts about whether I would enjoy serving in the chancellor role, and I also questioned my ability to fit smoothly into such a role. However, I thought it just might be fun to do this for a year, so I decided to accept the position if offered.

I subsequently had a couple of long telephone calls with President Bob Dynes, during the second of which, he offered to appoint me acting chancellor. Bob was clear with me that this in no way implied that I would have a leg up in the search for a permanent occupant of the chancellor's position. I, of course, already knew that since in each of several previous searches, the acting chancellor had not been selected for the permanent position. Nonetheless, as the months passed, I grew to enjoy being chancellor, and 14 months later, after a full nationwide search, I was appointed as the permanent chancellor at UCSC.

For me, the transition to being chancellor was astounding. I began my first day by just driving around the beautiful 2000-acre campus with its redwood forests and scenic views overlooking Monterey Bay. I remember thinking, "My God! To think that I'm in charge of all this. What a responsibility!" I soon learned that my days would be filled with meeting after meeting, and I was soon giving 7–10 speeches a week. I particularly wanted to reach out to faculty, students, staff, alumni, donors, and others to convey that the campus had committed leadership and that I would be pursuing three major goals: continuing and accelerating the campus's upward trajectory of excellence, moving toward a faculty and student population that better reflects the people of California, and making UCSC a primary destination for faculty, staff, and students. The fact that the campus was later invited to join the prestigious American Association of Universities and that we attained the status of Hispanic Serving Institution (HSI) during my tenure certainly suggests we met many of those goals.

I strongly felt that a key part of my role was to aggressively represent the campus in Sacramento, Washington D.C., among alumni and donors, and to the President and the other chancellors. A week or two after I first assumed office, I went to Oakland for my first monthly all-day meeting of the Council of Chancellors. I remember thinking that I had finally ascended the Mt. Olympus of Academia and that I had to strive mightily to hold my own in that setting. However, at that time the University was still reeling from the compensation "scandal" of 2006, and I was singularly unimpressed with the discussions at my first meeting. I remember walking out with Michael Drake, then the chancellor at UC Irvine and someone I knew fairly well. I told him I was really disappointed by the meeting, and he responded that this was the best meeting they'd had in months! Fortunately, that meeting turned out to be an aberration, and I usually enjoyed my meetings with the other chancellors a great deal.

At this point, I'd like to discuss a small subset of the important issues I faced in my thirteen years as chancellor.

University Growth and Town-Gown Relations

Back in the early 1960's when the city of Santa Cruz persuaded the UC Board of Regents to locate a new campus in their city rather than outside San Jose, the Santa Cruz community was rather conservative politically and very pro-growth. The original proposal for the campus as well as the first Long Range Development Plan (LRDP) called for a campus of 27,500 students, and the community fully supported that concept. By the 1980s, and certainly by the mid-2000s when I became chancellor, the city had changed dramatically. Some of that was due to changes in California's political landscape, and a great deal of it was the result of an influx of voting students, faculty, and staff. The community developed a very strong no-growth viewpoint about both the city and the university. The university continued to grow to around 14,000 students by the time I became chancellor, but neither the university nor the city had developed the infrastructure to support campus or community growth. Therefore, the relationship between campus leaders and community leaders had grown fraught by the time I assumed office. The city was frustrated that they had no direct control over university growth.

The timing of my appointment as acting chancellor in July was also awkward because the campus was slated to take a new LRDP to the regents in September, planning for a campus of 21,000 students. Community leaders were upset that the university had not adequately consulted with them before the development of that plan. Even the Santa Cruz academic senate was upset because they had not been consulted either. In fact, in May, the senate had passed a resolution calling on the administration not to bring the LRDP to the regents in September without signoff by the Senate Executive Committee, and guess what, I had very strongly and publicly supported that resolution at the time. Little did I know that in little over a month I would be the target of that resolution.

So, I responded in several ways. First, I issued orders that any and all documents concerning the LRDP should be turned over to the Senate Executive Committee. I met extensively with the Senate leadership, and ultimately, they agreed that we could move forward to the regents in

September.[7] I also went to meet with the city council on their turf, and I went alone as a way of signifying that I was my own man. I also met with community groups opposing university growth. I showed that I really did understand their concerns, most of which hinged on issues of traffic, water, and housing. I even decided to lower the LRDP planning target to 19,500 students in the hope (ultimately unjustified) that this might mitigate community opposition.

So, in September, I did bring the LRDP to the Board of Regents. Despite strongly negative public comments from city officials and community leaders, the regents approved it unanimously. One regent did criticize me for lowering the enrollment target to 19,500, but he sought me out after the meeting to let me know he was really sending a message to city leaders about the importance of educating California's youth.

Naturally, there were several lawsuits filed under California law challenging the viability of the Environmental Impact Report (EIR). After the matter was heard, the Santa Cruz court decided that the EIR was flawed and therefore invalid. We decided to appeal that decision feeling somewhat confident that we would win on appeal. Ultimately, we knew that even a flawed EIR could be corrected, so all these court cases could do is delay the inevitable implementation of our LRDP. But I wasn't very pleased. Although our ongoing building projects of a Digital Arts Building and our Library expansion weren't affected by these legal machinations, proceeding with our planned biomedical building did require the EIR to be valid. Furthermore, I really didn't want our relations with the community to depend on the courts – I really did want us to work together.

So, I approached city and community group leaders with the idea of trying to negotiate a settlement agreement. The mayor, Ryan Coonerty, was a tremendous ally in this effort. Most people (perhaps myself included) didn't think we would succeed, but I felt it was imperative to try. So, we brought in a mediator and started holding meetings with all stakeholders. There were dozens of meetings extending over six months. I recall one meeting that started in mid-afternoon and ended at 2:00 AM. But I attended all these meetings, along with the mayor, several city council members, county supervisors, and representatives of community groups. In the end, we reached a settlement agreement, which has survived for well over a decade.

The agreement had many elements, but there were three key issues within the settlement, which allowed the campus to grow to 19,500 students. (1) We agreed to stop growth if traffic to campus exceeded a certain level. Since I controlled parking on campus, I was confident I could control how many vehicles came to campus each day. In fact, despite continuing campus growth, we were able to reduce traffic to its level when the campus was two-thirds its present size. (2) We agreed to pay a premium for any water usage above the then current level. Again, I was confident that with extreme conservation measures, we could do that. In reality, we reduced water use to its level when the campus was half its size. (3) In addition to housing the same number of current students, we agreed to provide on-campus housing for half of all additional students above 15,000. UCSC already housed a higher percentage of students on campus than all but one public university[8] in California. Still, I was hopeful we could build more housing, and at least until now, we have maintained that commitment.

This agreement was hailed as historic by members of the community, and it did bring about a sea change in town-grown relations. Later, when after several failures by my predecessors to obtain approval for our Coastal Long Range Development Plan from the Coastal Commission for our Marine Sciences campus, support from many members of the community helped us get that through.

In the aftermath of the settlement agreement, we did have legal approval to move forward on the biomedical building, but there were other challenges. First, we had to endure a long tree sit by professional tree-sitters protesting our plan to remove a dozen trees to make way for the biomedical building. When we got permission from the state to remove the trees, I took the necessary steps to remove the tree-sitters as well as the trees in question. Then there was a problem with funding. Because of the great recession, we had a great bid from a contractor to build the building at a cost well below our estimates. We even had money from the California Institute for Regenerative Medicine to add a fourth floor to the building. But there was no state money to build the first three floors. I pleaded with UCOP to find the money before our bids expired, and with a couple of days to spare, they came through. Today, outstanding research and teaching occur there.

Inevitably, the campus continued to grow, and eventually, I realized that we needed to start a new LRDP process, but I was determined not to repeat the mistakes of the past. I set a campus planning limit of 28,000 students, consistent with the original agreement between the city and the Regents. I included the academic senate in the planning, and indeed, I appointed the senate chair to co-chair the LRDP committee. I established a Community Advisory Group composed of government leaders, community activists, and business leaders who met regularly to provide input to the LRDP process. I committed upfront to housing 100% of all students above 19.500 on campus, and I insisted that the plan be written in such a way that infrastructure had to be built as the student population grows. Of course, none of this will halt disagreements between community and campus leaders, but at least we can maintain communication and trust. I saw this process through its first two years until I retired as chancellor, and it was completed by my successor.

Rebenching

When I assumed office, I knew that financial considerations would play a key role in my success or failure as chancellor. I also knew that core funding for the campus on a per-student basis had decreased substantially over the years. So, I spent many hours with my Vice Chancellor of Planning & Budget, Meredith Michaels, going over the campus budget in great detail.

One day, at a cabinet meeting, I asked Meredith how UCSC's state funding per student compared to the other UC campuses. Her answer astonished me. She said she didn't know and couldn't know because UCOP refused to share budgetary information about other campuses. I was appalled by that. A few days later, she came by to show me some calculations she and her staff had done to answer my question. I should not have been surprised at the result that showed UCSC receiving about 30% less funding per student than the UC average. Having now done some forensic analysis of the history of this difference, I do understand its origins, but that origin was irrelevant. Every year, UCOP operated by giving every campus the same percentage increase or decrease to its previous year's budget so that any disparity was frozen in forever. Naturally, the big winners were campuses like UCLA and Berkeley. But the UC system was supposed to achieve the same high quality at all its campuses, so I was determined to bring about change.

As luck would have it, I was soon scheduled for my annual meeting with the President and executive vice presidents to discuss campus concerns. Many chancellors brought a large group to these meetings, but I was advised to bring only Meredith. When I asked her to join me, she said that was a bad idea since I already understood the issues deeply and since one strong voice was the best way to make the campus's case. So, I walked in with a large list (which I won't discuss here) of issues. First, I raised the issue of budgetary transparency. I said I was astonished that even chancellors couldn't get information about other campuses' budgets. UC had just hired a new CFO, Katie Lapp, and she was extremely receptive to that point. In fact, Katie phoned me several times over the next few weeks to discuss the best ways to achieve transparency. On the other issue, the disparity in the amount of state dollars per student going to the campuses, I made little progress. The President and the Provost were extremely interested in the results I showed them, but the President was already thinking of stepping down, and there was little stomach for taking on a potentially divisive issue among the campuses.

I soon became aware of another financial issue that disadvantaged the campus. UCOP was the entity that collected all tuition from students, but our campus was getting back only about two-thirds of the tuition that our students paid.[9] The unfairness of forcing our students to pay to educate students on richer campuses was so obvious that this policy was relatively easy to change. The new policy was that campuses get to keep what they collect. Of course, the larger campuses bought into this because they were increasing their nonresident student populations, and as a result, they were able to retain the much larger nonresident tuition paid by those students. Nonetheless, this was an important change for us.

Soon, UC had a new president, Mark Yudof, who had been the president of the University of Texas. I came to like and respect Mark very much, but for a couple of years, my complaints about the allocation of state funds fell on deaf ears. Every year, Mark held a budget meeting with each chancellor and their budget staff. Mark never expressed any concerns to me about our management of the budget.

After the Great Recession hit, I presented a budget to Mark that showed significant (30%) cuts to administrative services and student support but much smaller cuts to the academic enterprise. Mark didn't say anything, so I commented that this was important since he'd probably just fire me if I had cut every part of campus by the same percentage across the board. He reluctantly agreed with me that he expected me to use judgment in allocating campus resources. So, I said to him, "Why can't I have the same expectation of you in the allocation of state funding?" To his credit, Mark visibly winced and said OK, I'd finally convinced him to move forward with rebenching, which was the name I'd attached to this effort.

So, a rebenching committee was formed with representatives from each campus, and of course, I was a member. I definitely didn't get everything I wanted, but I did get a lot. We agreed that UCOP would provide state funds to the campuses on a formulaic basis. Every undergraduate and master's student, irrespective of level or major, would generate the same state funding. PhD students would generate 2.5 times the funding of undergraduates. And professional health sciences students would generate five times the funding of undergraduates. There was no data to support the health sciences number, but I had to argue to keep that number from being even higher. We also agreed that rebenching would be phased in over six years using only new money we received from the state, thereby avoiding serious cuts to any campus.

Overall, I was happy with these results, even if they weren't ideal. Rebenching helped my campus survive the aftermath of the Great Recession. When funding started to flow again from Sacramento, I was able to use the rebenching money to start new programs and establish the UCSC Silicon Valley campus. I was so grateful that we were able to benefit from the parity that came from rebenching.

Diversity and Inclusion

When I became chancellor, I knew that diversity and inclusion efforts were going to be a major priority, and I felt that my experiences in building Oakes College would serve me well in that regard. The dilemma I faced, however, was how to organize these efforts on the UCSC campus. At that time, UC Berkeley had just created a new office of diversity and inclusion led by my colleague Gibor Basri, who I knew would do a great job. However, I had a few concerns about recreating such a new structure on my campus. First, I did not want to put our diversity and inclusion efforts in a corner somewhere so that much of the campus could simply ignore them. I wanted to be able to hold the deans and vice chancellors responsible for diversity in their units. In other words, I wanted accountability. In addition, to establish such a position, I would have had to hire a ladder rank faculty member from the outside to fill the position, but for a small campus that would be a major commitment of resources.

So, we went a different route. I established two diversity and inclusion positions. I appointed our Vice Provost for Academic Affairs, Herbie Lee, to be our chief diversity officer for faculty. I knew that for faculty issues, diversity efforts had to be led by a faculty member, and Herbie was both committed to diversity efforts and already in charge of faculty advancement. In addition, I hired a well-trained chief diversity officer for students and staff who brought with her a wealth of experience in this area. This organization worked well for us, though today, I would probably favor a single office led by a vice chancellor of diversity and inclusion.

After a couple of years in office, I felt that I wanted to better communicate the importance of diversity and inclusion issues and to get more input from the broader university community. So, I formed the Chancellor's Diversity Advisory Committee, which I chaired[10] throughout the remainder of my chancellorship. We had representatives from faculty, staff, and students, as well as alumni and community members. We made sure there were representatives of all relevant groups on campus, including the resource centers, the disability center, and the interfaith council. This was an extremely collegial group that took on important and sometimes difficult issues for the campus.

At the top of our agenda for the Chancellor's Diversity Advisory Committee was to do a full campus climate survey. Actually, we did two such surveys – the first for ourselves and the second because the entire UC system was doing a uniform climate survey. I was impressed with both the response rates to the surveys and the quality of analysis that the subcommittees we formed were able to attain. Overall, we found a rather high assessment of the campus climate, but several areas would require work, such as beefing up our disability resource center. As a result of the surveys, we formed several task groups to work up specific suggestions the campus should implement. Just as one example, the Black Experience Team, which I formed at the recommendation of the Committee, made some recommendations to the campus, including building cultural proficiency across the campus, hiring a mental health professional who specializes in issues affecting the ABC community, hiring more admissions recruiters who specialize in improving the yield of Black students, and better publicizing our Hate/Bias Response program. These are all recommendations the campus was able to implement.

One program that we put in place even before the Diversity Advisory Council formed was a new Diversity Certificate program for staff. This was the brainchild of my chief of staff, Ashish Sahni. This was a two-year program for staff members who wished to have training on issues of diversity and inclusion in an increasingly multicultural university. The program was free and required participants to take six required core courses and an elective to receive their certificate, which I personally handed out each year. It was a great success! By the time I retired, about 450 people had attained the certificate. It was so successful that we subsequently opened it up to faculty and graduate students to participate as well. This is a program that has now been emulated elsewhere, and I remain impressed with the enthusiasm it has generated.

In fact, because of the success of the diversity certificate program, we decided to start a comparable program in sustainability, a topic that resonates on the UCSC campus. In fact, in our engagement of students in our various sustainability programs, we noticed that relatively few students of color were participating in those programs. So we initiated a People of Color Sustainability Collective to specifically attract such students and to recognize that there are sustainability practices of long standing in minority communities that we should recognize and incorporate into our strategies for the future.

All of these diversity efforts paid off for the campus. Within just a few years, our campus became an official Hispanic Serving Institution (HSI) after more than 25% of our students were of Hispanic Origin. But we didn't rest on our laurels there, we went out and got several large grants in partnership with community colleges to increase the numbers of underserved students who successfully transfer to UCSC, especially in STEM fields. Those grants have made a real difference already, as the number of such students has increased significantly.

By the time I stepped down as chancellor, the diversity of the campus had increased substantially. We had increased the percentage of underrepresented minority students by 50% and became an HSI university. Nearly half of our entering students qualified for Pell grants, and more than 40% of them were first-generation students. When I retired, we had the highest percentage of underrepresented minority faculty in the UC system and the second-highest percentage of women faculty. I am proud of those achievements, but I do feel compelled to add two important caveats. First, even with these improvements, neither our diversity of students nor our diversity of faculty is yet close to the diversity of the state of California, and that, of course, has to be the goal. Secondly, the diversity of students, staff, and faculty is not yet uniform throughout the campus. Some fields and divisions have done much better than others, and there is still work to do, particularly within certain disciplines.

Comprehensive Fundraising Campaign

When I stepped into the chancellor's office, I knew remarkably little about fundraising, but I did know that the campus had to step up its fundraising efforts. UCSC was bringing in only about 20 million dollars a year in philanthropy, and despite being over 40 years old, the campus had never done a comprehensive fundraising campaign. The number of endowed chairs on the campus was fewer than UC Merced had on the day it opened. So, I knew we had to make fundraising a key priority.

A couple of years earlier, when I was chair of the systemwide senate, I was told that the one invitation I should definitely accept was to UC San Francisco's Founders Day. So my wife and I attended the event, and was I ever impressed! They did a fantastic job running a black tie event that gave its large audience a real sense of pride in the campus's achievements and the direction it was headed. I was so impressed that I contacted the university relations office at UCSC to suggest that we put on a similar event. They probably just ignored this advice as coming from just another faculty member with a "great idea". Well, once I became chancellor, we started our own UCSC Founders Day event, which became an annual event to instill pride in our campus among friends and donors. At this event, we also handed out awards such as the annual outstanding faculty and alumni awards, our Fiat Lux award celebrating someone who has advanced the campus priorities, and our Foundation Medal which celebrates an internationally known figure whose contributions reflect our university's values. These events were always at capacity.

To move forward with the campaign, I proceeded on three fronts. First, in conjunction with our Vice Chancellor of University Relations, Donna Murphy, I brought in a consulting firm to assess our readiness for a campaign. They provided information on how we needed to beef up our development staff to run a successful campaign and how much they thought we would be able to raise. They suggested a campaign goal between 250 and 300 million dollars, so I immediately settled on the $300 million goal.

Secondly, I worked to gain campus buy-in to the idea of a campaign. I discussed it at virtually all events I spoke at. When I went around and visited every department on campus, I spoke about the financial picture of the campus and the need to run a successful campaign. I also emphasized that the faculty themselves would be a key component of our fundraising efforts. Some departments did push back on these ideas, but most were receptive. In fact, we ended up creating fundraising training workshops for faculty and staff, and these were very well received. Two years later, when I again went around and visited individual departments, I was gratified to see how many departments had established development committees and were putting on events for potential donors.

Thirdly, I wanted to establish a set of priorities for our fundraising. We started by asking every department, unit, and division on campus to send us their priorities for funding. Not surprisingly, we got back their wish lists totaling around $3 billion. I needed to extract from this several pillars, around which the campaign would be organized at the campus level. This was not easy, as I wanted to be as inclusive as possible, even though I knew that units on campus would have their own priorities. I am very grateful that when I created a list of pillars for the campaign, a group of our Foundation Board members took me to dinner to criticize the ideas I'd put forward. So I listened to their advice and with the help of my Provost, Alison Galloway, rewrote the list of campus pillars so that the Foundation would be more enthusiastic about the campaign. This was essential because instead of forming a separate campaign committee, we used our UCSC Foundation fundraising committee as our campaign committee.

Typically, fundraising campaigns begin with a silent phase, where the campaign is widely known but not formally announced, and a public phase where hopefully the campaign is well known. I decided that as this was our first comprehensive campaign, we should go public when we'd raised half of our $300 million goal. I wanted to announce the campaign in conjunction with our Founders Day celebration in the fall, so I held an event in the spring to encourage all of our development staff to accelerate our efforts so we could reach $150 million by the fall. We barely made it. During the morning, just before our formal announcement at a luncheon, I was literally on the phone with donors to raise the last 2 million dollars – and it worked! We had invited UC President Janet Napolitano and many community leaders to our announcement event, and it went off without a hitch.

I wanted to bring in a firm to handle our publicity during the public phase of the campaign. We interviewed several such companies with experience in higher education, and I was completely unimpressed. Each of them presented possible approaches that were so generic that they could have described a hundred universities. I was looking for something unique to our campus. So, we hired a New York firm, Fly Communications, which was run by a UCSC alum and had done excellent work for our social sciences division. They provided several options for a tagline for the campaign, and I chose "The Original Authority on Questioning Authority." I liked it because it recognized some of the groundbreaking work being done on campus, although others saw it as recognizing student protests, which have always been a part of UCSC's DNA. In any case, people either loved it or hated it, and as far as I was concerned that meant it was getting a lot of attention, which is what we wanted.

During the campaign, I attended perhaps several hundred events associated with the campaign. I traveled many times to New York and other cities to meet with alumni and donors. I was told many times by donors how well such visits were received. The campus also invested in development officers in Los Angeles, San Francisco, and Silicon Valley.

The campaign was a tremendous success. I decided to end the campaign six months earlier than planned as we had already raised more than $335 million, thereby exceeding our goal. More than two-thirds of the campaign's donors had never given to the campus before. We had raised funds to build a building, support programs such as our Genomics Institute, support needy students, and develop our quarry into an event center, among many other things. I am particularly proud that we doubled the number of endowed chairs on campus and that we endowed our environmental college, which will be henceforth called Rachel Carson College. As an added benefit of the campaign, our fundraising after the campaign had finished was double what it had been before the campaign. Clearly, these efforts will have a lasting effect on the campus.

Yes, Chancellors Do Have an Afterlife

After serving for thirteen years as the UC Santa Cruz chancellor, I came to believe that the campus deserved to have new vigorous leadership as I was feeling rather burned out. I felt that unless I could see these projects through, we needed a new chancellor to complete the LRDP and to successfully mount the next campaign. So I retired from the university, knowing that I would continue to update my books and start some interesting research projects.

I was also serving on several nonprofit boards, which I continued. I'd served for many years as the chair or vice chair of the board of the California Association for Research in Astronomy, which operates the Keck telescopes in Hawaii for UC and Caltech. Some years earlier, then Lt. Governor Gavin Newsom had appointed me to the board of the California Institute for Regenerative Medicine (the California stem cell board). I planned to continue that work since I was so impressed by the impact the Institute was having in developing innovative new treatments for diseases. As I was retiring, I was also asked to be one of the UC members of the board of the American University of Armenia. I was amused to be told that I would represent a youth movement among the UC trustees.

As I was gearing up to retire, I learned from a friend that Berkeley's Center for Studies in Higher Education (CSHE) was searching for a new director. That position had been vacant for two years. I had long been interested in the work being done at CSHE, so I applied and was appointed as the director of this renowned center. Even though I describe this as my first failed retirement, I've been absolutely delighted to lead the center. CSHE basically does two things. We do a lot of research on higher education, including our leadership in collecting and analyzing student survey data from universities around the world. We are also involved in policy analysis on a broad range of higher education issues, regularly publishing a series of online articles, and providing seminars and panel discussions to educate university communities on key issues facing higher education. We also run a program called the Gardner Seminar aimed at Ph.D. students from any department and any UC campus doing dissertations on higher education. Working with those students has been a joy.

Another program that CSHE has run for more than a decade is the Executive Leadership Academy (ELA). Still directed by its founder, Josie Baltodano, the ELA provides training for higher education leaders and potential leaders to further their careers in the multicultural environments of today's universities. Among its roughly 500 graduates, the ELA has trained deans, vice presidents, presidents, and system chancellors. I have truly enjoyed teaching in that program since joining CSHE.

One day, Josie came to me with a new idea. She had been speaking with a mutual friend, Mary Croughan, now the Provost at UC Davis, and Mary had spoken of how the two of us had met almost monthly for breakfast in Oakland for nearly a decade. She said these conversations were very helpful in advancing her career. So Josie suggested we start a new online program, called Breakfast with George, where I would mentor administrators whose next career step could be a university presidency. This would be the next step in training after ELA for participants. Despite my healthy skepticism, Josie was confident there would be enough willing participants in the program. She was right. In our first year, we had five cohorts of participants in Breakfast with George totaling 32 people. Several of them have already become university presidents, and I've greatly enjoyed participating in this endeavor.

So, even after retirement, I feel that I've been able to follow the principles that have governed my work from the beginning. I try to ensure that besides being of the highest quality, my work has a definite, meaningful impact and makes a real difference in people's lives. What more could I ask?

Chapter Questions

1 When he became Chancellor, Blumenthal had relatively little administrative experience. Do you think that impeded success? More generally, what are the attributes one should seek in a potential chancellor or president?
2 To what extent do you think the close working relationship Blumenthal developed with faculty and staff leadership before becoming chancellor contributed to his success? Do you think university leaders must have the experience of being faculty members?
3 This chapter discusses several major efforts to diversify the faculty and students at the university. Do you think other initiatives might have provided greater success? More generally, given the ban on affirmative action in US university admissions, what other initiatives should universities pursue to increase diversity?
4 It is clear that encouraging philanthropy and increasing funding from the state were major and time-consuming initiatives from the chancellor. In view of decreasing state spending per student at public universities and increasing tuition at both public and private universities, how can leaders ensure quality, access, and affordability at their universities? Is there another funding model that might work for higher education?

Notes

1 The satellite was launched in Kenya.
2 In those days, departments at UCSC were called boards of studies.
3 Originally, the college was called College VII.
4 Note that during that late afternoon earthquake, I was stuck alone in the elevator within that building for 45 minutes, an experience that felt like being caught in a milk shake machine. Later, when I got home, I told my wife that I had the best excuse she's ever heard for being late to dinner.

5 Preponderance of the evidence for grievances and clear and convincing evidence for faculty discipline and early termination.
6 Unlike most UC campuses, Santa Cruz does not have a representative assembly.
7 This may have disappointed those who had placed bets on what I would do if the Senate refused.
8 The California Maritime Academy
9 This is after accounting for money held back for student aid, the so-called return-to-aid.
10 Note that besides my chancellor's cabinet, this is the only committee I personally chaired.

2
HISPANIC CULTURE, FAITH, AND LEADERSHIP

A University President's Path from Philanthropy to Promoting Diversity and Inclusivity

Josefina Castillo Baltodano

Abstract

Josefina Castillo Baltodano exemplifies the leader who reconciles service above self that is rooted in family, creating opportunities and lessons learned from experiences. Merging her passions for social justice, advancing diversity, and the greater good with philanthropic and organizational skills learned from both volunteer and career fundraising, her story reveals the importance of finding joy, purpose, and meaning whatever the task. Family values and love rooted in strong religious spirituality led her to the presidency of a Catholic liberal arts college which she transitioned to a university. Her dedication to building structures for transformative change resulted in the founding and development of the Executive Leadership Academy at UC Berkeley's Center for the Studies in Higher Education under the Goldman School of Public Policy. Baltodano served at UC Berkeley for over 30 years, focusing not only on the big picture and goals but also on individuals, and their perceptions of and roles in said projects. Guiding principles that inform her personal and professional lives are based on understanding the possibilities and responsibilities of transformative leadership, reminding the reader that "a commitment to social justice is the lifeblood of humanity."

Early Life of Josefina Castillo Baltodano

I was born in San Antonio, Texas, but grew up in a predominantly white, working-class neighborhood in the Midwest - Racine, Wisconsin, to be exact. My parents were very proud of their Mexican-American heritage and instilled that same pride in me. Every year we would return to Texas for the summer, so part of me also feels like a Texan. We would visit with our relatives, and my father would always tell me that, as the oldest of nine, I was in charge of my siblings. My parents made it clear that, as the eldest, it was my responsibility to care for my siblings and ensure that they succeeded in life. To this day, I feel a sense of responsibility to ensure that my brothers and sisters know that I am here for them.

Although my father worked in a factory for all of his life, his dream was to save up enough money to open his little restaurant café in downtown Racine when he retired, which he accomplished. His second love, after his family, was cooking. My father made the best tacos I have ever had, and I was lucky to have learned his secret spice recipe. After all nine of us were in school, my mother completed high school and then went on to graduate from a community college with a degree in accounting. Ironically enough, from there she became an instructor of English for speakers of other languages, taught at a technical college, and retired after several years. My parents' philosophy was to study hard, work hard, get a good job – and you'll be rewarded. That really fell in line with the Midwestern moral code of working hard and helping your neighbors. Both of my parents were very community-minded and believed strongly in supporting the community. My father's lifelong message was always to share what you have because there will always be those less fortunate than you. He always reminded me that the person to the left of me and the person to the right of me should be better people for having met me. My parents believed in a Christ-centered family and, although we were Catholic, we attended all the activities of the First Church of God because it was just down the street to our house. However, we did attend mass at the Catholic church every Sunday.

Strikes were routine at the factory where he worked, so our finances were often affected. The Good Fellows, a foundation in the city of Racine, made sure that food baskets were always delivered to our doorstep for Thanksgiving and Christmas. They would drop off toys for the Christmas holiday as well. So, the value of philanthropy was instilled in me from the very beginning – I could see that others were giving to us and therefore we would give to others when we could as well. This idea of reciprocal philanthropy has stayed with me ever since I was a little girl.

Contributing to the greater good was so important that I began practicing this myself as a young teenager. When I was 15, I decided to get a job to earn money for school supplies and extras. A new store called Kohls had opened up in my hometown. You had to be 16 to work there, but it was just a few months before my 16th birthday, so I still went in for an interview. I got the job – a union job that paid a very good salary – and started in the bakery department. Every week, my father would drive me to work and pick me up at the end of my shift. And on every payday, I would hand over my entire check to my father and he would use it to buy groceries for the family that week. I would tell him that I was trying to save some of the money for college and my future, but I was also aware that my family needed the funds, and that's what came first.

A defining moment from my childhood that most distinctly shaped my character took place when I was in kindergarten. I was five years old and I could only really speak Spanish; English was my second language, so I knew a little, but not much at all. I was determined to make an impression on my classmates and show them that I was still worthy of notice even if I couldn't speak English. I was going to wear the prettiest, fluffiest dress that anyone had ever seen. So, my mother made me a stunning yellow, fluffy dress with lots of ruffles to wear to my kindergarten beginning-of-the-year party. When I woke up that day, there was a terrible thunderstorm outside. My mother and I proceeded to walk down to the bus stop, through the buckets of rain that were pouring down on us. Just as I was getting ready to board the bus, I fell directly into a mud puddle that was right in front of the school bus, and the bus drove away without me. When I stood up, my beautiful dress was covered in mud and ruined. I was soaking wet and very upset. My mother took me back home and I didn't think I was going to make it to my class party. I was stoic about it and I told my mom that we somehow needed to find a way to get me to school. But my mother didn't have a license, so that was impossible.

With my hands on my hips, I told her that from this day forward, I would never be left behind again in my life. From that point on, I was very competitive and always wanted to be the best, whether I was in school or on the playground, in sports or contests. This determination never to be left behind has stayed with me my entire life.

It surfaced again several years later when I was in middle school. I'd fallen madly and passionately in love with English history. There were huge volumes of English History books that contained information about all the dynasties that I enjoyed reading. So I would go to the library and fill up my backpack with massive volumes of English history that described all the royal dynasties and take them home to read. I would hide under my bed or in my closet with my little flashlight and read the texts that I had brought home. I would finish the book and go back to the library the next day to get the next volumes to continue my reading. I was such an avid reader that the library would bring in books for me from the other branches because I'd read everything my branch had on the shelves.

Sometimes my mother would tell me to stop reading and help out around the house. Of course, I wanted to continue reading, so I would fib a little and tell her that I couldn't help with the dishes or anything else because this reading was my homework for school. So she allowed me to continue my reading and got out of doing any chores. Later, during a parent-teacher conference, my mother asked my teacher, "Why do you give Josie so much homework? Those books you keep sending home with her are huge and very long." My teacher responded, "Oh, that's not Josie's homework, she does that all on her own! She loves reading English history, and, in fact, she just had a test and is reading at a college level!" To this day, I am confident that my ability to pay attention to detail, while at the same time seeing the big picture, stems from my early reading habits.

Education Background

I was blessed to go to a brand-new elementary school and middle school, under the Wisconsin State Educational System, which had been ranked one of the top public school systems in the country. Being enrolled in schools that had brand-new equipment, current books, and teachers who were excited to teach really made a significant difference in my early education. However, these schools weren't very diverse regarding the student body or faculty population. Growing up and not seeing other children or teachers in the classroom who looked like me opened a void in my life; it wasn't until high school, which was very diverse, that I began to have a deep appreciation for the value and importance of diversity and inclusion.

My high school counselor told me that I would never be able to go to college because I didn't have the intelligence or the money to attend. This experience undermined my confidence, especially with all my friends talking about the colleges they were applying to and planning to attend. At the same time, I was fortunate to have a caring social sciences teacher, Mr. Zerine, who believed in me. (He introduced our entire class to musicals by taking us on a field trip to Chicago to watch a live production of "The Fantasticks." From that day forward, musicals became a passion and love of mine.) This teacher's positive support encouraged me to continue to seek out funding for college. So, because I was determined never to be left behind, I went with a friend to the local recruitment office for the armed forces. There, I connected with a recruitment officer who assured me that they would cover the cost of my education after my tour of duty to Vietnam. I signed up for the Air Force in June 1966; the officer told me they would be sending me the final documents to sign in the mail. I felt this was an insurance policy that would allow me to attend college. While I was waiting to hear if I had been accepted into the Air Force, a friend of mine told me about financial aid grants and informed me that I could qualify. So I decided to sign up for financial aid and apply for admission to the University of Wisconsin. As with many Latin families, my parents were very proud that I was going into the Air Force and were bragging about it to our family and their friends. The same day that my final papers came in from the Air Force, I also received a letter of acceptance from the University of Wisconsin to go to school with a full scholarship. I had to decide between joining the Air Force or going to school full-time. I decided to take the scholarship offer because I could start going to school right away, whereas if I went into the Air Force, my schooling would be postponed until after I returned from my first tour. I started my undergraduate education at the University of Wisconsin that fall semester.

Everyone, including me, was amazed at how good my grades were in college – but that was because I was afraid that if I didn't do well, they might take away the scholarship and I wouldn't be able to continue my education. College was a wonderful experience. I joined a sorority and attended many events on campus and also had part-time jobs to help with finances. One of my favorite work-study jobs was in the Admissions Office. I enjoyed working with the new students who were just coming to campus and quickly became aware that there wasn't much diversity among the students being admitted. I became quite a leader on campus as well, participating in campus clubs and various other leadership activities. I co-founded a club of diverse students to create a recruitment plan to bring more underrepresented students onto the campus. We all gathered together and went to the chancellor at the time to ask for some money so we could pay our student recruiters. Campus leadership denied our request, so we went to the governor for funds to help support our initiative. The governor called the chancellor and told him to give our club the recruitment we needed. He also said that he would send the campus more money because we were on to something. And when I graduated, the chancellor came up to me and told me, "Josie, wherever you want to go in the country for law school, you let me know. I will be there for you."

As I mentioned before, since getting my first job at 16 years old, I always worked while going to school. It was very important to me that I had the funds needed to be able to go to school, so work and school naturally went hand in hand. When I was in college, my sorority friends would always tell me, "Just marry a lawyer and you'll be fine" and "just marry a lawyer and you'll have money." And coming from a disadvantaged family, I didn't grow up with a lot of extra money. So I thought, "Wait a minute... why should I marry the lawyer? I'll be the lawyer!" And when I told my friends this, they laughed and said, "Josie it's not that easy." But I said "Yes, it is; I can do it. Why should I worry about finding the right lawyer to marry? I'll become the lawyer, and then I won't have to worry about money." Because I wanted to grow up and become a philanthropist, that was my goal. And if I was going to give money away to people who needed it, I needed a way to make money and lots of it. Finally, I have always had a strong passion for social justice, and some of my professors convinced me that I had what it took to be a compelling lawyer and persuade others to share my social justice convictions. So with the understanding that I could make a difference and obtain the financial stability necessary to fulfill my dream of becoming a philanthropist, I decided to go to law school.

When I was getting ready to graduate from my undergraduate university, I applied and was accepted into three different law schools in the Midwest. I graduated mid-year and traveled to California for a brief vacation. While I was there, I met Carlos and fell madly in love. He was from California and had graduated from UC Berkeley with an architecture degree and a master's degree in city and regional planning. Hence, he was very much committed to staying in the state and the Bay Area. We got engaged fairly quickly and began thinking about our future together, trying to plan out our next steps. When it came time to decide what to do next, Carlos suggested that I apply to law schools in California instead of going back to Wisconsin, and that's what I tried to do. However, many of the law schools had already closed their applications for the year; I was interested in applying to Stanford, Berkeley, and Hastings (as of January 1, 2023, now University of California College of the Law, San Francisco), but none of them were accepting applications for the upcoming year. So, I was finding myself in a difficult position.

One night when Carlos and I were out having dinner, I ended up having a very serendipitous meeting with a young man who was very interested in me. We started talking and he asked me some questions, among them who I was and what I was doing in terms of school. It then turned out he was on the admissions committee of Hastings. He proceeded to explain that most of their applicants of color were local and that I was a unique case, being a Latina from the Midwest. He was impressed with my overall grades and test scores and said he would go to the dean of the law school and see if he might be willing to accept a late application from me. I was then introduced to the dean, who informed me there were still spaces available in the law school for low-income students who qualified for the Educational Opportunity Program.

These reserved spaces were very special, he said, and they preferred to select graduates who would be staying in the area and contributing back to the community. He was initially hesitant to accept me for fear that I would return to the Midwest after earning my degree. So I made my case to him and explained how I wanted to stay in California and make it my new home with my future husband, who was very much a Californian at heart. The dean was convinced and admitted me into the freshman class at the University of California, Hastings College of the Law. I'm happy to say that I kept my word and am still in California 49 years later.

My goal was to be community-minded, have a family, and create a successful career. One quote that has stuck with me was from Betty Friedan: "You can have it all, you just can't have it all at one time." My theory is that you can do it all, you just have to be very diligent in scheduling and managing your time. It's often assumed that the mother has to maintain the household, doing all the cleaning and cooking, etc. on her own. And sometimes women put that pressure on themselves, to maintain the household, take care of children, and develop a successful career. However, that doesn't have to be the case. I had a wonderful husband who was willing and able to devote his time to the children. I wanted to give my daughters the best opportunities possible, and everything I didn't have as a child, so they went to private schools and were involved with many extracurricular activities. All three of my daughters attended the Head Royce School in the Bay Area. And since I became a trustee of the school, I was honored to be able to endow a scholarship for future low-income students. I signed them up for everything: from tennis lessons to swim lessons, to golf and ballet, and Carlos was always dedicated to dropping them off and picking them up. I would not have been able to do any of that, as my work was demanding of my time. But marriage is a partnership that thrives with balance and shouldn't be restricted to perceived gender roles.

1980–1998 Developing Programs at UC Berkeley

Special appreciation goes to my husband Carlos for encouraging me to apply to the Equal Educational Opportunity Program/Affirmative Action Coordinator (EOP/AA) position at UC Berkeley because he knew how much I cared about social justice. I started at Berkeley in 1980 as the Coordinator of the EOP and was later promoted to the Assistant Director of the Student Learning Center and Director of the Summer Bridge Program. After a few years, I decided that I wanted to move up to department director. You have to have fundraising experience to become a director, and since Berkeley was preparing to launch its first-ever capital campaign, I decided that it was the perfect time to learn. I got involved by talking to the chancellor at the time, Michael Heyman, who agreed that his office would underwrite my training and give my department the money to cover my salary for a year. I did this so I could go off and train with the new vice chancellor for university relations, Kurt Simic, to learn how to raise money from the ground up. The campus had sent out a press release that said he was one of the top fundraisers in the country. Since he was the best, I wanted to learn from him. Why would the chancellor do this? In our discussion, I had told him that he was my role model, that I wanted to raise money and teach law and criminal justice at UCB, and that ultimately, I wanted to become a president or chancellor of a university. He saw my drive and commitment and was willing to take a chance on me. So, for one year, I went off to study from the new vice chancellor on how to create and run a capital campaign, including every aspect of fundraising from planned giving to class campaigns (or alumni giving). Berkeley's "Keeping the Promise" campaign ultimately raised $469 million. This first fundraising effort built a very strong foundation for future campaigns. Since then, Berkeley has gone on to run several very successful capital campaigns that have raised billions of dollars for the campus. From that experience, I learned that you can make a significant impact on an institution by raising money for student, faculty, and staff needs.

What really stuck with me about this training was the value of treating each donor as a special individual – every contribution is significant regardless of the amount. I remember coming into the office in the mornings and seeing a huge stack of thank-you cards on the vice chancellor's desk. He would be working away, hand-writing notes to each donor and signing the cards individually. Every day brought a new lesson plan on how to cover every single aspect of fundraising. One of the most rewarding times I have spent at Berkeley was working in that office and being paid to learn how to raise money. And as I was learning, I was teaching others how to raise money. When I returned to the student learning center at Berkeley, I went back to writing grants for my programs.

I was given the opportunity to become a member of the board of the public broadcasting system in San Francisco, KQED. I was also given the opportunity to serve as a trustee for the SF ballet. Both of these positions gave me the chance to use my newly developed fundraising skills.

Lessons and Learning from Mentors

While I was on the board of KQED, I was mentored by four outstanding philanthropists who were very familiar and very successful with fundraising. This group of philanthropists became my circle of friends and mentors at a time when KQED was going into its first capital campaign. This was an opening to put what I had learned from Berkeley to the test. I worked on two campaigns that had large endowment goals, so it was the perfect opportunity to apply my skills with continued guidance and support on how to do it and do it right from the right people. One of the most important aspects of fundraising, I learned, was the value of giving money first when you are in a campaign, so that you can ask others to join you. It was fun! I continued writing grants to bring in federal grant money and learned a lot.

Soon I was asked to join the Mills College board, and that is when my life changed forever. At this point, I was already a very accomplished fundraiser. Mills is located in Oakland, across the bay from San Francisco. After serving as a trustee for the college for approximately nine years, Janet

Holmgren, the president at the time, told me that it was obvious I needed to become a president too, because I kept trying to run Mills, jumping in to help with any issue or problem that arose. I was told by Jan that I was a natural leader and that I should consider moving on from Berkeley and becoming "the big fish in a small pond," which is exactly what I did.

1998–2006 Serving at John F. Kennedy University and Alliant International University

Soon after, Dr. Holmgren introduced me to Charles E. Glasser, who was the president of John F. Kennedy University in Pleasant Hill, California. At that time, JFK was running a campaign to raise money for a new building. During one of our early conversations, President Glasser encouraged me to leave Berkeley after 18 years and go work with him to serve as his vice president of research and the dean of the school of management. I didn't have any business or management experience, but I could teach strategic planning and business law with my background. I was very eager to learn and, in the meantime, I would help him raise the money necessary for the new building. So, in 1998 I left Berkeley and joined the leadership team at John F. Kennedy University. While I served there, I had a partnership with the president that was made in heaven. We accomplished many things in that time, including finishing up the campaign for the new building. I spent four years at JFK, eventually earning the position of vice president for university relations and dean of development. My successes, especially the development and fundraising work I did, were spreading through word of mouth by then. That's what led the president of Alliant International University in San Francisco to reach out to me and offer a new, exciting opportunity. She said, "You've done what you said you would do for the president at JFK, would you come help me now raise money and help me with strategic planning?" By that time, I had been teaching strategic planning for the School of Management at JFK and loved it. So, I happily accepted her offer and began my service as the executive vice president for strategic planning and advancement at Alliant. During my four years at Alliant, I was blessed to be able to count on President Jan and President Charles to continue with lessons on how to serve as a successful university president someday.

Giving Back to the Community – The Women's Office, American Council on Education

While I was serving at these various institutions, I had also been simultaneously involved with the Office of Women for the American

Council on Education, now known as the ACE Women's Network. I had been training many of the women in those programs on how to raise money and how to develop and secure grants, using all I had learned at Berkeley and from my mentors at KQED. Now I turned around and started teaching other women how to do it. I believe this experience was also key for my development; learning about fundraising as a student and then teaching fundraising strengthened my understanding and knowledge of fundraising even further. ACE was very important to me and my career aspirations because it had a variety of wonderful programs for women who were interested in becoming presidents and provosts. The workshops and networking I received through ACE were not only beneficial to me; the work I did there allowed me to help women and give back to others, which made it very special. At this time, my colleagues at the Women's Office were extremely supportive of my career advancement and began nominating me for presidential positions. Soon after, I started getting calls from search firms that were interested in me. A few inquiries came from private institutions, but most of the presidential positions I was being considered for were public ones. And while I am very supportive of public universities, I felt called to lead a Catholic university. As a lifelong, devout Catholic, the mission of Catholic colleges and universities aligns very well with my values, so I was confident that one of these institutions would be the best fit for me. So, I took matters into my own hands and began seeking out opportunities at Catholic universities.

2006–2009 Transforming a College into a University (Marian University)

Search firms were interested in me because, by this time, I had experience with 10 very successful fundraising campaigns, including one at Mills College. In addition to that, I was experienced as what you would call a "builder." There are different types of leaders in higher education; some leaders are sustainers and others are builders. I enjoyed all the elements of being a builder because you can nurture something from the ground up and incorporate your passion into taking it forward. Sometimes people are not comfortable moving too fast, so I would have to slow down, be thoughtful about plans to promote, and not push people too quickly. I had to learn how to establish measurable, reasonable, and achievable timelines and deadlines because these are extremely important to builders.

The biggest difficulty was motivating and inspiring people to move with me. I learned that the best way to do that was to spend quality time with each person. And when you spend quality time listening to them, it's much easier to get everyone to move forward together, because you can identify their strengths and passions. The book *From Good to Great* had a big impact on me and made me a fan of getting the right people on the bus. When I would gather my teams, I was always interested in people's volunteer work because through that you can see how serious they are – it's important to see what individuals do when they aren't getting paid to do it.

I was a builder at UC Berkeley when I created the Academic Achievement Division by bringing in grants to fund a new division, and again at JFK by completely transforming the School of Management, and at Alliant through successful fundraising. When it came time for me to decide where to go to become a president, my natural tendency was to select an opportunity to make a difference – a place where I could raise money, know I was needed, and there was a calling for me. I felt my calling was to lead a catholic university because of my faith and my appreciation for the deep commitment of religious universities to social justice. I wanted a school where I could apply my executive skills and whose mission I believed in and could follow.

I had two opportunities at the time – it became clear to me that I had to choose between serving as a chancellor at one of the University of Wisconsin campuses or serving as president of Marian College. Marian College was a Catholic institution in Wisconsin, my home state where I grew up, so that opportunity was very attractive to me. Marian wanted to make the transition from a college to a university, and they were looking for a president to lead that effort. The feat of turning a college into a university was also very attractive to me because I wanted the opportunity to help them with that transformation. So, I accepted the presidency at Marian College with a three-year contract agreement and went off to work with the Congregation of Sisters of St. Agnes.

I had a memorable and rewarding experience because the Congregation of Sisters of St. Agnes was very supportive of my tenure. During my three years in service, we were able to meet the goal and turn the college into a university. However, there were some difficulties that I experienced in my personal life that went along with my presidency that made it impossible for me to stay beyond the three-year contract.

When I moved back to Wisconsin to serve at Marian, I had already been married for thirty-three years and had three daughters. The youngest had just started college, so all three girls were adults when I started my presidency. My husband had decided to stay in California so that he could continue to be close to our daughters; one had just started at UC Santa Barbara and the other was a junior at the University of Southern California. So, while I was serving at Marian, we were dealing with a long-distance marriage, which became very difficult at times. I often felt very lonely and found it hard to deal with. My eldest daughter, who was a recent MBA graduate, would come visit me and stay with me in Wisconsin for a few months to try to make things a little easier for me. Towards the end of my contract, I decided it was time for me to return to UC Berkeley.

My ultimate points of pride while serving as president of Marian were as follows:

- In May 2008, Marian College became Marian University, one year ahead of the Strategic Plan schedule.
- Created five new schools and hired founding deans, one year ahead of the Strategic Plan schedule.
- Created an office of equity and inclusion and hired a founding vice president for equity and inclusion.
- Created an 8-point diversity program that resulted in substantial activity. The diversity program had a plan that included diversifying the board; creating an office for inclusion and diversity; and focusing on recruitment, retention, and graduation of all students, but particularly of students from diverse backgrounds.

While serving as President of Marian, in 2008, I was called to serve as an Associate of the Congregation of the Sisters of St. Agnes. I continued to serve as an associate for the congregation until 2022, which was a very important part of my life and who I am. My mission work has been around raising and donating money for hospitals in the Bay Area, including Alta Bates and the Alameda Health System Foundation. I also had the pleasure of raising money for the chapel, which was renamed the reflection room, at the Alameda Health System Highland Hospital in Oakland. Furthermore, as an associate, I was often called upon to join the sisters in prayer for those sick, injured, or in special need. I believe in the power of prayer, and, in addition to my prayers with the sisters, I make it a priority to find time each day to pray for others in need.

Christ and prayer are both very important parts of daily life. Each morning, I wake up and start my day with meditation and a prayer of thanks. It is very important to me to give thanks to God for my life and all the blessings he has bestowed upon me. I ask him to guide me to those who need the help and assistance that I might be able to offer them. The gifts that are bestowed upon you from the Lord should be shared with all so that they too can feel the joy that comes from his blessings. Equally important to my morning prayers are my evening prayers. Each night I pray with my daughter who lives with me. Our nightly prayers also center around appreciation and gratitude for the day. We also use that time to reflect on what we were able to do that day to help others live a better life. Because if we consider prayer to be the first step, action, then, would be the second step. Prayer has been very helpful to me, including conceptualizing action plans that help me identify ways to give back to the community and continue to advocate for social justice and equity.

2010 to present: Establishing a Transformative Development Program at UC Berkeley

When I returned to Berkeley after retiring from Marian, it was natural for me to go back to teaching law and criminal justice in the Ethnic Studies Department, which I could have done. However, I had a new idea and vision: to build a brand-new executive academy unlike any other in the country. I was familiar with what other leadership programs typically offered, as I had attended various development programs throughout the country. I recognized that they were missing the critical element of how to teach people all about diversity and the beauty of teaching in a multicultural and global environment. I attended a conference in 2010, which was sponsored by the American Association of Hispanics in Higher Education, Inc. (AAHHE), for Hispanic presidents throughout the country, at the invitation of Louis Olivas, the President of AAHHE. He wanted to bring us together to discuss ideas as to how he could help advance more Latinos into top executive positions. At that conference, I recommended that AAHHE create a program to support the concept of increasing diversity in higher education administration. Since I had established myself at UC Berkeley, having served there for 18 years, I trusted that Berkeley would be the ideal place to host this new diversity program. At that time, I went to Judson King, the Director of the Center for Studies in Higher Education at UC Berkeley, with my vision of a new and inclusive leadership academy that would be created in collaboration with AAHHE. The Director was very responsive and supportive of my new initiative, but informed me that the Center didn't have any money to sponsor the new program financially. I decided to reach out and gather some founding faculty[1] members for the program who believed in the mission so much that they were willing to volunteer their time and teach in the program that first year. And so, in 2011, ELA was born. For the first three years, the Executive Leadership Academy was presented in collaboration with AAHHE.

Knowing the importance of inclusivity, the ELA is very intentional in its recruitment of Fellows and Faculty, making use of, what we like to call, the "mirror impact." Since the start of the program, the priority has been to select 1/3 of Fellows from emerging executives, 1/3 from executives, and 1/3 from senior executives, all while maintaining a balance between genders and ethnicity as well. Emerging executives see themselves mirrored in executives, executives see themselves mirrored in senior executives, and senior executives see themselves mirrored in Faculty, which includes current or retired Presidents or Chancellors of institutions. The objective is to allow Fellows to mentor each other and for the faculty to serve as role models and mentors. Furthermore, another important aspect of this program is extensive mentorship that continues long after the Fellows have graduated from the program. We are fully invested in our Fellows and Alumni and offer support in various ways. We will coach the alums when they are in a search, submitting letters of recommendation and acting as a reference, among other things.

As of September 2023, 574 Fellows have graduated from the Academy, spanning across 36 states in the US and 10 countries. There have been numerous graduates who have contributed significantly to transforming higher education.

Interest in improving higher education and increasing diversity of students, administrators, and staff is growing around the world. We have seen this interest firsthand, as countries reach out to inquire about hosting their own Executive Leadership Academy program with our partnership. In November 2021, the ELA offered its very first international program in India, at Shiv Nadar University, Delhi NCR. Because of the Covid-19 pandemic, the ELA at Shiv Nadar University was held virtually, on an interactive videoconferencing platform, similar to all ELA programs offered in 2020 and 2021. We were honored to welcome 25 promising leaders from throughout India as the Founding Fellows of this historical program. We were also privileged to include distinguished scholars and executives from Shiv Nadar University in our renowned faculty line-up, which was comprised of 17 experts from the US and India.

In addition to the ELA program, which I administer for two days a week, I also serve as a high-performance executive coach for a major executive coaching firm, Archer-Martin Associates, for the remaining three days of the week. We offer high-performance executive coaching in the following areas: transitional leadership, budget & finance, accreditation, enrollment management, fundraising, board relations, community engagement, and entrepreneurial initiatives. Forty of the clients I have coached have secured positions as chancellor, president, or provost.

Passing the Baton: Advice and Practical Tips

"We become just by performing just actions. We become temperate by performing temperate actions. And we become brave by performing brave actions." – Aristotle

Being an authentic leader is one of the key aspects of being a successful leader. So, it is very important to find a role and an institution whose mission and values align with your own. It's very helpful to sit down and make a list of the values and principles that are most important and impactful to you. There are several values that I follow in my personal and professional life, which I call my fundamental guiding principles:

1 Clear of head, pure of heart
2 Be not afraid
3 Service above self
4 Treasure your moral compass
5 Volunteer work is a true measure of your success in life
6 Appreciative inquiry

Clear of head and pure of heart, to me, means to gather all the facts before making administrative decisions, and to make sure that you lead from the heart. "Be not afraid" are the words of Timothy M. Dolan, who is a cardinal of the Catholic Church and Archbishop of New York, who gave the homily at my presidential inaugural, which means that we must never be afraid to take action against social injustices and to stand up for the principle of social justice throughout our society. Service above self is one of the official mottos of the Rotary Club, and one that I have always lived by. In the context of higher education, service above self means that the mission of the institution we serve should be considered first, and that needs to be our guiding light in making decisions that will benefit the students, staff, faculty, and the community. Treasuring your moral compass serves as a reminder that the decisions we make must always be guided by a strong sense of moral responsibility. As mentioned earlier, volunteer work is extremely important to consider; it is the work that we do as volunteers that is the true measure of our success in life. When you give of yourself to others without expectation of financial remuneration, that is how you grow as a university administrator and as a professional. Appreciative inquiry can be understood as the ability to focus on and understand an individual's positive attributes and strengths. Through cultivating and celebrating those positive strengths, you motivate people to do more than they ever expected to accomplish. And never forget that a commitment to social justice is the lifeblood of humanity.

Discussion Questions

1 How can individuals in leadership roles authentically foster diversity and inclusivity within their institutions, drawing inspiration from the Executive Leadership Academy's guiding principles? How do examples

of these differ when they are "within" an institution versus "within" the larger community?
2 Reflecting on your experiences within your institution, can you identify specific instances where promoting diversity and inclusivity has led to positive outcomes in terms of organizational culture, student success, and community engagement? What examples have been more challenging? How can you leverage these less-than-positive outcomes to be opportunities to pivot or innovate creative solutions?
3 What challenges have you encountered while promoting diversity and inclusivity within your institution, and how have you addressed or overcome these challenges to create a more inclusive and equitable environment?
4 Considering your philanthropic experiences, how has volunteer work and giving back to the community influenced your personal and professional growth? In what ways has it informed your approach to leadership? What are some ways in which, reflecting on the journey discussed in this chapter, you can foster a culture of giving back at your institution?
5 Reflecting on the guiding principle of "service above self" and a commitment to social justice discussed in this chapter, what are some specific examples from your own experiences that speak to how your decisions as a leader have been guided by moral responsibility? How have these decisions impacted the well-being of students, staff, faculty, and the broader community?

Note

1 Founding Faculty Members: William Aguilar, Nancy Archer-Martin, Tomas Arciniega, Patricia Arredondo, Josefina Castillo Baltodano, Daniel Boggan, Diana Cordova, Ding-Jo Currie, Juan Gonzalez, C. Judson King, Loui Olivas, Tessa Martinez Pollack, Carlos Santiago, Ellen Switkes, Rose Tseng, Margaret Wilkerson, and Lloyd Williams

3
THE PATHFINDING ASIAN WOMAN PRESIDENT
Three Lessons for Leading an Inclusive College for the 21st Century

Ding-Jo H. Currie

Abstract

At one point in her story, Ding Jo Currie writes "Leadership matters, and who is leading matters even more. Who we are is how we lead." The story of her journey to the chancellorship and presidency of community colleges, and now distinguished faculty at Cal State Fullerton, is a forte of mindfulness, an example of how to mine one's experiences and culture to bridge and merge with others. Her early experience of living in Francophone Africa where her father worked, gave her a keen sense of the beauty of and sameness in difference. During high school and college in the United States, she "discovered the world of humanity through the liberal arts curriculum ... and began to search for and understand who [she] was as a person with multiple identities" Currie's story models the mindful search for diversity, equity, and inclusion in a beloved democracy and educational system on both the personal and institutional levels. This chapter serves as a primer for all of us who must navigate our own differences and those of others, as Currie melds the value of personal and sociocultural diversity with the significance and necessity of community colleges in our educational landscape.

Where It Began

Water buffalos standing in rice paddies backlit by the morning sun - this was my favorite sight as I walked the narrow path from our house to school. The farmers always began the day's work early. I was only four, but my mother accompanied me for only a couple of days on the walk to preschool. After that, I was on my own. I walked for nearly an hour from the middle of the rice paddies, across the swinging bridge, and into the little town of Shilin to our school.

The swinging bridge, built with suspended blocks of concrete strung together over the roiling river below, was full of holes where chunks had broken off from years of typhoons and the wear and tear of so many daily crossings. Every few steps, I saw the river rushing below me. One misstep and I would fall into the muddy rushing waters. If I even thought about the possibility of falling through every hole and crack as I went, I would have been frozen in place with fear. Turning around and going home was not an option. Mother would not be there anyway, busy with her regular chores to sustain a family. Overcoming the terror of crossing the bridge alone was my only choice, and the sooner the better.

I don't know where the courage came from, but it helped me learn to leap over those obstacles. On a sunny day in the summer, I hopped over those big cracks easily, even joyfully. But on bitterly cold, rainy, and blustery, windy winter days, my body felt paralyzed. The wind pushed me back and forced my eyes shut. I had seen the result of those that had been swallowed by that river. Not pretty, especially if you were the one to discover the floating bodies through the cracks. I learned about conquering fear on that bridge.

In this essay, I document my leadership journey as an Asian female in America. I share my journey from crossing the swinging bridge in Shilin, Taiwan, to serving as president of Coastline Community College and afterward chancellor of the Coast Community College District in California. The leadership lessons I have learned, I hope, will inspire and encourage future leaders working for equity, justice, and inclusion. I elaborate on a few of the many lessons I learned throughout my four-decade career in higher education:

- Lesson 1: Keep Your Soul Intact with Authenticity and Spiritual Anchors
- Lesson 2: Leaders Are Not Born, They Are Made
- Lesson 3: Understand the Importance of Power and Exercise it with Balance

In reliving this journey, I must include a statement of gratitude for all those who led, supported, and believed in me on my leadership journey. My gratitude is in applying their lessons and paying them forward. And I must apologize for the equity gaps I have not yet been able to fill, for the injustices I remained blind to, and for the times my words of inclusion were incongruent with actions that excluded some. Hindsight is always 20/20, and my vision is much clearer, sharper, and more panoramic now. As long as I can still breathe, think, learn, and act, I strive to devote my energy and effort to constructing a new just, equitable, inclusive system that is free of/from racism, classicism, sexism, and oppression.

The Foundation for My Leadership Journey
No One Told Me I Was Brave

No one told me I was brave to walk alone for an hour to and from school. No one told me that conquering the swinging bridge was an accomplishment. No one told me that chopping wood for Mother to cook over the fire was going to teach me life skills that would prove long invaluable.

Those early years of rural country living became life's laboratory where the most profound lessons grounded and anchored me. The river, floods, rice paddies, water buffalos, and farmers were my childhood education, and escaping death from typhoons and other disasters prepared me for the real tests of life. These and other elements became the constructs and preparation for a leadership journey that I could not have imagined then. The freedom to play with fighting crabs in the rice fields, the freedom to use the trees as ladders to climb to heaven, and the freedom to use my bed as my stage to enact every character of plays written in my head, all those carefree moments became my fondest memories of true freedom.

I might have felt free, but my parents did not. Stranded on the island of Taiwan without any support from or connection with our extended families was not what my parents had envisioned as they began to raise a family. Such are the casualties and consequences of the civil war between two political party regimes. "Our home in mainland China is on the other side of this island and we will return there one day," everyone pronounced as I was growing up. I am Chinese and I belong to that huge chunk of land called China across the ocean where I cannot go. The agony of separation due to China's civil war were the stories a young child could not understand but still remembers well. I learned early that war and conflicts have harsh consequences.

Experiencing Diversity in Africa

Before I was ten, my father began traveling abroad and later settled to work in Africa. His fluent French, which he had acquired while growing up in a French Catholic boarding school, served him as a cultural passport when working in French colonized African countries. Reading my father's letters with photos of him with Africans and collecting the colorful postcards and stamps on the envelopes from Africa became my first true hobby. The more than two decades my father worked in Africa, and my own brief time living there, became part of the journey that defined my perception and understanding of the diversity of the world and inspired my later work in justice and equity.

Going to the market in Abidjan, Ivory Coast in West Africa proved an experience far different from the trips to our open markets back home. The colorful vegetables and stinky fish looked and smelled the same, but the laughter, lively interactions, and vibrant energy exhibited by the local Ivorians, the color of their clothes, and the dynamic gestures were very different and fascinated me. The somber and quiet grocery stores operated by the French down the street seemed like a funeral compared to the local market scene. The African women carried the goods they bought on their heads, swinging their hips as they chatted and laughed while walking by our house. I became a curious sociologist observing and figuring out their moves as they passed by, danced to the drums, and took naps rolled up in their grass mats.

Somehow the heat of Africa in the summer was not as warm as the feelings I developed when surrounded by the African people. My first and early cross-cultural experience was stamped by loving a group of pure souls whose living habits and robust lives were so vastly different from mine. Who would know that the simple common love of daily rice and fish became an instant bond? The conclusion of the young sociologist was that Africans are fun-loving, insightful, wholesome, and generous people to a fault and despite the divergent differences, a common bond could still be found. I hated the giant flying cockroaches, but I fell in love with the Africans and their culture, their traditions, their history, an obsession that persists to this day.

Outsider in America

Leaving my friends behind in Taiwan as a teenager to join my father in Africa was not easy. But going to the foreign land of America became the most impactful experience of my young life. Father decided to send my older sister and me, two teenagers, 15 and 19, from Africa to the United States. He had visited America in 1963 and thought this country could offer us rich educational experiences for a better future. That decision altered my destiny and transformed my life. Not knowing much English, I prayed daily for the miracle that I would wake up being fluent in this new language. Much different from the fear I had faced on the swinging bridge, this was a fear of humiliation, of marginalization, of being perceived as dumb and inadequate without command of the language.

Living with my older sister in the inner-city section of Dayton, Ohio, without many resources or parents, mastery of the language, and cultural orientation became the test of a lifetime. Those first years of shocking acculturation were the education my parents never knew I received. Many of my life sessions came from that first studio living quarter my sister and I shared – one of eight such apartments converted from an old single-family house. Poverty, domestic violence, senior abuse, racism, sexism, alcoholism, scopophilia, single-mother struggles, etc. were among the ugly side of life witnessed and experienced contained in that house. That was my real-life education! My academic life at Stiver High School was nothing but normal either. The school's creativity was challenged to design a first-year program for someone like me whom they never had to deal with before. I had Typing class to minimize having to deal with lectures that I wouldn't understand; Boy's Cooking class to follow dummied down instructions; and of course, I soared in Math since all of the classes were simply reviews for me. It was the first time in my life that I felt my "B" grades on the report card were a teacher's pity gift – I couldn't possibly have earned them. The school counselors assured me that I deserved the B's for my effort while I sobbed holding my report card. They couldn't possibly understand how I felt.

A small liberal arts college in north Manchester, Indiana, eventually wanted me to be their student so much so that they offered me a full scholarship for four years.

Navigating the perceptions of being an outsider in a small, rural, white college town became my daily reality. For all I knew, the four Asian international students were probably also the only Asians in the entire town. Yet, at Manchester University, I discovered the world of humanity through the liberal arts curriculum that profoundly influenced my worldview and spiritual development. I began to search for and understand who I was as a person with multiple identities. This search was in contrast to my inculcation into what it meant to be Chinese and "Oriental," the label with which we were tagged. I recall liking the sound of the word Oriental, definitely better than the word on my entry visa identifying me as an "Alien" with an assigned number. I knew I was an outsider trying to figure out if there was room on the inside for me.

The math major, chosen for me by my father, would ameliorate my English language deficiency, he reasoned. Thus, my future would have been quite different if I had not taken a psychology class required for teaching credentials. The subject content dispelled so much mystery about our behaviors and showed how different yet so similar we are as human beings.

I graduated with a double major in math for my father and psychology to take care of my desire to become a psychologist.

Falling in Love in California

Moving to California in 1979 was the beginning of a new chapter for me personally and professionally. It was chosen for me again, not because I sought the sunshine, diversity, culture, or the West Coast lifestyle. I took a job teaching math at a North County San Diego middle school so I could take care of my father, by then hobbled by cancer.

I was the youngest teacher at the school, mistaken as a seventh grader and told to go to stand in the lunch line with the rest of the students. I avoided the teachers' lounge and retreated to my classroom where I felt needed. It didn't take me long to make enough progress with my Latinx students, who had all been told to sit at a separate table previously, that they caught up with work and were ready to move on to algebra. I was on a roll, thrilled by the joy of teaching, and ready to devote myself to teaching math for the rest of my life. My love for working in education started with a handful of Latinx students who had been deemed losers by the prior teacher. I made a difference, and that feeling hooked me.

Good things don't always last. Six months after I started, I was laid off due to the budget impact from the Prop 13 property tax shortfall – last to come and first to go. Any end is always the beginning of something else, though. I answered an ad in the *L.A. Times* for a counselor position at a community college.

What is a community college? Who attends community colleges? I wondered. I knew absolutely nothing except that I could do counseling because by then I had a master's degree in psychology. In the first job interview in 1980, I sold myself on being able to help the influx of Southeast Asian refugees in Long Beach. Even though the word "refugee" differed from the word "alien," I felt like a refugee many times. I was hired.

That was the beginning of an arranged marriage. I have always described my relationship with the community colleges as such. I knew nothing about community colleges and they did not know anything about me! Yet, I slowly fell in love as the years went by. After serving as a counselor and coordinator in the Refugee Assistance Program at Long Beach City College, I went on to become the matriculation coordinator at Saddleback College in 1990, and later in 1997 the vice president of economic and community development at Rio Hondo College before becoming the president of Coastline Community College in 2002, and then chancellor of Coast Community College District.

My aunt was right from her own experience: Love *can* grow in an arranged marriage if you're matched well.

Advancing Equity and Opportunity through California's Community Colleges

I discovered a profound and amazing alignment between a community college's mission of open access and Confucius's philosophy of "有教无类，因材施教" which means "everyone can be educated without discrimination, and we teach differently according to the diverse uniqueness of each person." In contrast to many elite four-year research universities, the community college system welcomes students of all ages, abilities, socioeconomic status, and academic readiness levels.

Community colleges are the democratic beacon of American higher education and an embodiment of American democracy and the American dream. According to the American Association of Community Colleges, in 2020, nearly half (46%) of all American undergraduate students attended community colleges because the doors are open to a wide range of diverse students, with vast programs including basic developmental courses, career technical training, lower-level courses for associate degrees, and curriculum that is transferable to four-year institutions.

For a significant portion of the US population, whether citizens or new immigrants, community college is the only door open, a destination of choice, or the safehouse for a second or third chance to achieve a college education and reach personal goals. Community colleges seek to equalize and level the playing field. I feel proud to belong to a system that has a distinct purpose and makes an outsized contribution to local communities. Community is the middle name that defines and brands this beautiful American invention. But navigating my career in the California Community College system is a different story. Like so many new immigrants and first-generation college professionals who enter their careers in higher education, there was no GPS for me, no guidebook.

My career in community colleges began on the outside perimeter of Long Beach City College in 1980. The refugee program operated like a micro-college, providing assessment, counseling, instruction, career technical training, job placement, and support in transitioning to college programs. Our goal was to help refugee students restart their lives from ground zero, and become self-sufficient, support them in continuing with their education, and ultimately help them build a career to succeed in their new lives.

I can't think of another higher education institution that exhibits such a zealous spirit in the practice of inclusion. The California Community Colleges accept and provide all that is needed for success to diverse students. For example, many Hmong refugees do not know the written version of their oral language, meaning their college education begins not only with learning English, but also learning to use written language. This amazing spirit of inclusion and equity-minded practice was my first lived experience of the importance and beauty of truly improving the human condition through education and service. Through immersion in this equity- and inclusion-minded system, I hewed many of the lessons that I will share with you.

Lesson 1: Keep Your Soul Intact with Authenticity and Spiritual Anchors
Find Work That Is Congruent with Your Values
Raised in a two-religion family, a Buddhist father and a Catholic mother, I later embraced the Bahá'í Faith, which incorporates the teachings of all major religions. The faith provided the anchors that grounded me with a set of core values congruent to those of community colleges. Whenever I come upon research that shows our work has made a difference, I feel spiritually inspired and rewarded. It is a soulful, purposeful, and necessary vocation. From working with both the internal and external constituencies of the college in the refugee program to coordinating matriculation processes with various sectors of the institution, the word "community" took on a whole different meaning. It's the engine of workforce development and an important bridge to earning baccalaureate degrees.

It's difficult to imagine this country without community colleges, often the *only* choice for too many. The system embodies the principle of equity – we meet you where you are and take you where you want to go. I'm passionate and compassionate about serving the students who represent the mosaic of diversity in America. I believe that to lead effectively, a leader must love the work she's doing, love the teams she works with, and love those she serves. As Mengzi said, "One who is benevolent has no enemy." I feel a deep sense of belonging when I can choose and strive to have a love-based model incorporating the many principles that feed my spirit. I often described my job in the community colleges as a life-transformation occupation.

If not for a pink slip, Long Beach City College might have been my home until I retired. Apparently, human resources alerted the college that all soft-funding program personnel must receive a lay-off notice by certified mail with no prior notification. I was incredulous. *After ten years? Really? So cold and without notice?* The harsh reality that institutions can be sterile and left-brained, devoid of empathy and ignorant of humanistic values, devastated me. Someone at the top of the institution had approved this procedure. With a feeling of betrayal, I vowed that I would never send a pink slip notice in such a way to anyone if I were in charge.

Bad news never is all bad news. My immediate job search turned up good news with more than one job offer from two different community colleges. In 1990, I became the matriculation coordinator at Saddleback College, with the responsibility of coordinating admission, orientation, assessment, counseling, follow-up, and research. I moved from the refugee assistance program on the outer fringes of a community college to the center of operations.

But I was such a novice coming to such a center, engaging instructional faculty, student affairs, and the various administrative areas of the college. There were no navigation systems. There were only real tests of relational ability, emotional intelligence, courageous integrity, and a lot of observing others and leaning into my cultural and spiritual strengths for assurance that my decisions had the clarity of the why and the what.

Create Your Own Authentic Leadership Style

It's difficult to understand how I became a leader when I juxtapose my personality to those of other leaders I have encountered. Many leaders share certain patterns of behaviors that I find difficult to imitate or emulate. I have often found myself at the crossroads between my Eastern cultural values and the dominant Western expectations.

In many of the leadership workshops, participants described me as "warm," "kind," and "nice." While I understood that these were narratives of positive personas, they were nevertheless not deemed characteristics that indicated I was perceived as a leader. My demeanor and behavior did not match others' leadership profiles, even after I began to see the leader in me. Not being confrontational, my vocal qualities, and my identity as an Asian woman became a veil.

Not conforming to Western conventional thinking or the dominant culture's approaches forced me to question whether climbing the career ladder meant that I had to strip off my core beliefs and values at each rung. What is the cost of remaining free and authentic? After being in the United States from teenage to adulthood, I stood at the crossroads of new American socialization intersecting with my past roots. As my poem written a few decades ago below shows, I ultimately found my way forward:

> *I am at the crossroads, must I choose?*
> *I look back, the road's fading away ...*
> *There's no going back.*
>
> *I'm at the crossroads, must I choose?*
> *Let me take the main road, but must I show my ID before you let me go?*
> *Why won't you let me take my mother's gold?*

Leave it behind, you say, or you can't pass.
Will my mother forgive me?
Will there still be honor in me?
I shed the gold and treasures, too, but why won't you let me through?

I'm at the crossroads, must I choose?
Let me take my road, but must I always be so bold?
Be different and go afar, you say,
Why won't you let me be me?
Why won't you accept me?
China doll, Susie Wong, dragon lady, very exotic.
Will you ever accept me?
Will you ever understand me?
I must hold on till I'm old. I can't give up, not now, since I don't know how!

I'm at the crossroads, must I choose?
I know what to do, roads that lead to a loop.
Let me take both, I can uphold.
Like the willow, strong yet soft when the wind blows.

I'm a traveler, to and fro ...
East and West, Never at rest ...
I'm a traveler, to and fro ...
West and East, Finally at ease ... Finally at Peace
I'm both, you see.

I was able to cross that intersection of authenticity and success. The power that came with each rung of the ladder gave me the opportunity to lift that veil to counter the stereotype threats and the freedom to demonstrate my authentic leadership without compromise. The more I leaned into being authentic, the more inner power and freedom I experienced in finding my style of leading.

As I ascended into positions of increasing responsibility, the stakes of integrity and authenticity rose. One of the first tests of my values came when I turned down a dean position, even though the college president who made the offer did everything possible to accommodate my needs with the hope that I would accept the job. On his third call, with teary eyes in front of my young daughter, I turned the job down for the last time. The position would have taken me away from my family and children at night and compromised my balance of work and family. Family came first. Experienced colleagues told me I had just put the nail in the coffin of my career.

The story ultimately did end well despite their predictions of doom. I was able to return to that district later as a president. Being authentic and true to my values is not always the easy road to choose. This was only one small example of many tests. However, staying true to my values has always rendered me an abundance of derivatives in trust, inner peace, and freedom. Leadership matters, and who is leading matters even more. Who we are is how we lead.

My immigrant journey equipped me with a different lens and vision to see the unprecedented challenges on college and university campuses with the influx and emergence of BIPOC students challenges for institutions to ensure their success. The refugee students at Long Beach City College were more than the evidence I needed to forecast our institutional void in awareness, response, and understanding of their needs. Whenever intersecting with such issues confronted by community colleges and higher education system during the recent decades. Those *issues* served as a prelude to the current era of diversity, justice, equity, and inclusion as we witnessed the demographic shifts of students, new emerging BIPOC leaders, and the crack in the open door for diverse faculty and staff. It was the start of an era for higher education and especially the community colleges to note and address the systems' DNA in structural racism, inequities, and exclusion under the umbrella of "multiculturalism." For many, that was the beginning of an end dying on the sword fighting for justice when the word wasn't even overtly used.

Choose Your Battles Wisely

My all-time favorite college president, Dr. Ned Doffoney, is one of those authentic leaders whose path crossed mine when I was at Saddleback College. He stopped me from going to the board to reason with the members when one of them tried to abolish the China study abroad program with the rationale that students must not study in a communist country. When the prejudice does not derive from logic, you cannot use logic to reason out of it. Ned's wise counsel stayed with me, "Choose your battles wisely and don't let yourself die on a hill. The key is to survive until you reach the mountaintop and then ..." you can have your say in every battle.

Ned would know, an African-American male, he served as a college president in the lily-white-flight part of the county. He would know, because being the target of hate incidents on our campus was not his first experience of overt racism but a common occurrence in his life. I learned from Ned, firsthand, how to confront and defy racism, fight it, dismantle it, and most importantly, to survive it first, and thrive later on that mountaintop.

Integrity Is Passing the Mirror Test

Dr. Ned Doffoney again was my guardian angel when he changed my mind about accepting the chancellor's job when I started the position in 2009 as the Interim Chancellor. I told him I was very happy being the President of Coastline and planned to turn down the offer later that afternoon. Without a second to waste, Ned told me I would do no such thing and that at the 2 p.m. meeting with the board chair, I was to accept the position. He proceeded to cite a long list of compelling reasons. I accepted the chancellor job and welcomed the new opportunity to test, challenge, and propel myself to find new frontiers as a leader for a three-college district. Moving from the president to the chancellor role provided an even more panoramic perspective, systemic insights, and ultimate accountability and responsibility when the shields between the chancellor and the board and other presidents are lifted. Instead of one college that I advocated for, it's now three colleges and the district office that I serve as the head of the household for this Coast family. The joy of my expanded impact is surprisingly something that I loved and feared simultaneously.

My chancellor experiences further demonstrated that leadership is both a science and an art. The principles of working with people remain the science regardless of the size of your team and organizational culture, starting with trust and then building unity by upholding justice and being equitable and inclusive. The art is when you integrate your free style into the leadership practice. Amid the economic downfall, I called for unity knowing that if we were together, united, we could confront any challenge. Divided we would surely fall apart. I focused on bringing the three colleges together and emphasizing collaboration instead of competition to overcome external financial threats. When the same academic senate president from one of the three colleges who expressed that she didn't see the point or value of three colleges coming together thanked me for bringing everyone together a year later after having experienced joint planning and working sessions, it was a moment of great validation for me. When your decision may not be popular, choosing to do the right thing is even more critical.

Long ago I was told that the fear of losing your job will keep you from doing the right thing. Instead, be excellent at what you do and jobs will come to you. As a chancellor who reported to a five-member publicly elected board, it became even more important for me to be free from the fear of losing my job to pass the integrity test of upholding my values.

I know I passed my test of integrity when I turned in my resignation to the board nearly three years after accepting the chancellor position. There are some things I simply could not compromise without losing my soul. While elected governing boards are entrusted by the citizens to develop policies and monitor operations, many chancellor colleagues agree with me privately that the crossroads of elected politicians and sound educational policy have often become a toxic or deadly intersection. When public servants are confronted with politics among board members and the threat of not being reelected, I have witnessed the purest intentions contaminated by the forces of the political power dynamics, structure, and system. Locally elected boards are not immune to the political virus that infects our national, state, and local level policy-making governing bodies. Political navigation is one of the chancellor's *must-have* competencies to protect the interests of the students and staff. And having one's own integrity test kit on hand is equally important for one's inner peace. The higher the position, the bigger the tests and the more at stake. I always have a mirror in my office and I passed my own mirror test – I can look at myself in the mirror and accept the woman in the reflection to go home with me. I surprised myself with how easy it was to make this decision to leave. The free agency and fearless spirit saved me once again.

I know how competent and effective I am as a chancellor leading a large organization, but I cannot report to a publicly elected board. Leadership 101, Principle 1: Know thyself. Principle 2: Know when to leave. And Principle 3: After departing, don't look back with regrets. When I do glance back, it will be to savor all the good memories of people and the satisfaction of being on the mountaintop. For a very brief moment only, because there is yet another mountain yonder to climb.

Lesson 2: Leaders Are Not Born, They Are Made

See Your Inner Lioness

Someone shared a graphic image of a kitten sitting in front of a mirror seeing her reflection in the mirror as a majestic lioness. I'm convinced that if the kitten cannot see herself as a majestic lioness in the mirror, someone else has to recognize it for her first. Perhaps that was the case when Dr. Beverly O'Neil, then president of Long Beach City College, sent me to participate in the National Institute for Leadership Development. Founded by one of the early pioneers in the field of women's leadership, Dr. Carolyn Desjardins, NILD is a leadership development program for women in community colleges.

Following Carol Gilligan's work revealing the male-oriented bias of earlier theories of moral development and conflict management, Carolyn researched the uniqueness of women's leadership characteristics. At every NILD session, female community college presidents presented on their work and leadership, shedding light on the unique challenges women face and their strategies to overcome them. I learned about Gilligan's studies regarding the differences between men's and women's perceptions and rationales, and how those differences impact decision-making and ideas about ethical behavior.

Enlightenment on the intersectionality of women and leadership led me to examine the intersectionality of my own identity as a woman, a leader, and an Asian-Chinese immigrant. Among this group of women, I first experienced unconditional acceptance and felt totally embraced. Carolyn took me under her wing and nurtured the leader in me.

Leadership study is a behavioral science, and behavior can be learned, shaped, and changed. Hence, leaders are not born, they are made as I came to understand with Carolyn's enlightenment. I was reminded of the Buddhist principle that everyone can be cultivated to achieve Buddhahood, so can anyone be developed to possess the leadership mindset and practice leadership behaviors. I began to learn more about being a lioness by becoming a student of leadership. If leadership is your chosen journey, then engage in perfecting this craft of leading the academy regardless of your current role. Practice leading from where you are now.

Having a Good Boss Teaches You Quality Leadership

After receiving the pink slip from Long Beach City College, I decided to take the matriculation coordinator position at Saddleback College because I chose Dr. Constance Carroll, president of Saddleback College at the time. We all know that hiring the right people is critical to your leadership success. I believe the reverse is true, too. She chose me and I also chose her since I had more than one job offer.

Constance was well known in the NILD circle. A young African-American female president in the deep south of Orange County – a white-flight destination for escape from Los Angeles – was a huge statement in itself of her talent and leadership. Even though I was several positions removed from reporting to Constance, following and modeling a first-class leader made a difference for me. Now decades later, like the relationship of the master monk and the young disciple in a martial arts film, Constance is still my abbot and I am her little grasshopper forever.

If you find lots of footprints on my back, they came from mentors. Next, I was kicked into the position of vice president of economic and community development at Rio Hondo College. The job announcement was hand-delivered to me by those who understood my passion and believed in my ability. At every zig-zag along my leadership journey, I was mentored, sponsored, and championed by many. Mentors saw things that I couldn't; sponsors mentioned my name to the right people at the right time; and my champions were like fans who constantly showed up to cheer me on. Being involved with leadership programs early on in my career was like having a secret key to a hidden passage that led to a room full of heroes and heroines. They noticed me and guided my way.

I am forever grateful to one of my mentors, Dr. Bill Vega, the chancellor who gave me the opportunity to prove my leadership in a presidency. I did prove, not to others as much as to myself, that staying true to who I am, not throwing away my family heirlooms and faith-based treasures along the way, was the right decision. Bill modeled, for the first time in my experience with a boss, how he supported me unconditionally to be authentic to myself and to let that guide my leadership navigation.

When I wanted to break past practice and not automatically renew the deans' two-year contracts, Bill inquired about my reasons, warned me of the shock wave it would cause, but supported me unconditionally. I couldn't, in good conscience, renew two-year contracts when the deans were asleep at the wheel. Instead, I woke one dean up, spurring him to use his talents to create an award-winning flagship program that became his legacy. As for the other dean, it simply was time to retire.

Bill was always there with me and for me, and most of all, he modeled loyalty and love. To this day, we can still say to each other, "Hey, love ya!" and understand that it is a love-based and heart-connected leadership that kept our relationship. Spirituality is love in action, a magic formula. So, like an arranged marriage, I started with loving Coastline first just like Bill did, and then again and again, fell deeper in love with all Coastliners. I found and felt the Coastliners' love in return. Having good bosses does matter!

Surround Yourself with Role Models Who Help You Believe in Yourself

Eventually, I did see a leader in the mirror, but I also saw the low ceiling above my head. After meeting so many women presidents at NILD, the possibility of being a president never entered my mind until I met Evelyn Wong, a Chinese-American female president. The powerful unforgettable moment of seeing someone with whom I could identify, in a position that I never consciously or even unconsciously thought was a remote possibility for me, is forever emblazoned in my mind. At that moment, I realized for the first time that someone who looks like me *can* be a college president. This is the phenomenal power of personal identification.

However, I knew that overcoming the biased perceptions would require extra work with intentionality to counter the long list of stereotype threats. While women were advised not to wear the color red to interviews, my women-of-color sister presidents gave me a push to wear my ultimate St. John's power suit, and in bright red! Who would know that inside that red suit was a soldier's body plastered with deep scars and marks from training and previous battlegrounds, and even with a few stab scars on her back. I survived because many on my journey understood, before I did, what I needed to do to overcome the challenges as a minority woman and gave me support and guidance.

I have been supported from the first job I had at Long Beach City College. I may have even been so naive as to not even realize I was being mentored at the time. The dean of Pacific Coast Campus, Bill Barnes, an African-American man who made it to the dean position and was revered as a hero in a lily-white world, was looking after me, guiding me. His voice is still in my ears, and his gentle smile of approval still warms my heart. Bill will not know how much I appreciated how he made me feel and neither does he know that I regret not giving him anything in return. Bill died in 2019, and I never told him that I could understand his plight as the only black administrator sent to lead a campus that others deemed a dumping ground in the middle of a downtrodden neighborhood of Long Beach. I now see how much it paid off that I was always surrounded by successful people, breathing their air, seeing with their vision, and being touched by their genuine care.

Keep Justice and Equity as Your Drivers

Many had already seen the image of me sitting in the president's chair before I even imagined it. And just because I began to see the possibility of becoming a president after meeting Evelyn Wong, it didn't mean that I wanted the job. When you're at the president's cabinet level, up close and personal, you can see how and what important decisions are made at such a level. But once I began having greater affirmation of my own values, clarity and belief in my leadership styles and approaches, I found it harder and harder to stay around people who didn't.

I'm certain that it was that urge to formulate opposing opinions, take alternative approaches, make different decisions, and forge different alignments based on my values that propelled me to climb toward the presidency. After realizing that *the presidency is possible,* there was one distinct moment when I experienced a definitive shift in my mindset.

That moment came when a brand-new Latino dean was facing full-frontal racist attacks. He was going to be put on the chopping block simply because, as the accuser told me, he was "too ethnic to fit in." I rallied some allies attempting to counter this unjust action. The six-foot-five white male temporary boss towering over me shouted in my face that it was none of my business to interfere with a personnel decision that had nothing to do with me. Excuse me, but injustice for one is injustice for all. The Latino dean thanked me and gave me a magnet with the quote by Emiliano Zapata that is still on my refrigerator. "I'd rather die on my feet than live on my knees." I had no choice but to stand up to that kind of bullying injustice and leave an institution that did not deserve my time. This incident ignited a fire in me with an unstoppable driving force that pushed me toward the ultimate power in decision-making for justice and equity. For the first time, I wanted that presidency!

Make Your Ancestors Proud

The Chinese have something to say about everything. "Such ancient wisdom to benefit a modern woman," as my father would say to me. "天时地利人和" (heavenly timing, the prime location, and with harmonious people) means that the synchronous intersection of those three elements indicates the preeminent conditions to seize perfection. According to that logic, Coastline Community College must have met all those conditions, or I would not have become their president, and their first Asian president.

As an Asian female in America, the chances of becoming the first Asian female leader in *anything* is very high because there is a 99% chance that one didn't exist beforehand. My presidency made the news, of course, especially in the Asian communities. If you are a person of color, you do not achieve something or become somebody just for yourself. Personal success always becomes a symbol for our people, a new possibility, a new hope.

I don't want to dismiss the rarity of becoming an Asian female college president. After all, according to the *American College President Study 2017* from the American Council on Education, only 2% of college presidents are Asian-American and a pitiful 5% are women of color. In 2002, the data looked even more grim with only 1% of college presidents being Asian-American.

I had heard of sponsors, those who bring your name up and vouch for you. And when they do, you have no idea what doors open to worlds that you did not even know existed. When I was nominated by Dr. Rita Cepeda, then president of Santa Ana College, to serve on the board of the American Association of Community Colleges, I could not have imagined entering into the ultimate CEO club of community colleges. Dr. Bill Vega, my chancellor at the time, told me that if I was elected by the presidents nationwide as a young budding president, it wouldn't be taken well by all the more senior presidents and chancellors. Not only was I nominated and won the seat, but I also was nominated again later to be the board chair. Like a fake bride being pushed into playing the role, I questioned myself.

The president of AACC at the time, Dr. George Boggs, may not know his words served as a lightning rod that got me in the game. "If elected as board chair, you will be one of the few females and certainly the first Asian to be elected to this position." Who would turn down an opportunity to make ten generations of your ancestors proud? I became chair and served proudly. Being involved with leaders at the national level came to be one of the most dynamic and meaningful professional development experiences I have had in my career, an opportunity to make a difference for others.

Diversity has always been my top agenda item. As board chair of the American Association of Community Colleges, I was not about to waste the opportunity. Working together with my counterpart at the Association of Community College Trustees, we published a joint statement on diversity. This statement shared the position on diversity that the community colleges embody, celebrate, and should be known for. It was a triumphant moment. But it did not come easily. It required working through the processes of two complex and very political organizations. For me, it's a huge validation that occupying a leadership seat provides the unique power required to create impact and enact the values we hold as sacred and non-negotiable. Be involved locally and nationally.

Lesson 3: Understand the Importance of Power and Exercise It with Balance

Garnering and Sustaining Power Is Not the Same Thing

Many view the college presidency as a bully pulpit from which to exert and shape your values and principles. I would go further. The presidency was my theatre, lab, and manufacturing plant to design, create, and implement changes I dreamed about to test out my psychological, social, and philosophical theories of people, leadership, and change.

Most importantly, for students' sake, the presidency was a golden opportunity with eminent power and responsibility to call the shots on implicit racism, injustices, inequities, and exclusion. I rejected hiring committees that were not diverse. I questioned the assumptions of quality associated with the color of one's skin or ethnicity. Even though I knew faculty had primacy on curriculum, I informed them when the curriculum was not inclusive of the identities of our students. I countered the academic senate's recommendations with explanations, evidence, and data. I challenged the practices and culture that disenfranchised our staff in a covert caste system. I called out inequities and dishonesty when I saw them. I righted the wrong for students who had been mistreated and simply wanted justice. I did all this and more because with my position came the power and responsibility of not only calling them out but also demanding change.

That list of joyful presidential rights, privileges, and responsibilities to stand up, speak up, and hold up for diversity, inclusion, and equity paid off. I had been once silenced but now I had a strong voice. I had been invisible but now I had a presence. I had been excluded but now I decided who was at the table and in the room where it happened.

The real challenge of the presidency is not in acquiring the seat, but in being a good president and maintaining the seat. In his book, *Good to Great*, Jim Collins outlines the principles of shaping good institutions to achieve greatness. Later in his sequel, *How the Mighty Fall*, he shares his discovery that greatness does not last if other principles are not applied to sustain it. I, too, have watched so many presidents of colleges and universities fall as fast as they have risen. I soon learned that what gets you to the presidency is not the same skills, capacities, and propensities required for being successful in the position.

Mistakes Are Empowering

As an immigrant, I have to keep my eyes and ears on high alert at all times. In those early days of my career when I was providing counseling services, I noticed the challenges the college was facing in serving an unplanned influx of Southeast Asian refugee students. These students were beginning their new lives here without language, financial means, cultural capital, or any of the other items on a long list of things that are important for success. Faculty, counselors, staff, and other students were showing signs of stress in adjusting to these students.

I had a brilliant idea: The college could create a multicultural center to educate and train faculty, staff, and students about Southeast Asian students, as well as students who are from other cultural origins. I thought if the vice president could be sold on the idea, we're done. I marched ahead without understanding any of the higher education political framework or the importance of participatory governance with stakeholders.

The vice president tried to help me but couldn't due to my lack of knowledge, skills, or experience to do the necessary groundwork before the seeds could be spread. "Today is about the life and death of a project," the vice president's words at the last planning meeting for the multicultural center are still a constant reminder of that fatal error I made. Losing face, trust, friends, and the boss' support left me believing that I could never go any lower than that.

The good thing is that I experienced this watershed moment so early in my career. I didn't see the hidden layers under the surface, nor did I tune in to hear the silence between the lines. I used a one-dimensional assessment in a multi-dimensional environment with a complex political context. To survive and thrive in higher education, as in any society, study the culture of the organization first before you plot out the strategy. Be absolutely enlightened about the culture of the academe so you can be empowered to reframe, recharge, and redesign in leading change effectively.

Zero + Zero Could Be Millions: Generate Resources and Work with Community Partner

My next big lesson in power and leadership came when I took the new vice president position at Rio Hondo College. Even though my title included "economic and community development," the position did not come with any funds to operate, let alone to create anything new. This gave the word *development* in my title multiple meanings: one of which was to *develop* my own funds.

When I went to the budget committee asking for funds to start new initiatives, the chuckles around the table came after the budget manager's mock, "Ding-Jo, zero plus zero is still zero." I won't forget that humiliation. But challenges can turn into strengths. In fact, challenges are the only thing that result in speedy growth. I soon learned how to garner external funding and coined it "OPM," other people's money. Developing and securing external funding streams from grants, contracts, partnerships, and state, federal, and local support became fun, rewarding, and also the fuel needed for change and innovation.

Thanks to that budget manager who challenged me and granted me the opportunity to learn how to make zero plus zero into millions. Yet, leaving that post with multi-million-dollar annual revenues was not my proudest moment there. Venturing down from the hills where the college sat to partner with the community in addressing real needs was the trophy.

Of the many programs we launched, our "I Am Going to College" program spawned wide-ranging community support, providing strong evidence of *la familia* that has been there in the culture all along. In a ninety percent Latinx community, the college-going rate was extremely low. We researched the critical school-grade level and classes that determined whether a youth was headed on a college-bound track or not.

We gathered community partners from local government, businesses, schools, churches, and funding partners with a call to work together and make a college-going culture in the community. The thrill of witnessing such united action was exhilarating and validating. Experiencing the college-going culture shift gave me the affirmation that the most valuable resources that can be generated are from communities united toward the goal of making a difference for future generations. That's real power!

A House Divided Cannot Stand: Unity Is the Nucleus of Power

My love story with the community colleges is not all rosy. It did not take long after becoming president at Coastline to discover that the college was a divided house. Many faculty were polarized into two camps over a curricular issue, which was central to the institution's brand identity. Some colleague presidents advised me not to get involved in faculty conflicts because they were not shooting arrows at my administration. However, these horizontal forces were not only a big distraction, but also a major impediment to the college's momentum in moving forward and upward. As Abraham Lincoln said, "A house divided against itself cannot stand."

Central to my Bahá'í Faith's teaching is building unity: "The light of unity is so powerful that it can illuminate the whole world." Accompanying it, and fundamental to my cultural anchoring values, is harmony. I made this my top priority and first order of business as president. I was able to incorporate both my spiritual and cultural teachings to mend the broken relationships.

The process led to a final meeting to erase the line that divides the two camps. The preparations were full of care, down to the last details, including the intentional setting design at the Sherman Gardens. If, by the end of the meeting, the two camps showed authentic signs of choosing the path toward unity together, I had a basket of beautiful decorative eggs to give to each of them, symbolizing a new life together as a unified team. If the meeting ended with them continuing on separate paths, I would go home with a basket of Easter eggs to give to my neighbors' kids. I went home with an empty basket.

Inspiring the vision of greatness for Coastline and building a stronger foundation for unity remained my central theme as president. Coastline was the youngest and smallest college in the three-college district, but we had *the power of one* to achieve record enrollments, an abundance of external revenues, multiple national and international awards for our innovative education courses, and the mission to serve members of the military as well as incarcerated students in different ways. *The power of one* had a double meaning: The power of oneness in our integration as a united whole; and, the power of one individual, meaning everyone counts and everyone can make a difference.

Lead with the Power of Tai Chi

I have often been questioned whether I can handle conflicts because my "niceness" is interpreted as not possessing what it takes to confront or resolve conflicts. Conflicts, when ill-managed, become energy zappers that tax everyone's time, physical energy, and mental capacity, and oftentimes sow the seeds of a toxic work environment. The drain of poorly managed conflicts can be witnessed in higher education institutions across the country. We are certainly seeing the consequences of unresolved differences ending up with extreme irreconcilable polarities in political, social, and financial realities today.

As a Chinese culturally and Bahá'í spiritually, I have learned that unity is the central foundation of a thriving family, organization, and community. When achieved in a diverse context, unity in diversity is a spiritual principle that is a constant intentional goal. Therefore, detecting potential conflicts, avoiding unnecessary conflicts, and resolving conflicts are essential preludes and conditions to achieve unity in diversity. When confronting conflicts, the inculcation of Confucius's philosophies anchored me in finding the middle way by staying away from polarities. By standing in the middle and center, I can lead by bringing others closer to the middle common ground. When one stands at the edge of extremes, there's no space for others, and with often little room to turn around.

I recall a conflict over a new policy that required intrusive proactive programs and enforcement of course prerequisites. My peers were worried about how I would handle certain faculty's strong opposition to the new policy. The opposition was seen as "troublemakers." I was advised to keep them at a far range and to not engage with them. Instead, I wanted to understand their point of view, and the Bahá'í consultation process became my secret weapon. I found that at its core, the conflict was fundamentally a disagreement over whether students have a right to success versus a right to failure. I used some of the Chinese martial arts Tai Chi principles of staying loose to diffuse and send off the negative energy.

Many principles of Tai Chi are perfectly suited for leadership. While the soft-flowing movements of Tai Chi are seemingly not perceived as forceful, the power comes from leveraging and deflecting the attacking force while letting the opponent's energy flow through you. This can happen only if you follow a few principles: #1 anchor yourself, #2 maintain balance, and #3 remain completely soft, loose, and flowing. That may sound abstract, but you can observe this in real physical confrontations. I simply adopted the same principles into leadership practices. So rather than ostracizing or attacking the troublemakers, I invited them to serve on the steering committee. I leaned into their passionate energy, channeled it with the consultation process, and received a 180-degree about-face with those faculty changing from opponents to champions of my efforts. Indeed, this "nice" and "kind" Asian female can handle my conflicts just fine.

Conclusion: Leading with Wholeness

Meaningful Accomplishments Are Not Always Quantifiable

Like the shift in self-perception I experienced from meeting Evelyn Wong, I hope that my story might encourage others, especially Asian women, to discover and believe in their inner leaders. That innate leader in me defines what my accomplishments of purpose are. While there are quantifiable metrics that one can show, such as enrollment, graduation rates, flagship programs, institutions' awards, revenue streams, innovations, demographic shifts, or faculty's votes of confidence, I do not consider them my significant successes. The following are a few samples of my accomplishments that transform lives, raise critical consciousness, and unify communities:

Building Bridges for Life Transformation

At Long Beach City College, while I was serving the refugees, we took students with absolutely nothing left in their lives and gave them hope and home again by designing and building solid bridges that helped them cross over to new lives. There is no quantifiable measure to account for these successful life transformations.

Instilling Critical Conscientiousness

At Saddleback College, I also developed and taught courses like *Psychology of Prejudice* and *Ethnic Cultures of the United States*. These types of curricula, programs, and activities are essential in helping students examine their own socialization of racism, classicism, and sexism across cultures and diverse backgrounds. Again, there are no measures to tabulate the elevation in students' critical consciousness. Once enlightened, they carry that consciousness for life.

Win-Win-Win Partnerships

At Rio Hondo College, we galvanized the communities to come together for a common goal in the *I'm Going to College* program. The spirit of *de la familia* came alive, making it a win-win-win partnership uniting the community, students, and college in changing to a college-going culture. While we could count the increase in student admissions to college, there is no way to measure the generational rippling effect of such community pride.

Leaving No One Behind

At Coastline College, I aimed to serve as diverse students as possible: new immigrants with very limited English, developmentally delayed, the brained injured, sailors in the submarines, coast guards on cutters, soldiers in foxholes, early college high school students, the unemployed, centenarians, incarcerated students and more! We proved that if your mission is to be inclusive, then you leave no one behind.

Focus on Unity

When I arrived as Chancellor, the three colleges under the Coast Community College District umbrella operated independently of each other with much autonomy. Sensing a missed opportunity, I implemented cross-college strategic planning, district-wide budget planning structure, and piloted curriculum alignment with joint faculty coordination. This new culture of collaboration empowered each institution to lean into the other's strengths in a synergistic way that cannot be measured, especially during a period of economic downturn.

Embrace Diversity as a Value and a Way of Life

I'm not sure if my father knew the name he gave me in Ding-Jo was spot on. The Chinese give thoughtful consideration to names. Some names commemorate the moment of birth, such as the first rain of the spring season, or convey the special meaning of the mountain peak where the parents first met. Then there are names like mine that represent some quality or character that the parents wish upon the child.

Ding-Jo came from one of the ultimate states of being in Buddhism. Ding is the Buddhist concept of reaching a state of profound tranquility and stillness. Jo is the inner wisdom derived from that serenity. I've been working on first achieving that stillness ever since the name was bestowed upon me. I naturally seek action, delight in different experiences, and love adventure. To put it simply, I get bored easily.

That ability to create fun out of diverse possibilities transferred to the thrill in any job I have taken on, seeking to create new and interesting frontiers, breaking old rules, pushing the norm, and fathoming innovative designs. My zig-zagging career journey has given me many diverse and stimulating experiences. From my first jobs selling roast beef sandwiches at Arby's, cooking tacos and burritos, being a janitor for women's restrooms, to serving refugees, leading career technical programs, virtual college, and serving as chancellor of three Coast Colleges, I have discovered my love of and need for diversity start in my own life.

My early adolescence in Africa combined with my experience as a new immigrant living in the inner city, low SES neighborhood of Dayton, Ohio, resisting the socialization of racism, particularly against the African American communities became the foundation for my convictions and core values. Those early experiences shaped my multidimensional identities and passion in this life-transforming work of education.

No books, classes, or degrees could have taught me the insights I gained from my diverse experiences working and living with people, students, and colleagues of all socio-economic statuses, cultures, abilities, backgrounds, and so many unique identities. I have come to understand the kinds of diverse elements I need to live, work, learn, lead, and thrive for my soul.

Leading with Inner Peace

I might be accused of toxic positivity if I say the road to the presidency and chancellorship is not that difficult. It's arduous and full of growing pains, but it is not unbearable or with unrealistic exigent demands. Wanting the presidency too desperately may land you at the wrong institution at the wrong time. The chancellor or president positions come with personal costs and sacrifices, so proceeding with clarity on what you are willing to trade off is critical.

Finally, I want to convey here my wish for future leaders to obtain the same inner peace, contentment, and satisfaction I have found as a leader. Unfortunately, so many of my colleagues in leadership roles are worn out, frazzled, and fatigued from all the battles they have fought. I know I am not a perfect leader by far; I'm still growing daily. However, I've found that if I'm anchored deep in my roots with positive authentic energy, if my leadership comes from my heart and is founded on the values of justice, equity, diversity, and inclusion, if I invest in the bank of trusts, then that leadership gives me power and hope for change, immense pleasure, and ultimate freedom to implement important and necessary changes to the system. This style of leadership feeds me, nourishes me, and revives me. May you develop your own authentic inner leader and experience rich joy and nourishment in your leadership journey to the next peak. Just don't forget to have some fun and sprinkle with love along the way!

Chapter Questions

1 Carefully consider the various viewpoints and identities discussed in this chapter; in what ways is the concept of intersectionality important to current leadership roles within higher education? What does it mean to be an "authentic leader"? What does it mean to be an authentic Asian Female leader in higher education? How is this leadership memoir interwoven with a personal, autobiographic reflection on identity?
2 Lesson 2 describes an example of blatant race-based discrimination and the potential termination of a Latino dean for the reason of being "too ethnic to fit in" as well as the outcry and counter-measures taken to fight this injustice. How does the following passage from Lesson 1: *"when your decision may not be popular, choosing the right thing to do is even more critical"* apply to this example? What are some examples from your institutions and your leadership roles that underscore this point? How

would you have responded to this if this occurred at your institution? Why?
3 Reflect on leading authenticity as discussed earlier in this chapter. How do you balance the demands of leadership roles with your values? On what do you anchor your approach to leadership while focusing on equity, diversity, and inclusion? How can your leadership style empower you and others around you while avoiding compromising your authentic self? In what ways does this resonate with the "mirror test" that is described in Lesson 1?
4 Think about your journey to leadership and the instances where you've sought to create new frontiers, break old rules, and push the norm. Reflect on the example offered in Lesson 2 where two deans were "asleep at the wheel" and the issue of breaking tradition and not renewing their two-year contracts was raised. What would you have done in this scenario? How could this be seen as an opportunity to express your own authentic leadership style? What role does the "status quo" have within your leadership framework?
5 Consider your experiences in implementing unity through cross-college strategic planning, joint faculty coordination, and collaborative initiatives (such as the "I Am Going to College" program that served the Latinx community discussed in Lesson 3). How can you work to foster a culture of collaboration to empower your institution and the broader community it serves? How can you measure the impact of this, especially in challenging times?
6 Reflect on the following passage from Lesson 3: "*I soon learned that what gets you to the presidency is not the same skills, capacities, and propensities required for being successful in the position.*" What are the skills, capacities, and propensities discussed in this chapter? What are the differences and similarities between them? Which are helpful for the "climb" to the presidency and which are helpful for the actual position?
7 Conflicts, especially poorly managed conflicts, can be a significant drain in leadership positions. What are some examples from your own leadership experiences that speak to this point? Considering the wide array of experiences discussed in this chapter, what are creative, innovative, peacemaking, and unity-based conflict resolution processes that you can exercise and implement in the face of these issues?

4
CREATIVE LEADERSHIP IN INSTITUTION BUILDING

The Unconventional Journey of a Woman Quantum Physicist in India

Rupamanjari Ghosh

Abstract

In a departure from the classic debate of breadth versus depth, Ghosh's career starts from a deep understanding of quantum physics, both in its structure and its preternatural content, supported by a love of music, humanities, and literature that instilled "the sense of logic, the essence of rhythm and the value of life ..." in her; and goes on to encompass an innate sense of justice and equity in her administrative roles, demolishing silos, and blurring boundaries of action. Moving from a teaching, research, and administrative career at a prestigious public university to a newly established private university meant embracing an educational experiment of focusing uncompromisingly on quality while addressing structural problems of inequality and poverty at a critical time of growth in India's higher education. Dr. Ghosh's story is one of the pursuit of excellence, intellectual diversity, and social justice, grounded in the sociocultural and technological changes and challenges before and after the COVID-19 pandemic in India. Besides practical advice and examples from her professional life, this chapter clarifies the potential leadership wellspring in the synergy among disciplines; the personal and professional; and conscious, and unconscious bias and policy changes in the context of "the essential human quality of compassion to fellow human beings ... to all living creatures."

I have often found myself faced with challenges in structurally complex or changing situations and was able to turn these into exciting opportunities to create and realize innovative solutions. When there is a vacuum, or everything is shifting and new approaches are yet unknown, or rigidity in the system is opposing progress, I needed to ensure clarity of purpose for my teams. How did it work, and how do I define success for me and my people? Let me tell you the story.

On my return from the USA after my Ph.D. in Quantum Optics, I spent 24 eventful years as a physics faculty and academic administrator in a prestigious but small public university located in the Indian capital, New Delhi. It was a rich journey, contributing to and leading the growth of the institution in several dimensions, and I could have continued on that path safely till my official retirement. But I took a risky turn when I was invited to join a new private university in nearby Uttar Pradesh. The record of private colleges/universities in India till that time was not very impressive. My decision to join the new private university meant a commitment to a model experiment in higher education in India at a critical stage of its growth, and a challenge to keep an uncompromising focus on quality while dealing with some of India's structural problems of inequality and poverty. After an exciting but strenuous tenure of 10 years, establishing & leading this private university's ambitious quest to become a globally acclaimed center for holistic learning, and multidisciplinary research and innovation, I am now getting ready to take on another challenging leadership role. This narrative is an attempt to capture the essence of these experiments along my creative leadership path, shaped by my convictions, and driven by my desire to impact the lives of people. Let me start at the beginning.

Early Days

I was born in a middle-class family in Calcutta (now Kolkata), India. I was the third and the youngest child of my parents, and it helped – as it happened, when my elder sister and brother were struggling with their studies, I got to learn by being in the background, by osmosis! By the time it was my turn at school, I sailed through the regular curriculum. I had the time to do my own things after school work. I was an avid reader. Our house was full of books, stacks and stacks of every possible Bengali and English literature work, Indian classics, and Greek epics, and I read each and every one. I added my collection too, gathered as gifts or bought from my prize money. The philosophical, cultural, and social influences of the *Bengal Renaissance*, which ended with Rabindranath Tagore, Asia's first Nobel laureate, were deeply rooted in the family. Music was an essential part of our everyday life. Nobody in my immediate family was in science; but I think I imbibed the sense of logic, the essence of rhythm, and the value of life from music and literature – in a sense everything that you probably need for a later career in physics. It was seeded in that very humanities-oriented family of mine. I have heard my father speaking extempore in public events in the locality – he was quite creative. My mother was, and is still (at 93), extremely bright, and embodies a rare grace. I was pampered by both my maternal and paternal grandmothers – not with toys but with their time and affection. Both were very strong and generous characters. I also had the constant support of my aunt, my father's sister, who specialized in history and museology and was a teacher and lead administrator in a remote school.

I loved mathematics, and I loved the logical deductions I saw in science. I also loved music … and literature. For a brief period, I found a mentor in the Principal of my higher secondary school, who came from the island country of Malta, and again was more into English language and literature, with a deep interest in philosophy. By the time I was in grade 9, I already knew that there were some things one had to go through in a structured manner. I would not be able to learn physics on my own. But maybe if I tried, I could learn history on my own; maybe if I tried, I would enjoy literature and music on my own, with a little help. I realized that the way physics was built if you did not cross the steps as designed, you could get lost – my scientific journey had to follow a "system."

Education

In what seemed a logical transition, I received my B.Sc. (Physics honors) and M.Sc. (Physics) degrees from the University of Calcutta. I received prizes for standing first in Bethune College, University of Calcutta, among the B.Sc. Honors graduates as well as in the overall B.Sc. examination. I again received the Silver Medal award in the M.Sc. in physics at the University of Calcutta.

My science was not in silos, not insular from Social Sciences and Humanities. I continued taking part in inter-college debates and elocution competitions on social issues and winning! Interestingly, I attended a convocation of the University of Calcutta to receive the "Dr. Shyamaprasad Mookerjee Memorial Debate Medal" awarded by the University for best performance in an All India Debating Competition, in my first/second year of undergraduate studies, and that was the only convocation of the University I ever attended. It was inspiring, to say the least. During my undergraduate days, I gave talks on contemporary issues in my native tongue, Bengali, on *Yuvavani* (Voice of the Youth), All India Radio, Calcutta. I got elected as the General Secretary of the college Student Union – it was an apolitical organization, and I tried to make the forum active and responsive.

I did not have anybody to guide me for the next phase after my master's, but I saw that my M.Sc. classmates were appearing for the GRE (Graduate Record Examinations) and TOEFL (Test of English as a Foreign Language), and applying for admissions in graduate schools abroad. I was curious to know my "market value," and was truly interested in exploring a research career in physics. Late in getting started, I could not get early dates to appear for the GRE (general and subject) and TOEFL at the USEFI (United States Educational Foundation in India, now called United States-India Educational Foundation, USIEF) in Kolkata. The application deadlines in the top US universities were over by December/mid-January, and I was yet to get my GRE scores, or even appear for the TOEFL. My mother's cousin, who was in physics and had completed his Ph.D. from Rochester, NY, was visiting home, and I had a chance discussion with him about his experiences – he was impressed with my intuitive way of doing physics on my own, and encouraged me to apply to a few places including Rochester. As it turned out, it was the best time to join Rochester to do Quantum Optics.

The University of Rochester had a Department of Physics & Astronomy, with a stellar group in Quantum Optics. The University also had a unique Institute of Optics. Outside the University, there were headquarters of Xerox, Kodak, and Bausch & Lomb in Rochester. I applied to the University of Rochester and a select few other places for my Ph.D., and early in February 1981, I received an admission offer from Rochester with a tuition-fee waiver and a good teaching/research assistantship. Within two weeks, I received another letter from Rochester offering me their prestigious Rush Rhees Fellowship on top of my research assistantship, chosen for *"outstanding scholarly ability and the promise of exceptional contributions to scholarship and teaching."* By then, I had received offers from a couple of more places too (one offer was subject to submission of my GRE scores), but I decided to join Rochester. My father, in his non-interfering way, was a big support. My mother was a bit worried, but she always wished me the best. I wanted to get into Quantum Optics and master experimental techniques. I finished my M.Sc. final examinations at the University of Calcutta, and set out at the end of August 1981 on my first move outside our Kolkata home all the way to Rochester – the one-way flight started from Kolkata, stopped at Bombay (now Mumbai), then Abu Dhabi, London Heathrow, New York JFK, and finally I landed in Rochester, exhausted.

The atmosphere for learning and practicing optics in Rochester was highly energizing. Optics is the subject that deals with the generation, propagation, detection, manipulation, and application of light. Our principal contact with the world around us is through light. But what is light? There was a period in our recent history in which one had to know which experiment one was analyzing to tell if light was waves or particles – that's not the way a physics theory is supposed to work! Quantum Optics finally gave a single framework that reconciles the particle properties of light with the wave nature. My work with Prof. Leonard Mandel on two-photon interference was groundbreaking and has yielded a new direction in quantum optics and quantum information.[1] In the creation and use of a source of entangled photon pairs, and of single photons, this work is at the forefront of research even today.

Professional Life

There is a wide range of challenging, exciting, and productive careers open to people who study physics. In universities or research institutes, you have intellectual freedom – you get to study the research problems that you want. Few other careers can be as intellectually flexible. My life with physics has been truly fascinating and fulfilling! Most people work just to earn a living, but as a physicist, I had the luxury of pursuing a hobby at my workplace, and it was wonderful to get paid for a hobby! People ask me why I chose this career, how the journey has been, particularly as a woman in physics, and what changes I would like to see in the policies to enable more women to choose and be successful in careers in sciences and take leadership positions. To be honest, I was never very ambitious myself, but I wanted to give my very best in all the diverse and interesting things that came my way.

After my Ph.D., I wanted to return to India. I joined the brand new School of Physical Sciences at Jawaharlal Nehru University (JNU). It was a prestigious, small-scale public university situated in New Delhi, and funded by the Central Government. The University was established in 1969, and named after Jawaharlal Nehru, the first Prime Minister of India. It was already known for several forward-looking *interdisciplinary* Schools. The need for *basic* sciences was felt much later, and the School of Physical Sciences was conceived in 1986, initiated in 1987, and I joined the School as an Assistant Professor on November 1, 1988.

The University has been "the best" in the country in terms of its academics – we believed in excellence without compromise. I have always enjoyed research and teaching – I learn and I grow every day. My students are my pride. For my research, I worked on various fundamental and applied problems in the domains of Experimental and Theoretical Quantum Optics, Laser Physics, Nonlinear Optics, and Quantum Information.

I had very productive international collaborations. It was an interesting start when I was invited by the French Government for a month-long lecture tour of France in July 1999. I was based at Laboratoire Kastler Brossel, ENS, Paris, at the invitation of *Nobel Laureate* Prof. Claude Cohen-Tannoudji. Though Claude offered me a visiting position at the Collège de France, I could not take it up because there was no possibility of leave from JNU at that stage. I picked up a collaboration with Dr. Fabien Bretenaker, and we had a joyful and fruitful collaboration over the years, even with changing institutions, playing with atoms and light. The collaboration, supported initially through an initiative of the Department of Science & Technology (DST) and then by the Indo-French Centre for the Promotion of Advanced Research (IFCPAR/CEFIPRA), led to breakthroughs and quality publications and opened new perspectives. It contributed to the training and subsequent placement of several Ph.D. students and post-doctoral researchers, both in France and India. It is not just academic complementarity based on each other's strengths, but shared values and culture, a bond between families across continents, and deep friendship define this grand and successful Indo-French partnership. Fabien-Fabienne's little daughter has the middle name "Amrita," which is the name of my foster daughter!

I contributed to the development and coordination of the academic programs in JNU's School of Physical Sciences from the very beginning and became its Dean in December 2007. In the initial days, I was terribly busy teaching, developing teaching laboratories, and setting up my own research facilities in a new place, and was hesitant to take up general administration. There were a lot of processes to be put in place, and with an established central administration, changes were hard and at best incremental. The Dean of the School had assigned some administrative work to me, which I presume, I performed reasonably well, and he came back to me sometime later with another administrative assignment. I wanted to be excused from taking the extra load, and he made a comment to me that has stayed with me till today: "If you do not do it, someone *with no understanding* [words in *italics* are mine – he used harsher words!] may get to do it, and then you will have to suffer the consequences." Well, I accepted the job.

More Leadership

At JNU, outside the School of Physical Sciences, I had to share many responsibilities, one important role was as the Chairperson of the new Gender Sensitization Committee against Sexual Harassment (GSCASH). My experience in the Gender Committee became a critical one. The Supreme Court of India had passed a historic judgment (on *Vishaka & others vs. the State of Rajasthan & others*) in August 1997 stating that every instance of sexual harassment is a violation of "Fundamental Rights" accorded in the Constitution of India, and amounts to a violation of the "Right to Freedom," and pronounced the guidelines on the prevention and deterrence of sexual harassment in the workplace. The guidelines became mandatory for every employer to follow. After some serious groundwork at JNU, GSCASH was set up in April 1999, but for it to be operational and effective, its rules and procedures were to be drafted and approved by the University's Executive Council. I became a member of GSCASH in 2001, and in a few months, was elected the Chairperson when the incumbent Chairperson fell seriously ill. I had to learn on the job, negotiated with all stakeholders without compromise, edited and placed the complete Rules and Procedures of the GSCASH before the JNU Executive Council – it was a great moment when these got approved in September 2001. The Rules of course followed the spirit of the Supreme Court judgments but covered a wider spectrum in consonance with the requirements of a residential institution of higher education. The JNU model became a standard for other educational institutions in the country to follow. I got involved in many inquiries and appeals in complicated cases of sexual harassment in that one year. As things progressed, I was made the Chairperson of Committees to review the Rules and Procedures of GSCASH in 2002 and again in 2006. There were controversies that my Committees needed to straighten out to the satisfaction of/acceptance by all sections of the JNU community.

I was elected the President of the JNU Teachers Association (Faculty Council) for two consecutive terms. Starting in December 2004, it became a very busy time – my main agenda was to get the principle of *participatory management* implemented at all levels of JNU. I was proud to be leading the JNU faculty, the intellectual stalwarts of the country. There were frequent communications with the faculty, extensive coordination with non-teaching staff and students, select communication with the external media for public awareness on relevant issues, and we often worked with the central administration as part of the JNU team, bringing to the fore and supporting bigger causes with our intellectual strengths. In these two years, we resolved several long-pending issues and placed new issues of academic planning, gender, environment, and sustainability on the agenda.

I held many other academic and administrative positions over 24 years at JNU. Starting August 2009, I served as the Director of the Academic Staff College (ASC) at JNU for a term of 2 years. ASCs were autonomous institutions set up in suitable universities in the country by the University Grants Commission (UGC), Government of India, to aid the professional and career development of faculty in the region. Throughout the year, the ASC ran residential month-long "Orientation" and subject-specific

"Refresher" programs for select college and university faculty in the country. I had introduced a Refresher program in Physics at JNU in 2000, and coordinated and lectured in many such programs. Later as the Director, I streamlined the processes, made sure that the academic standard of the programs kept on rising, and also introduced a workshop for Academic Administrators at ASC-JNU, as I felt the need for a dialogue and understanding to bridge the gap between the academic and the administrative sides of functioning in a university.

Let me share how I got the opportunity to guide school-level science training. I was made the Chief Advisor for Science textbooks for grades 9 and 10, to be developed afresh by the NCERT (National Council of Educational Research and Training) in 2005–2006. There was a lot of excitement about the new National Curriculum Framework, but it was to be implemented on the ground. My only professional link with school education till that point was as an expert/Delhi Coordinator in the interviews for the selection of meritorious students under the *Kishore Vaigyanik Protsahan Yojana (KVPY)* of the Department of Science & Technology, Government of India, since its initiation in 1999 – it was a prestigious scheme for award of fellowships to select school-leaving students interested (or to make them interested) in science research careers. Every year, I would assemble a multidisciplinary team of faculty from JNU and neighboring institutions to interact with these bright young students, and I aimed to make the interview enjoyable and illuminating for each one of them (and also for the faculty!).

The NCERT task was of a completely different scale. The NCERT was established by the Government of India in 1961 to design and support a common system of education, which is national in character, enabling and encouraging the diverse culture across the country. The textbooks I was tasked to develop were to serve more than 400,000 students in grades 9 and 10 in the country. I was given a mixed group of school teachers and a few subject experts to complete the task of planning and writing the new textbooks, within a seemingly impossible timeframe. In the course of the first couple of months of giving shape to the Grade 9 Science textbook, the group developed into a team. We interpreted the syllabus to present a coherent coverage of scientific concepts related to daily life. It was an integrated approach to science at that level, with no sharp divisions into disciplines such as physics, chemistry, biology, and environmental science. The entire approach of the books was activity based – the students were required to construct knowledge themselves from these activities. The old school at NCERT was opposed to my approach. Unlike the previous versions, the emphasis was not on definitions and technical terms, but on the concepts (or the "stories") involved. Special care had to be taken so that the rigor of science was not lost while simplifying the language. There was also a conscious attempt to address the relevant social concerns wherever possible – the concerns for people with special needs, the issues of gender discrimination, energy, and the environment. Students were encouraged to get into the debates on some of the management concerns (for sustainable development, for example) so that they could arrive at their own decisions after a scientific analysis of all the facts. It was a massive task of leading from the front and taking my team along, and in the process, I made some life-long connections. The books were very well received by the students, and till date, I receive appreciative notes from school students and teachers, often alongside a science query or two! The main learning for me was an understanding of the essential link between secondary and tertiary education that is often broken.

Because I did my Ph.D. abroad, I did not have a godfather or a godmother in India, a network sorely needed as you take your first steps in the professional domain. I am a product of a generation where some of us have "made it" *in spite* of the system and *not because* of the system. More and more, I wanted to change this for the next generation.

Since physics is about discovering the "why" and "how" behind things, a physics graduate is uniquely qualified to tackle all kinds of business challenges as well. Even today, I gain clarity of purpose and perspective, and then formulate plans in almost all the situations I face by asking the three basic questions of "what," "why," and "how." Physics training makes you logical, teaches you the value of integrity, and encourages you to look beyond the mundane in life. If you come to administrative leadership positions from serious academia, you have the advantage of knowing the nuances of this system of excellence, which is open-ended by design. At JNU, I was never a full-time administrator. Even as the Dean of the School of Physical Sciences, I was quite productive in research and took more than my fair share of teaching. As more and more administration came my way, I learned the critical lesson of time management, and I was astonished to experience the expanse and flexibility humans are capable of.

A New Inning

In 2011, I was contacted by people involved in setting up a new private State University in Uttar Pradesh, adjoining Delhi. At that time, "private" in India was the last option for students and good faculty. This new one was created out of the philanthropic trust of Mr. Shiv Nadar. I did not personally know Shiv, the founder of HCL, a USD-10-billion global technology enterprise. A meeting was finally set up, I did some homework on Shiv and his institutions, and I met Shiv at his residence to hear his vision of a research-led university first-hand. It was a very engaging meeting, and I was struck by his simplicity, wisdom, and depth of experience. The Shiv Nadar Foundation, which he established in 1994, was committed to the creation of a more equitable, merit-based society by empowering individuals through transformational education, and to bridge the socio-economic divide. The Shiv Nadar University was to be his most ambitious (and most expensive!) plan. The only question he asked me was: if I had students like me in the class, how would I make a system?! This was a fundamental issue in the higher education space in India. There is always a fine line between the exercise of freedom and anarchy, and that needs to be navigated very carefully. While the institutions were to be held accountable, I was keen to build an atmosphere where the rules of the system did not suffocate excellence.

I decided to take up the challenge and join the new university. It was a risky decision. I had a secure government job in hand for at least 11 more years. Private philanthropy was a new concept. Most donations in India go unreported even today, especially by donors who are themselves at the bottom of the pyramid. Also, India has been a nation of "quiet givers," mostly in health, education, and religion. It did not help develop the culture, policy, or infrastructure to promote or incentivize philanthropy. *"Give a man a fish, you feed him for a day; teach a man to fish* (or to form a fishery cooperative!), *you feed him for a lifetime."* This saying captures what is at the heart of the difference between charity and philanthropy. After my meeting with Shiv, I came back realizing that an independent philanthropic sector can take (calculated) risks and experiment towards excellence – something the government sector, using taxpayers' money, may not be free to do. It was difficult because the corporate brass, while focused and efficient in their domains, were new to higher education. Shiv was an exception. I felt positive that philanthropy from successful industrial houses would naturally create industry-academia relations and much-needed two-way, equitable collaborations. We still need both the public and the private. Philanthropy should not be about the government "outsourcing" its responsibilities – the State should of course be accountable for its roles and responsibilities in resolving structural problems of inequality and poverty, etc. at this stage of India's growth.

I joined Shiv Nadar University as the founding Director of the School of Natural Sciences, which had the Departments of Physics, Chemistry, Life Sciences, and Mathematics. I later started a Center for Environmental Sciences (and added "Engineering" to the name). The Foundation had acquired 286 acres of land for the university campus – such a large piece of land had to be slightly outside of Delhi. During my very first visit to the campus when it was just about starting its operations, I was struck by the abundant natural wealth of the area. There were also visible signs of the pressures of development or economic growth, increasing population, and growing consumerism, taking a rapid toll on the health of this rich environment. I started searching for an answer as to what was really "worth" conserving in the face of these pressures, and the first step towards the answer was proper scientific documentation of the local biodiversity, which would then help formulate a much-needed strategy for conservation. An urgent, focused research on the documentation of plant and animal diversity was to be carried out so that the inevitable human intervention could be informed, integrated, and holistic. This was the first big project that I pushed at the University starting in 2013. This initiative led by the Center for Environmental Sciences & Engineering, yielded some quality publications, information handbooks, and a Biodiversity Garden at the campus. It is in line with our vision of a *"glocal"* university – global in its outlook but deeply rooted in its local context. It also laid the ground for our future push for creating a sustainable campus. The Center also got involved in several other interdisciplinary explorations.

When I started at Shiv Nadar University, I had a fresh experiment in my hand, with the ambition of a research university, in a new model of private funding. Everything had to be built from scratch. The vision and mission of the School/University were to be shaped. We needed sustainable resources – both financial and intellectual, to enable the vision and mission. The only way forward was to choose a team with an *alignment of purposes*. Once this alignment is established, each individual will work for what is good for them, and it will automatically be good for the institution as a whole, and my job will be done!

The overall challenge was that the Indian higher education system was large and complicated with many layers. 17th Century coexisted with the 21st Century, one could not just cater to the millennials or Gen Z, and innovative, contextual solutions needed to be thought through. Despite a glorious past, and the fact that some of the top scientists, technologists, and CEOs of the world are the products of India's science and policy ecosystem, the massive system of higher education in India faced problems of quality, access, and affordability. There was a severe shortage of quality faculty, and a large number of graduates remained unemployable. There was also a worldwide *existential* issue. With the advent of "Industry 4.0," there has been large-scale panic about the "Future of Work." Today's young students are going to face a complex world with uncertainties about jobs. We no longer need University graduates to contribute to the labor force of the country. Machines can perform rote jobs, and thinking jobs too, thanks to Artificial Intelligence. So will an algorithm take away the available jobs? What are humans still good for? What are the things that machines still cannot do? Now "Industry 5.0" is here – the focus lies on the interaction between humans and machines. Industry 5.0 must leverage the collaboration between increasingly powerful and accurate machinery and the unique creative potential of the human being. It adds a personal human touch to the Industry 4.0 pillars of automation and efficiency.

Education had to move too. We needed to change our focus: from "Make in India" to "Make by India," from aiming to be a country of factory workers to a country of innovators, from creating the labor force to producing creative leaders, who will have the ability to generate innovative solutions, especially in the face of complex or changing situations. If our young have this ability, they will never be jobless. What is the "right kind" of university education that will prepare them and give them this ability? In the last century, innovation remained strongly coupled with STEM (Science, Technology, Engineering & Mathematics) subjects. But now, I felt an integrated "STEAM" curriculum, with the extra "A" for Art & Design (and more), and the "E" standing for Enterprise education, was needed to give our students a clear advantage in the face of world-wide challenges of "Future of Work."

The university curriculum needed to have a multidisciplinary breadth and a disciplinary depth. The traditional boundaries of disciplines and education *in silos* have proved to be irrelevant. Be it food, energy, healthcare, climate change, transportation, or housing, real-life problems need real-life solutions that are not restricted to any one discipline. The students must have a multidisciplinary breadth, allowing them to handle interdisciplinary areas of importance. But multidisciplinarity, and hence interdisciplinarity, should not be at the cost of "disciplinarity" – the students should be trained to go deep into at least one discipline. The method of delivery should be such that the students learn "how to think" in a research or exploration-based setting, and then they will be able to re-learn a new stream that the unknown future may demand of them.

With the support we had from Mr. Shiv Nadar and his Foundation, we could not afford to fail in our mission, and we had to deliver *the dream*. I made a plan (a Plan A, and always, a Plan B). My own experiences gave me the advantage of understanding and prioritizing research, and soon excellence started attracting excellence. Buildings started coming up with our design, and facilities were open 24×7. What we did inside the beautiful buildings was more beautiful! With purposeful mentoring, the research by the young Natural Sciences faculty started gaining visibility, and the faculty started attracting external funding for research, not only individual grants but all four Departments of Natural Sciences received prestigious infrastructure grants from the Department of Science & Technology, Government of India, and the School started drawing the attention of the world community in a very short period.

Today in the higher education space, it is fashionable to talk about Liberal Arts (literature, philosophy, social sciences) on one hand, and disruptive technologies of AI (Artificial Intelligence), ML (Machine Learning), and VR (Virtual Reality) on the other. But, we must remember that Liberal Arts is incomplete without physical sciences, and disruptive technologies alone, without sciences, will not be able to solve all societal problems. Technologies such as AI will be enablers and multipliers only when physical solutions are there. That's the importance of a serious Science curriculum. The recent global pandemic has reinstated the importance of basic and applied scientific research, and also of stable research infrastructure and funding, for survival. Our leading universities ought to be in the driver's seat of a robust ecosystem of research, with strong, equitable, and credible partnerships – national & international, academic & industrial, and public & private. Given the unavoidable disruptions, now and in the future, the task is to cultivate generations of visionaries, thinkers, and academics who can change the world, before it changes them.

As an extension of my role in the School to the University level, I became the founding Dean of Research & Graduate Studies in 2012. I strongly believe in exploiting the synergy between teaching and research, and I think research need not be restricted to only faculty, post-doctoral fellows, and Ph.D. students. Universities need to catch the students young – expose undergraduate students to research, providing them with training in research-oriented exploration to address societal and industrial needs. We introduced research in the regular undergraduate curriculum. Also, outside the curriculum, I introduced a program in 2013, fondly called OUR ("Opportunities for Undergraduate Research") program. This opportunity was not restricted to the students' disciplines – they could find a faculty mentor anywhere in the University, and work on a research problem of their choice to experience the nuances of research. Despite the skepticism of many at the beginning, in these few years, the OUR program has become a differentiator!

The critical stakeholder for these initiatives was no doubt the faculty, whose role ought to be of guidance and mentorship. Quality faculty was still in short supply. In the competitive scenario, perceived insecurity in a private place became a deterrent. I kept my focus on hiring the right kind of faculty, working with them shoulder to shoulder, and retaining them by empowering them to do their work in the best possible way. It was also important for the faculty to have avenues of recharging, and stay life-long learners. In 2013, I became the founding Head of a Faculty Development Center, which recognized faculty as "professionals." Much of the learnings in the faculty development workshops happened from the sharing of "best practices" by peers from all over the world.

At the University campus, fully residential for students, there were some instances of problem behaviors. It took quite an effort from my side to change the mindset of people in charge of student discipline, as I wanted less reliance on reactive and punitive practices – in particular, hefty monetary penalties causing hardship to poor or middle-class parents, which did not aid reform but caused resentment. I put more emphasis on reducing misbehavior through a structured system of positive interventions. The principle of freedom with responsibility was to be practiced by everyone – we needed to openly address regional and other disparities, and actively promote a culture of tolerance, respect for individuals, dignity of labor, and celebration of diversity. This is always a work in progress, but the trend has caught on.

I was the founding Chairperson of the "Gender Committee," established in July 2012 as the Committee on Sensitization of Gender, Prevention, and Redressal of Sexual Harassment, now called the Internal Complaints Committee (ICC) by government order, and later, for a brief period, the Director of the School of Engineering. I worked to bring all my myriad experiences together in a cohesive whole, leading up to, but not ending with the Vice-Chancellorship of Shiv Nadar University starting February 1, 2016, for the maximum allowed two terms. In Indian universities, the Vice-Chancellor is the principal executive and academic officer of the university and exercises overall supervision and control over the affairs of the university. I aspired to build an "intelligent" institution, which is agile, flexible, resilient, diverse yet integrated. Institution building is in fact synonymous with community building – I wanted to build a community where people are not just satisfied or happy, but inspired and engaged. It was the *collective dream* of the University that did not let us sleep!

The University started delivering results slowly but steadily. The first two-day inspection by the regulatory authorities (UGC) in 2016 was a grand success. The University won the "University of the Year" award (*"in existence for less than 10 years"* category) from FICCI (Federation of Indian Chambers of Commerce and Industry, the largest such entity in the country) in 2016. The graduating students started getting well-placed. We started participating in the "National Institutional Ranking Framework," launched by the Government of India, and the University has been the youngest institution in the top-100 "Overall" list every year. In 2020, the University became one of the few university campuses in the country to have received two ISO certifications: ISO 14001:2015 for Environment Management System, and ISO 45001:2018 for Occupational Health & Safety Management System.

We proposed in 2017 to set up an incubator under the prestigious AIM (Atal Incubation Mission) program of Niti Aayog, the think-tank of the

Government of India, and defended it in four grueling rounds of evaluation. From 1719 academic and 1939 non-academic applications, only 10 green-field institutions were selected in the first round in June 2017, with Shiv Nadar University being the youngest institution chosen. It was my first exposure to the nascent ecosystem of incubators/accelerators in the country, but I felt that we were ahead of the curve with all our experiences creating the University itself as a start-up! The incubator's mission was to serve as an active knowledge and resource catalyst for the development of promising entrepreneurs and to incubate and accelerate their early-stage organizations from ideation to marketplace success. This Atal Incubation Center (AIC), an "independent" company named "Shiv Nadar AIC Research Foundation" hosted by the University, has since been a boon to the community.

In this short period of ten years of its existence, Shiv Nadar University has started distinguishing itself from other private universities by having a *"public mission"* at its core, a concomitant and equal focus on education, research, and innovation, and by comprehensive and equitable coverage of disciplines, ranging from the natural and social sciences, humanities, to engineering, and management. In a broad sense, the "public mission" of a university gets manifested through its engagement with and service to the external professional community as well as the society, at national and international levels, in responsible education and research. For Shiv Nadar University, the public mission started with making quality education accessible and affordable for all, in a merit-based admission system, with reasonable fees (comparable to the per-capita GDP of the country), further enabled by generous scholarship schemes such as Gifted Student Scholarship, Merit-cum-Means Scholarship, Rural Scholarship, Sports Scholarship. We needed to make sure that our elite higher education institution did not become *elitist*. It was, however, meant to be a deep-intervention model, and its spread in terms of student and faculty numbers was limited by design. The public mission was amplified by the University's ability to create positive impacts on society through translational aspects of research and innovation, and also through science-driven policy-making, of the kind of the national water policy. Given the immediate environment of Shiv Nadar University, its public mission also included engagement and collaboration with the local communities through a range of short-term and long-term initiatives.

Education without quality serves no purpose. Accreditation of programs and courses is a must so that our students are assured of the minimum prescribed standards. We went through an elaborate process of accreditation of Shiv Nadar University (with Grade "A") by the National Assessment and Accreditation Council in 2019. I think the very definition and assessment of educational quality and excellence need re-imagination today. Higher education needs the "surprise" elements – not all to fit in the "standard" statistics or standardized tests. Judging by uniform standards, trying to mimic another institution, or ranking by uniform parameters, makes our universities risk-averse, and it also stops growth catering to contextual issues. The world needs several different kinds of rankings, and an institution should be allowed to choose the one that suits its journey. The different sets of parameters for evaluation/assessment can be set very carefully.

We also need to combine the priorities of abstract knowledge generation and excellence with "relevant" or contextual research and innovation linked with an economic agenda. The often-unexpected benefits of blue-sky, abstract, or futuristic research cannot be understated, and are essential in the country's quest to become a leader in today's knowledge economy. A competent peer review process is the only way forward.

The University applied for the coveted *"Institution of Eminence"* (IoE) status introduced by the Government of India in December 2017, with credible projections of the current status into 5-year, 10-year, and 15-year milestones in global ranking parameters, and I defended a 10-slide presentation in front of the Empowered Expert Committee[2] in April 2018. A three-day campus visit by a 10-member IoE expert committee happened in early March 2020, just before the COVID outbreak, and at the end of this long process, the University was granted the IoE status, envisioned to elevate Indian higher education to the global stage.

The Culture

The COVID-19 pandemic has shown the necessity of responding to the VUCA (volatile, uncertain, complex, and ambiguous) world with *vision, understanding, clarity, and agility* (VUCA). This was already being built as the culture of the University. The country went into a nationwide lockdown on the evening of March 24, 2020. At the University, we had anticipated and seamlessly shifted to a completely online mode of delivery of courses on Monday, March 16, 2020, right after our mid-semester break, without losing a single day. In the unprecedented, harsh, alarming, almost existentially threatening context, we continued to keep the University rising, thanks to the faculty, staff, students, parents, and well-wishers. We kept taking feedback & innovating. We engaged with and learned from our peers all over the world. And we never stopped thinking big! Our strategy helped us navigate these unusual challenges, ensuring that our commitment to education and research stays firm. For the students on campus during lockdown and students returning to the campus, isolation and quarantine wards were made operational. All essentials of daily need, including medicines, were made available to the campus residents. Two months of the second wave of COVID-19 were particularly hard. Even I contracted the infection. A dedicated team worked round the clock to provide all possible support to members of our community in those very dark days, including oxygen cylinders, hospitalization assistance, medicines, and a lot more. HCL and the Shiv Nadar Foundation extended their full support, standing by every member of the University community, and later organized a vaccination drive covering students on campus, faculty, staff, and their families.

In this post-COVID era, everyone is trying to navigate the maze of online and hybrid teaching and learning models, and there is a lot of speculation on the future. Does the future of education lie in the digital? Will classroom teaching still be relevant? Will brick-and-mortar universities cease to exist? Will, as they show in those edgy science-fiction movies, all teachers be replaced with their electronic versions? What will the jobs of the future look like? I strongly believe that *"Technology will never replace great teachers, but technology in the hands of a great teacher can be transformational."*[3]

Technology can tune and customize/personalize education as needed; it can make processes efficient and transparent. We need to create *digital enablers* to generate and integrate new technology, and *digital literates* to use the power of technology effectively, but *not* be slaves of digital technology.

In a fair system, the University should mirror the society at large – the (eligible part of the) country's demography. It has been proven that diverse teams are smarter![4] Diversity and inclusivity are thus not just the right, morally correct principles, but it makes perfect business sense to promote them. I am very proud of the fact that in India, officially stated hiring policies have no gender bias, and the official norms and procedures are not discriminatory. But unfortunately, discrimination here is subtle and indirect. My main concerns are the conscious and unconscious biases and unstated discriminations.

We need to prevent a division of men and women into two opposing interest groups. We need to understand that each *individual* is unique, and capture and nurture the uniqueness of individuals. The real challenge is to frame and support policies and systems that cater to and respect the uniqueness and choices of an individual – whether a woman or any other gender. It is not about treating everyone equally – it is about understanding the differences rationally, ensuring equity, and making the best of everyone's abilities and choices.

A career in science often demands long hours, there are issues of lack of security and basic amenities that affect women more adversely than men in this society. I faced the issues myself and later tried to pay active attention to these preventable problems. Starting out a career in science, women often face the challenge of balancing the demands of career and family – this "balance" is an elusive concept, which can only lead to mediocrity/career break and dissatisfaction on both fronts. The key is to find the right kind of support. Policies need to be fair, and, ideally, gender-blind (or should we say, gender-rich?).

UNESCO estimates women represent only 33% of STEM researchers globally. UK's Intellectual Property Office estimates women inventors account for 13% of worldwide patent applications. There is still a long way to go. I participated in several discussions over the years organized mainly by the Department of Science and Technology, Government of India, leading to the formulation of some action-oriented programs and schemes, benchmarked with exemplary international practices. However, some policy-level interventions, while having the right intentions, may not be serving the purpose. For example, in April 2017, the length of maternity leave was increased from 12 to 26 weeks through an amendment to the Maternity Benefit Act, 1961. According to a survey in 2020, small firms in India admitted to hiring fewer women because of maternity leave costs, and the 2017 Act was pointed to as a major reason for this reduction in women hires. Not only do women continue to face discrimination – forcing many to quit work, they also remain fearful of using their full quota of maternity leave. As long as the maternity leave policy remains gendered, it harms women by raising the cost of hiring them. I strongly believe that *maternity leave* should be changed to *family leave*, which can be shared by the parents, based on their needs, medical requirements, and demands at the workplace such that all key needs, including the infant's welfare, can be served well.

What Has Worked for Me?

Let me list some of the principles that have been significant for me in my journey.

I believe in leading from the front and leading by example. For instance, I never set deadlines on projects that I do not know every step of. This may not be very practical in every situation, but while building a new institution and a new community, I saw my role as *hands-on, minds-on,* and *hearts-on.* While I was involved with my people at the individual level, I was confident about my ability to manage scale and complexities across intra- and inter-institutional functions.

I always envision and anticipate the future, and allow myself to be proactive, and not just reactive. A related principle is to put out the fire *before* it breaks out. This way I may not be getting a lot of credit because others may not be aware of the danger that was awaiting, but the interests of my institution and my people are best safeguarded.

In many higher education institutions, policies are archaic and rigid. People usually feel safe operating under such "established" frameworks. But for *progress*, some norms need to be broken, and policies therefore need to be impersonal but fluid. As the last two years have shown, we need to be prepared to *expect the unexpected*. The flexibility and autonomy I am talking about should propel excellence in higher education, and not be used to shield mediocrity.

Leaders are *not* coded computers, and I think discretion needs to be applied as liberally as needed. According to me, this judgment call is what defines a leader. I tell my people, *"Give me a good reason to violate a rule!"* Having the right reason for using discretion is very important. You show your authority or "power" by saying "yes" to a "good" proposal & finding a way to support it, and not by saying "no" to off-the-curve thoughts, which happens to be the usual response in many official situations. A leader should not be the gatekeeper, but the gateway! The system of course needs working structures, and one cannot invent a new policy at every turn, but the structures should be kept at the minimum level.

The judgment call I talked about is often based on a leader's ideology. For me, the broad ideology is *humanity*, seeking and chasing the "greater good." Doing the right thing (even when nobody is watching) is *not* always the most convenient thing, but for me, that's the only way forward. I do not have to explain my philosophy – I must embody it. The ideology matters, as one cannot be a leader without convictions. Intellectuals can debate every issue, and come up with two sides of an argument. A leader then has to take a step "forward," based on her/his judgment or philosophy or conviction. In hindsight, if the step is proven to be wrong, that's part of life, but a leader who does not take a step is not a leader. I like the fact that I am accountable, and I take ownership of my actions.

It is important to have clear communication with all the stakeholders at every important turn. But I am conscious of not overdoing or manipulating this bit, out of sheer respect for the intelligence of my people. An important aspect is consistency while dealing with different stakeholders – while the language of communication often needs to be tweaked for different segments of the community, and one may leave out some details for some, the core message should be consistent and honest. I feel comfortable creating and working in an environment of trust. When I was young, I read a saying by a Bengali sage, *"it is better to trust and be proven wrong than to mistrust and be proven wrong"* – I completely agree!

Can you teach/learn Leadership? Are leaders born or made? While leadership traits come naturally to some people, I think these traits can be inculcated. How do you improve in the practice of leadership? Like everything else, to get better, you need to constantly improve on three elements: (a) knowledge, (b) skills, and (c) attitude. I would like to stay a lifelong learner, with humility.

I have been fortunate to be associated with the first *international* Executive Leadership Academy (ELA) of the Center for Studies in Higher Education (CSHE), University of California-Berkeley, hosted by Shiv Nadar University in November 2021. The program was directed by ELA's founder, Josefina Castillo Baltodano, and steered by CSHE Director, Dr. George Blumenthal, on the theme of "Leading in a Multicultural & Global Environment." Josie and George prompted me to share my story, and I would like to record my deep admiration and appreciation.

My working style has been based on the understanding that life is short – if something is worth doing, it's worth doing well. If you are lucky to find your passion, you are likely to excel in it. Passion with commitment is all that it takes to be successful and happy. Starting from the idealism and optimism I inherited, I have been self-driven with the desire to impact the lives of people – creative leadership was the only way forward in the large, complex, and mostly unexplored higher education scene in India. I have been fortunate to see the effects of my efforts in real-time. In the process of a somewhat lone journey as a leader, while one needs to cultivate detachment, one should never lose the essential human quality of compassion to fellow human beings, in fact, to all living creatures – vulnerable or strong, and to all of nature surrounding us, and there will not be any regrets in life.

Discussion Questions

1 What would you look for in a potential leadership role? How would you assess what is right for you?
2 Ghosh's *ikigai* ("life purpose" or "raison d'être") – shaped by her convictions and driven by her desire to impact the lives of people – has been a daily guide rather than an end goal. What is your *ikigai*? How can *ikigai*'s four elements of what you love (your passion), what your professional world needs (your mission), what you are good at (your vocation), and what you can get paid for (your profession) converge for you?
3 Research has been an integral part of Ghosh's journey in higher education. Do you think it is important for a university leader to have this experience first-hand?

4 The most defining leadership trait is the ability to inspire and motivate others. Can this trait be learned? If not, why? If yes, how?
5 Have you encountered a situation in which the "right thing to do" clashed with the "convenient thing to do"?

Notes

1 You will find a clear description of the work and its importance in some popular books, for example, in *"The Quantum Challenge: Modern Research on the Foundations of Quantum Mechanics,"* G. Greenstein and A.G. Zajonc, Jones and Bartlett Publishers, 2006, pp.169-173.
2 The committee tasked with the selection and subsequent monitoring of the "Institutions of Eminence" was called the Empowered Expert Committee in the UGC Guidelines 2017.
3 George Couros on Twitter, 11 September 2014.
4 See, for example, *"Why Diverse Teams Are Smarter,"* D. Rock and H. Grant, Harvard Business Review, 4 November 2016.

5
A LATINO PRESIDENT'S RETROSPECTIVE

Diversity, Ethnicity, and Race in American Higher Education

Alexander Gonzalez

Abstract

Gonzalez held two presidencies and one provost position in the Cal State system. As a Latino, ethnicity and diversity were always factors, positive or negative. As a member of the "firsts" generation in higher education during the Civil Rights and Chicano movements, he points out early on that it will take many years to achieve parity between students and leadership that resembles them and sees as a major issue whether there will be minority leaders to fill leadership positions. Gonzalez's experience growing up in East L.A. and being *bien educados* from the barrio during the 1960s taught him to "balance [his] notions of morality with strict adherence to societal norms" and became the "crucible that forged [his] identity and career in higher education." His journey from department chair to president provides useful insight and commentary on institutional structure and organizational behavior. Taking a position as assistant to the president at Fresno State led to the provost position that prepared him for a presidency. Throughout his presidencies, he dealt with the proverbial us-them of faculty and administration, connected community and campus, developed community support, and fundraised. Transparency in budgeting and use of funds, improvement of campus operations, all this and more, Gonzalez's story models leadership, emphasizing context and communication in overcoming barriers and opposition.

Introduction

Being able to contribute to this volume provides an opportunity to share what was for me an interesting, challenging, and fulfilling career in higher education. And, given the current social, political, and racial situation in this country, I can also look at it through the lens of a president of color. Having served in a large public university system for over forty years, on three campuses and as president at two of them, I want to share my thoughts about the condition of higher education for minorities as well as how I managed to achieve some administrative success. I hope it informs those who may want to follow this career path. Finally, I want to answer the question that I'm frequently asked: How did someone like you become a university president?

Well, I certainly did not attend "presidents' school" and I was not anointed by anyone. But there was a definite path as well as goals I set along the way. And while I learned from my successes, I probably learned more from my mistakes and failures.

Throughout my career, my ethnicity was always a factor. Also, the issue of diversity was always present. Sometimes it was a positive influence but often it was negative. Nevertheless, I had to deal with both; especially during the time I began my career in higher education.

In many ways my path was deliberate, but a great part of it was serendipitous. In that sense, it's probably not much different from the other stories you will read in this collection of professional life histories. However, I think the key to understanding my career path is to recognize the role other people played in its development, how I recognized opportunity, and that I had the presence of mind to take a risk.

The State of Diversity and the Presidency in Higher Education

Since 1986, the American Council on Education (ACE) has conducted a comprehensive study of American college and university presidents (American College President Study) and published the first report in 1988. Since then, it has completed the study about every five years; the latest report was published in 2017. Broad in scope, it provides an important view of the American college presidency at all levels, including background, demographics, and the institutions they serve. According to ACE:

> *College and university presidents occupy a leadership role unlike any other. They play a critical role in ensuring their institution's success, especially as internal and external pressures have grown at a time of resource instability and demographic change.*

Since it was first published in 1988, the American College President Study (ACPS) has remained the most comprehensive source of information about the college presidency and higher education leadership pipeline. (https://www.aceacps.org/)

A few findings from the 2017 study focused on the diversity of college presidents. According to the results, 83% of the presidents in the study were White and 17% were Minority. Of the White group, 58% were men and 25% were women. For the Minority group of presidents, 12% were men and 5% were women. Overall, men still held 70% of the presidencies.

While African Americans comprised 8% of the presidents in the study, Latinos held only 4% of the presidencies in the country. Moreover, Asian or Asian Americans accounted for only 2%, and American Indian/Alaskan Native led only 1% of the country's institutions of higher education. The study also found that the majority of Minority presidents led public institutions (71%) and that 36% of them were at the Associates degree level (https://www.aceacps.org/minority-presidents/).

Based on the findings, the study concluded that while some progress has been made in diversifying the presidency, it is clear that the number of minority presidents has not kept pace with the growing number of minority students attending higher education institutions across the country. In fact, the data suggest that if minority student enrollment continues to grow at the current rate, it will take many years to achieve parity between students and leadership that resembles them. In the broader context, however, the issue is whether there will be sufficient numbers of leaders from minority populations who can fill the positions that will be needed in the future.

The Context for My Experience and Perspective

The California Master Plan for Higher Education was established in 1960 and was the envy of systems of higher education around the world. Comprised of three different segments, it promised access to a free education for all citizens of California who qualified for admission. The three segments include the University of California (UC), The California State University (CSU), and the California Community Colleges.

My higher education career was spent in the California State University. Today it is the nation's largest four-year public university. It educates 482,000 students on twenty-three campuses in California from Humboldt near the Oregon border to San Diego, literally a few minutes from the Mexican border city of Tijuana. In addition, courses are offered in eight off-campus centers as well as online.

The CSU employs 53,000 faculty and staff and nearly three-quarters of CSU students are students of color. Nearly one-third of the undergraduates are the first in their families to attend college. Women comprise 57% of the student body while Hispanic/Latinx students are the largest single group totaling over 207,000 (43%). African American (4%), White (22.4), Asian/Pacific Islander (15.7), and students of Mixed Race (4.4%) also contribute significantly to the overall diversity of the student body within the CSU. More important, 95% of all enrolled students come from California. (The California State University Fact Book 2020).

My Path to Academe or How I Ended Up in Higher Education

Growing up in Los Angeles during the 1950s was much different than it is today. The tallest building then was the City Hall, the downtown area was busy and bustling and even the streetcars still operated and made their scheduled rounds.

I was born and raised in East L.A., a few miles east of downtown. It was geographically defined, and in many ways, it was a closed and parochial society. While still diverse with a few Anglo, Japanese, Armenian, and Russian families, the majority of the people who lived in East L.A. were Mexican. Some had been there for generations, while others were immigrants from Mexico, and still others had moved to Los Angeles from other parts of the Southwest. During World War II, many were drawn to Los Angeles to work in the factories and other industries as part of the war effort. In the aftermath of the war, Los Angeles was developing around new industries as well as becoming a new melting pot of peoples.

Like so many others in East L.A., my parents came from Mexico; my father because of the Mexican Revolution, and my mother to start a new life with him. My father was born in Aguascalientes, Mexico in 1912, but because of the Mexican Revolution, his family was forced to flee the country while he was still a toddler. They settled in Kansas and worked for the railroad for a while but when things calmed down, the family returned to Mexico. But a pattern of leaving and returning to Mexico played out several times during that period with the family relocating to Arizona and California and back to Mexico. Eventually, during the early 1930s, my father settled permanently in Los Angeles. Later, while visiting his family in Mexico, he met my mother, they were married, and returned to Los Angeles, where they began life together in what was part of Boyle Heights. All but one of their seven children were born in East Los Angeles. That is where we grew up and attended school.

The school system in Los Angeles and California post World War II was one of the best in the country. Along with a developing economy, the schools focused on providing the best education at the time.

As the middle child of seven, when I began school, I was fortunate that I had two older sisters and a brother who were already in the school system. Even though my first language was Spanish when I entered school, because of my older siblings' experience, I had already developed English as a second language. The entire time I was in elementary school, not one of my teachers was other than white. And even though my mother did not speak English, we served as her translators, got along, and did well in school.

Those were my formative years, both at home and school. My parents were hard-working and independent and instilled in us those values (hard work, honesty, respect, and family) that are at the core of what my siblings and I are today. These values have their basis in Mexican culture and are common in Latin America. In addition, my parents were good Catholics, so religion played an integral part in our lives while we were growing up.

We may have been poor, but we were well-behaved and were "*bien educados*" (well-educated, in the social sense) and respected not only our elders but those in the community. We learned that with age came a sense of wisdom and respect that was accorded to those individuals who were older and had earned it. In addition, we learned to respect those in authority. This respect for authority was not subservience, but rather a way to transact everyday behaviors and interactions within a defined scope of what was acceptable and expected. So we obeyed our teachers and the police as well as anyone else who was in a position of authority.

The reason I raise this is that this view of respect for legitimate authority later played a significant role in my development during my undergraduate years during a time of great turmoil in this country. While I had grown up respecting authority, within a few years everything was being called into question. My ability to balance my notions of morality with strict adherence to societal norms and authority was the crucible that forged my identity and career in higher education. To this day, understanding the roles that legitimate authority, respect, cooperation, and shared governance play in higher education is at the core of my approach to administration and the role of the president.

But let me focus on another important aspect of my early development. Despite growing up in East LA, I became aware of inequality, racism, and prejudice rather early. Living in East LA was an environment that was known and, to a great extent, comfortable. It was comprised of different neighborhoods, and everyone knew their roles. As a young boy, I learned early on what was and what was not acceptable behavior.

But when you left the geographic boundaries of East LA, there was a palpable difference. Not only did the structures look different (they were clearly newer and more expensive), the people were different as well. Venturing out of East LA meant confronting this reality and experiencing that things were different and other people lived and worked differently. The stares and glances also communicated clearly that you were not at the same level, neither socially nor economically. So along with living in the *barrio* came the understanding that one knew one's place and that the world was different outside the confines of the familiar time and place. While unspoken, it was clear to me that there was both an informal as well as formal stratification that one had to learn to navigate.

I attended Garfield High School, made famous by the actor Edward James Olmos in the movie *Stand and Deliver*. At the end of my senior year in high school, I made one of the most momentous decisions of my life that would have repercussions and influence my life's path forever.

The year was 1963 and graduation was rapidly approaching. While I was a good student, the opportunities to attend college were limited. It was common for only a very small number of graduates to go on to the local community college and then on to the local state university. In reality, the path taken by most of my peers who did manage to graduate from high school was to find a job, get married, and start a family.

Faced with these prospects for the future, my best friend and I decided we would take a different route and join the Navy and, of course, see the world. So, one day just a few weeks before graduation, we went to the recruitment office to sign up. But it was during lunch and the Navy recruiter was not there. However, the recruiter for the Air Force was, so we decided that a different shade of blue would work just as well for us, and we signed up. Of course, we were only seventeen at the time and needed our parents' signatures. That accomplished, we joined on the "buddy system." Unfortunately, after basic training, we did not see one another again for another four years!

While often challenging, the four years I spent in the Air Force taught me some vital life lessons. I was exposed to different peoples and places. In the military, I was thrown into the same experience with other young men from diverse geographic, racial, and socioeconomic backgrounds. Moreover, as part of my assignments, I was fortunate to have traveled within the United States and overseas. Notwithstanding the fact that the Vietnam War was building at the time, given the circumstances, I did manage to have as positive an experience as I could.

During that time, I also learned several things that would influence my life and career. First, I learned about discipline and about *being* disciplined. It is critical for any endeavor but especially in the world of academe.

Without setting goals and being disciplined to achieve those goals it is very difficult to succeed. For example, as an undergraduate and later as a graduate student, I had to have the discipline to complete each step in the path to the degree. I learned that many very smart people did not complete the degree primarily because they did not have the discipline to stick to the task and achieve the objective they had set. Second, I learned about setting goals and how to achieve them. Third, I learned about leadership and how to develop and exercise it. But most significant, was that I learned that even though I had come from East LA, I could compete with anyone. The military for me was the great democratizer. It reinforced the idea that I could succeed and not be afraid to compete at any level. It was while I was in the military that I decided that after I completed my service, I would return to school and pursue a college education.

Upon my discharge from the Air Force, I returned to Los Angeles and began working where I had worked while in high school. I began driving a truck delivering laundry. I did that for a few months but a short time later, I realized that I was not getting much out of the job. While working, I also took my first course at the local community college (East Los Angeles College) at night. It was a course in psychology, and when I completed it, I decided to quit my job and return to school full-time under the G.I. Bill. The following semester I was fully enrolled and thoroughly interested in my studies. It was during that semester at the community college that I met an alumnus of Pomona College who convinced me to apply. I did, and surprisingly, was admitted.

Pomona College is the founding college of the Claremont Colleges located in Claremont, a city 30 miles east of Los Angeles. It is a small liberal arts institution that prides itself not only on the quality of its curriculum, but its faculty and students. When I enrolled, the college had a student body of around 1,200, and of those, probably no more than a dozen students were Mexican American (the term used then). However, that same year some minority students were admitted at the other colleges so there was a critical mass of us emerging at the Claremont Colleges. The year was 1968 and the country was experiencing not only the war in Vietnam, but also the Civil Rights Movement and the Women's Movement, all at the same time. It was not long after I arrived that the status quo was being challenged across the nation, and by the end of the year at the Claremont Colleges, we had founded a Chicano student group and had successfully made the argument to start a Chicano Studies program.

The establishment of the Chicano Studies program at the Claremont Colleges was significant because it signaled the impact that Latinos were having in California. Programs in Chicano Studies had been established at California State University, Northridge and others were being developed at

San Francisco State and Fresno State. In addition, the Civil Rights and Chicano movements were developing across California and the Southwest. At the same time, immigration from Mexico and Latin America was increasing. Not only was the status quo being challenged, it was changing.

I majored in history at Pomona but maintained my interest in psychology. Then during my junior year, I learned that a Latino professor had recently arrived at Pitzer College, another of the Claremont Colleges. Because we could take classes at the other colleges, I signed up for his course. It turned out that the professor was Manuel Ramirez, at that time one of a handful of Latino psychologists in the country. He was originally from Texas, and his class focused on issues affecting Latinos at all educational levels. We covered a wide array of topics that included bilingualism and cultural influences on learning. The scope was broad and included both anthropological and psychological perspectives. I was certainly affected by the course and the professor. It was so interesting and novel. All of a sudden it made sense. There was a context for how to understand the uniqueness and the importance of differences and how they interact within the broader social context.

My time at Pomona College was very significant for me both intellectually and professionally. Originally my goal was to obtain the bachelor's degree and enter the workforce but, as the time to graduate drew near, I found myself thinking of continuing my education. While graduate school was a possibility, I was also encouraged by some of my professors to think of law school as an option. I applied to both and was admitted. After weighing my options with my wife of less than a year, Gloria, we both agreed that I would attend Harvard.

My first year at Harvard Law School was pretty much what I expected. It was very different from undergraduate school, and of course, it was Harvard. It involved a tremendous amount of reading and the Socratic method wasn't all that inspiring. But I managed to get through the first year and made a lot of friends along the way. What I hadn't expected was that there was a core of Latino students from across the country at the law school who identified and interacted as a group and provided support to one another. The significance was clear and the impact was long-lasting.

After my first year of law school, I was fortunate to land a summer job with a law firm in Los Angeles. My wife and I returned home for the summer. I worked twelve-hour days and saw what practicing law was going to be like. By the end of that summer, I had a good idea of what to expect as I began my second year of law school. What I did not expect was that I would become disenchanted with law school and the profession. After months of thought and questioning, I concluded that I just could not see myself practicing law. One day halfway through the second year, I decided to take a leave from law school and regroup. It was a tough choice, but with my wife's unconditional support, I decided to take the time to really assess and explore what I wanted to do.

My experience with Manuel Ramirez and the work I had done with him at the Claremont Colleges convinced me that I wanted to pursue graduate studies in psychology. After I took a leave from law school, it made sense to reconnect with Manuel and work with him at the graduate level. At the time he was moving to the University of California, Santa Cruz. I applied and was accepted into the graduate program where I completed a Ph.D. in Social Psychology.

While at Santa Cruz, I became absolutely certain of the choice I had made. Psychology as a discipline was clearly what I wanted to do. In addition, other events happened that would impact my future. During my second year, my wife and I moved to the campus where we were preceptors at a dorm that was specifically "themed" for Chicano students. Many of them were from the Central Valley of California and were from rural backgrounds. These students were great to work with and taught me quite a bit. We enjoyed it so much that we stayed in the dorm for three years. I think living and working with students on a daily basis further convinced me that I wanted a career in higher education as a faculty member. The other significant event was when I met my mentor, Elliot Aronson, who introduced me to social psychology through his work, and who would influence and inspire me throughout my career. Finally, as a graduate student, I was able to pursue my interest in how psychology and social factors influence Latinos differently. As a result, I was able to develop and teach my course in the developing subfield of Psychology that focused on Latinos. For me, the opportunity reinforced the career choice I had made.

When I was about to complete my dissertation in 1979, I began to look for a job. Unfortunately, it was one of those periods in the country, but especially in California, when the economy was headed in a downward direction, and there were few employment opportunities available. In California, there was nothing for a neophyte social psychologist. I was very fortunate in that I had interviewed and gotten an offer to do research and teach at the Center for the Social Organization of Schools at Johns Hopkins University in Baltimore.

As luck would have it, I ran into an old friend from Harvard Law School, Hugo Morales, while walking in downtown Santa Cruz. He told me he was teaching at Fresno State and how much he enjoyed it. He also told me he was in the process of starting a bilingual radio station. Within a few weeks of seeing him, I saw an advertisement for a job at Fresno State, applied, and was invited for an interview. What I found at Fresno State resonated with me. The students were very good, the faculty I was to work with was a tightly knit group who were focused on their students, and the mission of the university was something I could believe in and work to achieve. Even though I knew very little else about California State University or Fresno, I took the job at Fresno State instead of Johns Hopkins.

The Academic Ladder (or Treadmill)

I began my teaching career at Fresno State in La Raza Studies where I taught courses related to psychology and Chicano Studies. During my first year there, I also wrote a grant that was funded for three years to assist the Hollister School District (near San Jose) in implementing a program focused on a cooperative learning approach to bilingual education. After my second year, however, I moved to the Psychology Department and continued with the grant. During my third year in the Psychology Department, I received a postdoctoral fellowship from the National Research Council and spent the following year at Stanford University where I worked with Phil Zimbardo conducting research on the psychology of time.

While at Stanford, the opportunity to move from Fresno State to another position arose. However, after weighing what I would gain as well as lose, I decided to stay at Fresno State. I think the deciding factor for me was the fact that the CSU mission was so compelling that I decided that I wanted to be part of it for the long term. I understood clearly how important the role of the CSU was for the state and its people – especially for the growing Hispanic/Latino population. In that dorm at UC Santa Cruz, I witnessed the impact that higher education has on the everyday lives of Latinos from low-income backgrounds. At Fresno State, I found the work in the classroom very rewarding, and the students and colleagues I worked with were among the best anywhere. As a result, after a year of post-doctoral experience at Stanford, I returned to Fresno State. To my astonishment, I returned as a tenured professor.

I guess a lot can be said for being at the right time and place, but for me, it was a wonderful surprise to return to campus and learn that I had been granted tenure and promoted to professor. As it turned out, being away certainly helped. I was very active in pursuing grants and other opportunities, and I think the value I brought to the department was clear. But more significant, was the fact that Tomas Arciniega (who would later become President of CSU Bakersfield) was the Vice President for Academic Affairs at Fresno State. Again, it was because of his support and mentoring that I was a viable candidate for promotion. As a result, I returned and continued to teach, do research, and work with students. It was a great life!

The time I spent after my return to the faculty at Fresno State was the most important in my career. I became active in the life of the university and broadened the sphere of colleagues with whom I interacted and worked. I served on committees and was exposed to shared governance and the politics that are part of any campus. I learned about the importance of scholarship and teaching as well as the fundamental values of the academy. I also learned from experience that, in many ways, being a faculty member is not only often a solitary experience, but also that this individualistic approach to success is what is rewarded. Being cooperative and working for the good of the whole is, in many ways, contrary to the basic motivational structure of the university. Later as an administrator, I learned the importance of this observation. Very often, behavior that would seem individually focused and motivated, was in reality, consistent as a frame of reference. Again, integrating my faculty experience with my administrative role was useful and critical to my success as an academic leader.

It was also a time when I worked closely with students both at the undergraduate and graduate levels. Perhaps the most important lesson I learned during this time was the importance of being a role model and mentoring students. With any relationship, there has to be balance, but there is an inherently unequal relationship between a professor and a student. It is crucial that this interaction be positive. As I worked with students, I learned to appreciate this relationship. I learned a lot from my students, just as I hope they learned from me. As a result, I formed very strong bonds with students who, to this day, stay in contact with me. I guess the axiom here is that whether a faculty member or president, students come first and are the reason we exist.

Four years after my return to the department I was asked by my colleagues to stand for chairman. After some thought, I agreed and began a three-year term as the leader of the department. This was my first foray into administration. I had no idea what it was about or what I was supposed to do from a technical point of view. However, I learned very quickly that the department chair was only one among equals and that the role of the chair was critical since he/she oversaw at the closest level, the operations of the department and interactions of the faculty and students. In addition, I learned early on that control of resources was critical, as well as the ability to guide and weigh in on the hiring process. I also came to understand the importance of being able to control resources and exert influence on the processes that are part of every department. More importantly, however, I recognized the long-term effects this influence could have. For me, that was the first real sense I had of the importance of leadership in an organization.

Fortunately, very quickly I experienced success as department chair. It was good sized, with about 35 faculty members, many of whom had worked with one another for years. In many ways, the tensions that existed among the members had developed over the years. As chair, I used common sense and my ability to interpret the behaviors, both good and bad, that were part of departmental life. The result was that I addressed many long-standing issues and helped the department develop into what was arguably one of the best at the university. The number of majors doubled in size and it became one of the most popular and respected departments at Fresno State. For me, the most significant aspect of this change was the realization that the leader of a unit could help both faculty and students so directly.

My initial success in administration had not gone unnoticed by the president of the university. During my tenure at Fresno State the President and I came to know one another. He was always very cordial and showed interest in my work. Over time he had indicated to me that I should seriously consider administration. I declined. I just couldn't understand how any job could be better than being a faculty member. However, when my term as department chair was about to end, he made me an offer I could not refuse. He wanted me to work for him as the assistant to the president. He promised to mentor me, and at the end of the year, if I didn't find administration to be something I wanted to do, I would then return to the department as a member of the faculty.

The president, Harold Haak, lived up to his word. My experience working with him was what he said it would be. Every morning we would meet and spend time discussing the previous day as well as what was ahead. He explained to me the significance (or insignificance) of meetings, events, and actions both at the campus and system level. He was a great teacher and mentor, and I learned a great deal about university administration from him. Unfortunately, I only was to work with him for that year because, after a few months, he announced that he was stepping down at the end of the year. He had been president at Fresno State for eleven years and he was feeling tired. At the time he did not know that he was suffering from a major health issue. He thought he was just exhausted and that it was time to step down. However, because of his decision, my role as his assistant was greatly expanded and I learned quite a lot from representing him at various functions on and off the campus. It was an opportunity that was unexpected but extremely valuable.

When the search for a new president was concluded, I was able to take advantage of an unexpected opportunity. The search for President Haak's successor yielded several candidates, among them the Vice President for Academic Affairs at Fresno State. The Vice President was not selected, however, and in the end, opted to take a presidency somewhere else. As a result, the vice president position was open, and after an on-campus search, I was appointed to the position as the interim under the new president.

In retrospect, I can say that the provost position was difficult but also very rewarding. In terms of learning and day-to-day operations, the provost is at the center of the academic enterprise and is where the major academic decisions are made – not just about the curriculum but about everything. It allowed me to work with the faculty at all levels and taught me the value and importance of having the support of those around me. While much is said of leadership, being the academic leader of an institution is much more than being an administrator. It means being the leader and often the arbiter. The members of the faculty expect you to assert their academic values just as they would. Moreover, they also reserve the right to correct you when you are wrong. In many ways, the provost position prepared me for the scope of responsibility and issues I would encounter as a president.

The Presidency

I was fortunate that I served as president of two institutions in the California State University. While some things are similar because these campuses are both part of the same system and at some level, higher education institutions share many things in common, each is very different and presents a different set of issues.

The first time I was named president it was to lead Cal State San Marcos, a new campus in north San Diego County. It was founded in 1989 and began its operations in a rented space next to a furniture store. Faculty members had to be hired, academic programs had to be developed and the plans for the permanent campus had to be drawn up. These initial tasks were accomplished by the founding president and faculty. The first buildings on campus were opened for the 1992–93 academic year. I arrived as the second president for the 1997–98 academic year.

The San Marcos campus had been developed initially during a time of fiscal constraint for the State of California. However, the decision was made to build out the campus, and sufficient funding was allocated to proceed. In order to do so, faculty members were given a reduced teaching load to develop the curriculum and the organizational structure. It may sound fairly straightforward but in actuality, it was very difficult.

Along with developing the basic structures on the academic side, the operations of the campus had to be developed. Payroll, human resources and facilities, and maintenance were all part of the day-to-day work that had to be accomplished.

When I arrived at San Marcos, much of the basic infrastructure had been completed. The six years I was there were spent building out the campus; not only the buildings and facilities, but also policies and procedures that had to be in place. In addition, operations including university advancement and fund raising had to be developed. I even had to start intramural sports and competitive athletics. All this was going on while we were building enrollment and programs.

After six years, enrollment was strong, community support had increased dramatically, and what was once a chicken ranch was now a real campus with new buildings and classrooms, a science building, and a beautiful library. In addition, the campus had become a very important part of the social and economic development of the region.

The experience at San Marcos taught me a great deal about being a campus president. Paramount was the importance of working with all members of the campus community and having a clear set of goals. But perhaps the most important lesson I learned while at San Marcos, was the role the community plays in the development and functioning of a campus. In this instance, much of the community had actually been against the establishment of the university. The area was a very popular retirement destination. Many of the residents were former military. It was not until the campus reached out and brought them into the university and demonstrated its value to the community and them personally, that things changed. Today the campus is thriving and a critical player in the area.

In contrast, when I arrived in 2003 as its eleventh president, the Sacramento State campus presented a different set of challenges and opportunities. Established after World War II (1947), the campus is located at the state capitol and along with San Jose State and San Francisco State, is considered one of the larger campuses in northern California. A comprehensive university, 85% of its students come from the region.

My predecessor at Sacramento State had led the campus for nineteen years, from 1984 until my arrival in 2003. During that time, many changes had occurred both at the campus and system levels. For example, in the early 80s the faculty and staff unionized. Nevertheless, the Board of Trustees decided to continue the practice of shared governance. Over time, this decision became an exceedingly difficult issue since the faculty union is technically the bargaining agent for the faculty, yet the academic/faculty senates continue to exercise control over the curriculum. This has been a point of conflict that has not been resolved and has played out differently on the campuses across the system.

Over the years, the faculty members of Sacramento State had been fairly aggressive and had asserted their role as part of the shared governance of the university. In fact, the relations between the faculty and administration could be aptly described as being very contentious. After the founding president served from 1947 until 1965 (18 years) there was a series of eight presidents who served various terms, each of them either short or very short.

There had been a long history of conflict between the faculty and the administration on the campus. In fact, a few years before I arrived, the faculty had changed the name of the governance body from the "Academic Senate" to the "Faculty Senate" and had taken all voting rights away from administrators. That is the environment into which I entered in 2003.

At the outset, my approach was to attempt to change the most obvious things that needed attention. Very quickly, I developed an initiative to move the campus forward. It was called *Destination 2010* and had four cornerstones. The first was to develop outstanding academic and student programs. The second was to have a welcoming campus environment. This was aimed at bringing the community onto the campus and making it part of the greater region. For years, people knew of the university but had never been on the campus or taken part in activities. Third was to have a dynamic physical environment. The need for renovation and some new facilities was obvious. And the fourth was to develop community support for the University. Clearly, there was a need for fundraising and community involvement.

While the initiative was very well received both on and off the campus, of course, it was still a matter of implementation before there would be believers. Very quickly we began the process of implementation and developed plans for physical changes to the campus as well as strategic planning. For the first three years, things moved along rapidly and we built a new parking structure, new student housing, a new bookstore, a new building to house information technology and resources, a new field house for athletics, and the students had passed a referendum to build a new recreation and wellness center. By any measure, the changes that were being implemented on the campus were transformational.

On the operational side, I was in the process of implementing a more transparent approach to budget allocation and governance. At first, I experienced some resistance from the faculty leadership of the Faculty Senate because of the sheer complexity of the budget process of a large public university in the CSU system. In fact, for years the allocation process on campus remained relatively unchanged. However, the year I assumed the presidency was the beginning of a period of recurring budget reductions California would experience over the next decade. Nevertheless, I attempted to include faculty and students in the budget discussions.

After three years however, it was obvious to me that the leadership of the faculty and the faculty union were displeased with the lack of progress with the collective bargaining process at the system level because contract negotiations were rancorous and had stalled. That was when I along with three other presidents, were targeted for votes of no confidence. Needless to say, it was a time of stress and conflict. I saw what raw politics and communication could do to one's image and position. In the end, the vote passed against me and my colleague presidents at the other CSU campuses.

That being the result, however, the very next day the local newspaper carried a full-page ad developed and paid for by local businesses and other supporters thanking me for my leadership and the changes I had brought to the campus. In addition, the Board of Trustees and the Chancellor not only supported but praised me as well.

This was the watershed moment that really changed the campus. In the past, the almost inevitable conflict with the faculty had essentially resulted in the presidents leaving the university. With the community's reaction and the Board's action, it was clear that it was a new day. It is important to note that during all of this, I essentially did not get into a contest with the detractors but rode it out. In the end, that was the best course of action, and it allowed us to move forward.

The accusation against me was that I was somehow misusing funds, so almost immediately I established a committee to review the budget. The committee was comprised of faculty, staff, and students. Within a few weeks, the committee issued its findings and stated that they agreed with my actions and that I had proceeded correctly. Subsequently, I established the committee (called the University Budget Advisory Committee) permanently, and it has operated very effectively ever since.

During the twelve years I was president of Sacramento State, the initiative I put into play at my arrival was completed successfully, the operations of the campus changed substantially and the campus' status in the community improved dramatically. But perhaps one of the most significant changes that came about was a statement on shared governance that was developed jointly by the faculty and administration and endorsed by the Faculty Senate. That statement and the clarification of roles led to a greater understanding of shared governance in a collective bargaining environment and allowed the university to move forward in a way that was not possible before. Because of the involvement and leadership of the Faculty Senate and the general faculty membership as well, a review of the academic programs was also completed successfully. This was the first major step in meeting head-on the issues that existed and would continue to face the campus and state.

On a personal note, the Faculty Senate passed a resolution commending me on my leadership. Specifically, they noted the implementation of the University Budget Advisory Committee, the Statement on Shared Governance, and the level of communication and cooperation that existed. In addition, the commendation was shared with the CSU Board of Trustees, the Chancellor, and all campus presidents.

Most Significant Achievements

In retrospect, while there were many achievements during my tenure as president, for me, three are salient. First, was the fact that I was able to lead two campuses that were not making progress and that were essentially "stuck," to turn around and make significant changes that in many ways, transformed the campuses. Clearly, the situations at both campuses were filled with challenges and roadblocks. However, overcoming barriers and opposition resulted in many positive outcomes and set the course for the future for both campuses. Sometimes being a "change agent" is what is required for an organization to move forward in a positive direction. I served that role and, despite the challenges, enjoyed the engagement and results. Today, both campuses are thriving.

Just as vital, but not as focused an activity, was the effort to diversify the student body, faculty, and staff at each of the campuses where I served. As a faculty member, I engaged as many students as possible, especially those from underrepresented groups. Later as department chair, in addition to attracting as many minority students as possible, I was able to hire both women and faculty of color and diversify what had been a predominantly white male department. As Provost, I led the effort to attain the designation of a Hispanic Serving Institution (HSI) for Fresno State. The threshold to receive the designation was an enrollment of at least 25% of the student body that was Hispanic. As president of San Marcos, I set the same goal and the campus achieved HSI status as well. Finally, in Sacramento the campus not only reached the threshold to become an HSI, but it also was recognized as an Asian American and Pacific Islander (AAPI) serving institution. In addition, the campus was recognized as a Minority Serving Institution based on the overall minority student enrollment.

Being designated a minority-serving institution is significant in many ways. Not only does the institution enjoy benefits from the federal government as a result of its designation, but the students can avail themselves of internships and positions within the federal employment system. More important, however, is that minority students are also attracted to the institution because they know the student body reflects who they are. As a result, diversity becomes part of the campus' character and has an impact on all aspects of its operation and reputation.

Perhaps, what I feel was most important throughout my career, was the fact that I was able to mentor and assist many people. As a faculty member, I tried to be a mentor to all the students who worked with me. Many of them went on to complete advanced degrees and develop successful careers in a variety of fields including law, medicine, business, and education. Later as a provost and president, I was fortunate to be able to work with faculty and others aspiring to secure leadership positions. I did this informally and through programs such as the ACE Fellows and ASSCU programs, the Executive Leadership Academy as well as through programs at the campus and system levels. Several of the people I mentored went on to serve as provosts and presidents at campuses in California and other parts of the country.

Lessons Learned

Throughout my career, I learned many lessons – some that were easy and others that were very difficult. However, certain themes emerged that I'd like to share.

To begin, there is no one single path to the presidency. While there are perhaps more people filling the president's position who have come from the academic side of the house, there are also others who have come from student affairs, business and administration, and other non-traditional areas. This observation supports the view that it really is about "fit" more than anything else. Leadership can be exercised in many forms and there is certainly no dearth of books and publications that give advice or even a "how to" approach to leading and managing an organization. But in the end, what counts is your leadership style and the "fit" with the institution and its people.

Regardless of what path you may be pursuing, people are still the secret ingredient to achieving success. You do not operate in a vacuum, so it's the support and interaction with people that ultimately will help you achieve your goal(s). In reviewing my path to becoming a university president, it would have never happened without the advice, support, and influence of key people at each stage of my development.

Ultimately, it all begins with you. One of the most important lessons you can learn is about your true self. You must ask yourself who you are and what motivates you to want to become a college or university president. Whatever the reason, you need to explore and determine what drives you and whether are willing to take on one of these jobs. At the core, you have to know yourself.

However, knowing yourself is not necessarily a one-time experience where you achieve an "aha" moment as a culminating experience. On the contrary, I've found that what is most important is that you need to develop a sense of self, of who you are, relative to the position you are in and what you aspire to be professionally. You are shaped by your environment and your experiences and, if you are aware of that fact, then your ascendency to the presidency will come a lot easier and will be much more rewarding.

Another important lesson I have come to realize is that to be a successful president, there has to be balance in not only your approach to the job and the task at hand, but also in your life generally. Most presidencies are, or can be, all-consuming. It is not an exaggeration to say that the job can be 24/7. With the day-to-day issues and demands on your time, it is easy to be consumed by the role and exigencies of the situation. Nevertheless, there also has to be a counter to this constant pressure and being "on" all the time. With the help of my wife and family, I found that it's critical to set time aside for family and activities that are focused on you and not the job. Over the years I tried to incorporate much of the job as part of what we did as a family or a couple. Unfortunately, that doesn't always work. So, you have to look for ways to separate yourself from the role of president and leader to one of the other roles you may have. The key is to find a balance that will allow you to achieve both the yin and yang of life.

On the other hand, harmony isn't what is always best for you or the institution. I've learned that if you want to succeed in higher education in general and, specifically as a president, you must be able to take risks. In other words, sometimes you need to do the unexpected and move beyond the safe path. Academe is very conservative and is very slow to change. Moreover, being a member of the faculty within a discipline is a very individualistic endeavor. As faculty, we get rewarded for being competitive and succeeding individually. With this type of structure, it is often difficult to move the enterprise forward. Sometimes you have to focus on the big picture and risk the repercussions from challenging the status quo. But, if you weigh the alternatives and the possible outcomes, I've found that sometimes the best approach is to take the risk.

But taking risks does not imply that you have to be a gambler. I think the best approach is one that takes into account two things, what I always use as the litmus test. First is to use common sense. While everyone wants to succeed and move forward, sometimes common sense dictates what is the more prudent approach to solving a problem or making a decision. Often what may seem like a good and thoughtful approach may turn out to be not so good after looking at it through the lens of common sense.

The second is to always have in mind those individuals who will be affected by your decision. For me, the best example I can use is that I always have students in mind when I make decisions. For example, if the Faculty Senate is reviewing the policy on repeat courses or if a department is applying to add another fee for a lab course, I always weigh the consequences of such action. Very often, once the intended and unintended consequences of an action are considered, the decision is to not approve going forward. In either event, I've found that considering as many aspects as possible of an issue and the consequences leads to better decision-making.

In this era of mass communications and technology, the lessons I've learned and apply each day are to be transparent in all my activities and to communicate as often as possible with the various constituencies on campus. I think the times when a president was viewed as someone who was somehow separate and, in many ways unreachable, have changed. Today's president has to be public, approachable, and, in many ways, transparent. Presidents who do not understand the power of *Twitter* and *Facebook* as well as the media generally, will have a difficult time meeting the need to be transparent in what they do and say. On the other hand, being aware is simply not enough. You must communicate as often as needed and to those people and groups that are necessary to achieve a level of transparency that will heighten your ability to lead the university. This is a very difficult lesson for some and can have severe negative consequences.

Given the state of Hispanics/Latinx and other minorities in this country relative to higher education and its future leaders, I would have to say that the lesson I've learned is that diversity in leadership doesn't just happen. It must be purposeful and focused. Consequently, the most important issue for me has been the identification and mentoring of future leaders. Being mentored and becoming a mentor is critical to the development of future leaders who will be both able and willing to take on the role of leaders of our country's institutions of higher education. If we hope to succeed in the future, we need to plan and act now for the crisis in succession that is already taking place across the country.

Finally, the most important lesson I learned is that race and ethnicity (still) matter. It's not enough to champion diversity, you have to fight for it. Throughout my career, racism and prejudice were present. Sometimes it was subtle but very often it was raw and overt. What I learned early on was that I had to work harder and be more focused than everyone else if I was to succeed. As a university president, that lesson was reinforced for me almost daily.

As I mentioned earlier, academe is very conservative and resistant to change. While the diversity of the student body has changed dramatically during my career, many of the issues facing students have not changed. Barriers to achieving student success must be addressed and goals have to be set so that every student can accomplish their goals.

Conclusion

So how have the values I learned so many years ago influenced my career and role as university president? Overall, I think the values relate to the notion of access and helping all students better their lives through education. A college or university is a marketplace of ideas. Exposing students to those ideas and providing them with the vehicle to explore and move forward is what education has meant to me. But while access to higher education and exposure to ideas is the ideal, it is only half the equation. Along with access, there has to be success. And I think that's where one's values come into play.

Students must be secure in the fact that we are there to help them succeed. That is what the president and those who support higher education must accomplish. Our programs should be sensitive to differences as well as to those things we all hold in common. The value of respect for people, both as individuals and groups, has helped me develop programs that are inclusive as well as academically sound. In other words, while students are engaged in learning and developing the foundation for a good, quality education, they should have the opportunity to explore and feel that they can be successful. That means providing them with support both in and outside the classroom.

In addition, students' backgrounds and needs should be taken into account, and where necessary, accommodations should be made to ensure success. For example, today's students in the CSU are very different than they were in 1960 when the California Master Plan was developed. There are now more women than men who are students; the average age of our students is in the upper twenties rather than between the ages of 18–22; returning veterans are enrolling in great numbers; and the economy has left many people out of work and as a result, many have decided to either enter college or return to school for further education. And finally, the demographics of our country have changed dramatically and will continue to do so over the next two decades.

In retrospect, being in higher education over the past forty years has been interesting and personally rewarding. However, it is the future that will provide not only the greatest challenges but also the greatest potential rewards. In my view, public higher education is currently in a critical period. Although the university is one of the institutions most resistant to change, the pressure to change is clear and is coming from different quarters. The use of technology, for example, is changing not only the delivery of programs but pedagogy and content as well. Government regulation and oversight have clearly increased. The economic pressures we are all witnessing are shifting the focus to job preparedness and away from the liberal arts-based approach to the undergraduate degree. The public attention on transparency and efficiency as well as executive compensation are all issues that will continue to be salient and will clearly have an impact on the leadership and operations of all institutions. Finally, increased costs and rising tuition are defining more and more the gap between those who will have access to higher education and those who will be effectively shut out. In sum, the issues and problems are many, and the solutions so far, are few.

On the other hand, looking to the future provides many possibilities for positive change. For example, adapting the use of technology as an adjunct for learning can be very beneficial for the future of higher education. The students now and in the future expect technology to be part of their lives and it has already become an integral part of how they learn. And changing the curriculum can also be positive and can enhance the offerings of any institution. Change doesn't have to occur at the expense of quality and a "dumbing down" of the institution's curriculum. Ultimately, what is needed is a positive outlook and creativity.

I began this chapter by focusing on the California Master Plan and my career in one of its segments. I'd like to end by reaffirming my belief in the Master Plan and public higher education as an organizational structure that is still viable. However, it will only work if two critical conditions are met. The first is that the public has to continue to believe in the value of public higher education and, in turn, support it. The second is that the best and most appropriate leadership will be available for the next phase of American public higher education. I am hopeful and optimistic that both will be met.

Discussion Questions

1 The author states that for him, ethnicity was always a factor during his tenure as president. What do you think he meant by that? In what ways do you think it was manifested? Do you think his ethnicity lessened or enhanced his effectiveness as a leader?
2 A theme that runs through the essay is the importance of mentoring. The author highlights the mentors he had and the many people who helped him on his journey. Do you think mentoring is necessary and important for someone who seeks a presidency or other position of leadership? Aren't leaders supposed to be independent, visionary, and driven? How would you mentor someone?
3 The author stressed the importance of having a basic set of values as a guide for effective leadership. In his case, he focused on family values as well as what he learned in his many roles that required discipline, respect for others, and the authority inherent in the position of the presidency. Do you think having a clear set of values is important to be a good leader? Do you need to articulate what they are? What would constitute your core set of values and how do you use them?
4 The author states that "Today's president has to be public, approachable, and in many ways transparent." How is this different from what

presidents in higher education have always done? Has the social, political, and economic situation in this country changed so much that it requires new approaches to leadership in higher education? What evidence can you give that would argue or support the author's point?

5 Taking into account the results of the ACE study on the American College and University Presidents presented in this chapter, and the current emphasis on diversity, equity, and inclusion (DEI), what do you expect the results would be if a similar study was conducted today? Do you think there would be more or less diversity among college and university presidents? Why? What factors do you think mitigate against DEI? What factors would you consider if you were attempting to increase diversity among presidents and other top leadership positions? How would you go about devising a plan to achieve this goal or should things develop "organically"?

References

American College President Study 2017. Washington, DC: American Council on Education (2012). Retrieved from http://www.aceacps.org.

California State University Data Insights/CSU (2021). Long Beach, CA: California State University Office of the Chancellor. Retrieved from http://www2.calstste.edu/data-central.

6
ONE WOMAN'S PATH TO THE PRESIDENCY OF A WOMEN'S COLLEGE

Janet L. Holmgren

Abstract

A first-generation college graduate, Holmgren grew up during the first wave of baby boomer women who sought a college education to enable them to achieve professionally while at the same time having a family and community life. Her educational and life experiences of the late 1960s and early 1970s made her aware of the profound inequities in US society and the world and of the possibilities that education offered to drive progressive social change "despite clear evidence of how hard those changes would be." As a graduate student at Princeton University, she experienced the challenges of a woman in a male-dominated professional world. Holmgren's professional career in higher education included faculty and administrative positions in public and private institutions, research universities, and liberal arts colleges, culminating in a 20-year presidency of Mills College. Her leadership extended to national and international organizations supporting educational opportunity and social change. Many lessons are embedded in her narrative, including the challenges of balancing work and family life, taking on leadership roles in institutions and organizations traditionally reserved for men, and matching her values grounded in equity and social responsibility to the leadership positions she filled.

My presidential profile centers on my twenty-year presidency at Mills College in Oakland, California. Mills is a beautiful 135-acre oasis in the middle of Oakland with an undergraduate enrollment of about 1000 – all

DOI: 10.4324/9781003465812-6

women or women-identifying students – and a graduate enrollment of both women and men of about 600 at its peak. Mills is the first higher education institution to grant baccalaureate degrees to women in California in the late 19th century. The college was founded in 1852, making it the second-oldest higher educational institution in California.

When I arrived in 1991, Mills was experiencing major challenges. Like many women's colleges in the United States, Mills was challenged to recruit students to an all-women educational environment and had gone through a major period of soul-searching and Board and administrative upheaval in 1989–1990. The Board had determined that to preserve and enhance Mills, the College should become co-educational at the undergraduate level. Students, alumnae, friends, donors, and others joined in a nationally publicized strike. Based on commitments of increased giving and enrollment, the Board reversed itself two weeks after its original decision and vowed that Mills would remain a women's college at the undergraduate level.

The upshot of this tumultuous historic moment for Mills was the resignation of most of the senior administration and an intense national search for a new president during the academic year 1990–91 while a member of the Board served as acting president. At the time of the celebrated strike, I was working as Vice Provost of Princeton University and living in Princeton, New Jersey with my two young daughters. My knowledge of Mills was limited to what I saw and read – passionate, articulate women believing in themselves and wanting to secure the opportunities they had for future students – and I was moved and impressed. Little did I know at the time of watching the televised coverage that in a little over a year, Mills would be my new home.

In the summer of 1991, I moved to the President's house on campus with my family and began my presidency. I was 42 years old with 18 years of teaching experience at public and private universities and 9 years of administrative experience overlapping with my teaching. I was a single mother of two daughters, 8 and 12. I had never attended, worked at, or spent much time at a women's college. I had never even visited the California Bay area before my first Mills interview, and while I had served as Vice Provost of Princeton University, this was my first presidency and my first experience of reporting directly to a Board. Parenthetically, I had not aspired to become a college president, and the Mills search was the first that interested me and that I agreed to get involved in as a consequence of several nominations. On the advice of a mentor at the American Council on Education, Donna Shavlik, I also entered another women's college presidential search to be able to make an informed decision about whether to move forward with a presidency. I was offered the other presidency as well and also encouraged to stay at Princeton, but Mills presented an opportunity to make an impact and explore a whole new world.

In taking on the presidency of Mills, I inherited the very real effects of a major institutional upheaval that had challenged trust and left many constituencies counting on the new president to deliver on a long list of aspirations and hopes. In some ways, I couldn't have found a tougher assignment, and yet, I felt then as I do now that it was the right match and that this presidency was going to bring out the very best of my leadership abilities. I was intent on building on Mills' extraordinary legacy and strength to expand its capacity and reputation as a beacon for women's empowerment as well as a model for equity and excellence in higher education. Despite my lack of administrative and academic experience in the women's college context, I believed my personal history leading up to this moment was the preparation I needed to engage and meet the challenge.

Early Years: Family and Education

My story of finding my way to leadership in American higher education coincides with the profound social changes in our society since the middle of the 20th century, in particular the changes that have affected me as a heterosexual white first-generation college-educated woman. It's difficult to tell this story without interweaving the personal and professional experience of growing up in this time and place and being among the first generation of women who dared to dream of "having it all" (or as we might now phrase it "doing it all") in terms of opportunities in professional life but also in terms of family and personal growth.

I grew up in the white, middle-class suburbs of Chicago – a baby boomer – the first child of parents who came from first-generation American immigrant backgrounds and whose families had struggled during the Depression. My parents were determined that their children (I have a younger sister who is a distinguished scholar) would have every opportunity that had eluded them – first and foremost, a college education. Their highest priority in life was providing a safe and secure home and a quality education for us, including a degree from a four-year undergraduate college or university.

In my family and in the idealized white middle-class version of American society that marked the post-WWII era, the marriage plot – that one meets the right person, has a romantic relationship, marries, has a family, and lives happily ever after – was the prevailing expectation for women. I don't remember ever discussing a choice between motherhood and career with anyone as I was growing up. It was simply assumed that girls who had the socioeconomic choice would grow up to be wives and mothers and if there was to be more to life, the choices were quite limited to traditional female roles of nurse, teacher, or secretary, often work that ended with childbearing. It was still the case that education, high school and college, for women was expected to prepare us to be better wives and mothers. If by some circumstance, we needed to support ourselves and maybe even others, then we should also have professional possibilities that a higher education could enable.

Yet I dreamed too of the quest plot – going into the "public" world to make a mark. The models for me came from books. I was a voracious reader from a young age and I looked for and found stories of bravery and heroism, superheroes – Clara Barton, Abraham Lincoln, Sacajawea. Not surprisingly, the women's stories I encountered were largely about nurses or the rare "female" doctor.

The only "working women" I knew were my mother and my teachers in elementary and a few in high school. My mother worked as a neonatal nurse for most of her adult life, and she was proud of her accomplishment and her work ethic. Her biggest regret was that she became a nurse without a college education, and she was determined that neither I nor my sister would miss out on the opportunity for a four-year college education. For my mother, working outside the home was complicated by her value system. Men were the providers; women were the homemakers. She always made the point that her earnings were for the extras; she didn't have to work; and working outside the home could never be her priority if it took precedence over her primary reason for being as a wife and mother.

Although my father was proud of my mother, they both considered her professional life as something not to be much discussed publicly or privately, but I had absorbed the message that my mother loved her work and that it was important to our family. When I was planning to go to college, I had my heart set on becoming a nurse like my mother but with a college degree. I sent away for catalogs of schools I could think of that had such programs, but when I laid out my plan to my father, he said "You don't want to be a nurse, you want to be a doctor." He saw that as a step up in the world and as a natural consequence of my high achievements in school, which both my parents supported wholeheartedly. He also, I believe, did not see me leading my life in the recognized "career" paths for women. He wanted me to "shoot the moon," and I doubt that he ever thought about how that might work with the wife/mother roles that were also my destiny and desire. While surprising, I found that his pronouncement opened a door into possibilities in life that I had never considered. I would go to college, and I wasn't really interested in becoming a doctor, so now I could go to college and think about other ways to make my mark in the world.

Higher Education

I went to a large, well-respected high school, Hinsdale Township, in the southwest suburbs of Chicago. There were nearly 800 students in my class alone, and I was placed in honors classes with high-achieving peers whom I didn't know, since I came from one of the smaller elementary schools on the outskirts of the district. I had a few friends, and while I had been a leader in elementary/middle school years, in high school I was a joiner and occasionally a leader in academic settings. By going to summer school and increasing my semester load, I qualified to finish in three rather than four years, a not insignificant dilemma for the school's administration, since it had never been done before (my sister was the second student to do it seven years later). As a further complication, I would as a result of changing class years become valedictorian of a class I was not even in, displacing a high-achieving young man from that spot.

Both because of my gender and my not really having a senior year, I got very little advice about college from counselors, and my parents had limited knowledge drawn from their own experiences of attending junior colleges in the Chicago area. Additionally, my parents were worried that as a 16-year-old, I was too young to go far away from home. The radius they defined was the Midwest and the campus had to be within a day's driving distance round trip if I were going to live there.

I had the good fortune to have a high school French teacher who was going to the faculty of a new four-year liberal arts college in Michigan, Oakland University, established in the 1960s as a "brain trust" for Michigan State University. Oakland was in the formative stages, and it had the benefit of many talented faculty members – many newly minted PhDs who were committed to shaping the future of public higher education in the liberal arts mold. Of course, they were majority white males. I had two white women and one African American man as professors in my eight semesters. But the culture was liberal for those times – no fraternities or sororities, no revenue sports, no honors college (emphasis on equity) – small classes and intense mentoring for all with a diverse (for those times) student body, recruitment efforts that brought in students from around the country as well as Michigan and an engaged leadership committed to the ideals of high quality public higher education. It was a transformative experience for me and made me a true believer in the life-changing potential of a first-rate liberal arts education in a community that embraced the ideals of equality and excellence. In those undergraduate years, I did not experience being limited as a woman in a co-educational academic environment, but I quickly became more aware of the inequities in American society and started my engagement in both racial justice and feminist activism. It was the 60s and it did seem possible that the world or, at least, the country was on the precipice of progressive social change despite the clear evidence of how hard those changes would be.

A Princeton Woman

Oakland was on a trimester system, and with persistence and family support, I did several three semester years to finish my undergraduate degree in three calendar years. As I approached the next phase of life, I had abandoned the dream I had moved to after giving up on nursing. I had wanted to be a foreign service officer – a diplomat who traveled the world. At the same time, I was in a serious relationship and planned to marry upon graduation. Career foreign service women, of which there were very few, could not be married – so simply by regulation (as well as societal norms and practical considerations) that path was ruled out if I chose to marry. I had shifted from a French major to a double major in English and Linguistics. My professors encouraged me to go to graduate school and teaching in higher education seemed like a possible career path for a woman in the 1970s that would take me professionally beyond the proscribed boundaries for women, while keeping open the opportunity for marriage and children. Linguistics was a hot subject at that time because of the amount of government money flowing into language study and the developing interest in the "science" of language as well as its uses. Graduate programs in linguistics were growing rapidly to educate new professors and scholars in the field. For me, in that moment the marriage plot and quest plot intersected. My fiancé, also graduating from Oakland, and I decided that we could get married if I got a fellowship and he got support in his field as well, and we could go to graduate school in the same place.

Of the universities I applied to and received acceptance and potential support from, I chose Princeton. It was not my personal first choice, but Princeton had given me a very encouraging visit – I liked the faculty – and my husband-to-be had his heart set on going to the Princeton Theological Seminary. So, at 19, almost 20, I married and started graduate school in a part of the country that I knew little about, in an Ivy League institution that still didn't have undergraduate women and had only recently admitted graduate women. I was now an aspiring scholar, a co-provider, a wife, and a homemaker (of sorts).

It was at Princeton that I first learned about the academy from the perspective of a potential faculty member as well as a student, and it was an academic community that confronted me daily with embedded gender discrimination. I had never felt like a minority before nor really like an outsider. I was used to being distinguished by my intellectual gifts and to having a balance of women and men in my classrooms. In graduate school, I was one among a tiny number of women in two graduate programs, English and Linguistics, in an institution that did not yet admit undergraduate women. For the first time in my life, I was cautious about speaking out in class. I had difficulty imagining for myself a career like those of the professors (all white men) who taught and advised me; I was always aware of my difference.

When I began my job search for a faculty position, after four years of graduate school, I was finishing my dissertation in Washington, D.C., at the Library of Congress and my Princeton advisor was on leave and teaching and researching at Georgetown University in D.C. He invited me (and my spouse) to meet him at the Cosmos Club to discuss my prospects. I knew I was in trouble when I discovered that this white male-only membership club required women to enter through the side door! This was to be a male experience – quite thoughtfully designed on my advisor's part in the traditional male model. In the course of the dinner, he announced that he had researched the job market and matched my research and teaching interests with the University of California, Irvine, then a relatively new institution. He had secured an assistant professorship for me there for the fall. My mouth dropped open and I blurted out, "But I can't move to California. I live in Washington." The look of consternation that crossed his face captured the dilemma. His students went where he sent them, and this was the way the academy worked. This was a good opportunity – now what? For my part, I hadn't really given much thought to location except to believe that I had to be able to commute from D.C. since that's where my husband and I lived now and he was established in his job.

That first experience of going on the job market made me realize that I had to make my own way, so I started to scour the metropolitan Washington, D.C., area and felt fortunate when I was offered an assistant professorship at Federal City College. Like my undergraduate alma mater, this was a relatively young higher educational institution. Unlike Oakland University, however, this public liberal arts college was established in 1968 for largely political reasons in direct response to the riots that ripped through Washington, D.C., in the aftermath of Martin Luther King, Jr.'s assassination and in response to the public outcry that there were no open admission or community college opportunities publicly offered to the citizens of the District of Columbia.

FCC opened a door for me into a new academic and social world. There was no central campus, and the various departments were spread across the city. The Humanities – administration, faculty, and classrooms - were housed in a temporary building (later to become a homeless shelter) nestled among a group of Federal court buildings in the shadow of the U.S. Capitol. The English department dominated the building. The faculty was more diverse than any I have ever encountered since – an array of scholars and writers, African American and Caucasian, American and international, women and men, gay and straight, fledgling and experienced with degrees from a wide range of institutions drawn to this experimental environment for the opportunity to build a new brand of urban liberal arts education and simply for employment as many were not welcome elsewhere. There was also daring in the plan to create this new place. The jazz musician and poet, Gil Scott-Heron, and I were hired in the same year to the English faculty. Students ranged from working adults with families to traditional undergraduates. The student body, all commuters, was over 90% African American and largely part-time as many were working full-time. There was no tuition, but for many students, the expense of buying books, paying for transportation, and paying fees was a hurdle that caused them to attend intermittently and often not complete their degrees.

To move from the privileged and homogeneous white patriarchal world of Princeton to the urban, politicized, diverse, and often disorganized world of Federal City College was both daunting and exciting. My more experienced colleagues educated me in how to teach and how to incorporate into my teaching and research both writers and scholarship that represented the diversity and vitality of a much bigger swath of American society than the traditional canon ever imagined. My classes ranged from remedial vocabulary building to upper-division history of the English language. During my years at FCC (1972–1976) there were intense, sometimes bitter arguments, among our faculty about curricular change and the most effective ways to educate African American students in an urban higher educational institution. The majority of our students lived within the predominantly African American community of Washington, D.C., and their spoken language was what had then only recently been labeled Black English.

The institutional leadership was eager for all faculty, no matter how junior, to take a hand in administration. Shortly after I arrived at FCC, the college was accredited for the first time, and we all had a role in writing the documents needed to achieve this major and essential accomplishment. In my second year at FCC, I agreed to chair a committee in the English department to revise radically the required first- and second-year humanities curriculum. The introduction of authors and materials from African American and African diaspora writers was revolutionary at the time. The work of chairing that committee and then educating myself to teach with that curriculum were two big growth experiences that I continue to draw on. Getting a group of faculty with widely disparate points of view to agree (sometimes alluded to as "herding cats" in academic administrative circles) and then executing the consequences of those decisions in my teaching and administrative work, particularly in terms of making social change through expanding knowledge, are core skills within academic leadership that I have drawn on over many years. Beyond the collegial experience, I learned through my first teaching experiences to respect and listen to my students, to gain from them knowledge and skills that I lacked, and to appreciate the drive that brought them to class and motivated them to learn.

University of Maryland College Park

In 1976, I was recruited to the University of Maryland College Park as an assistant professor in the English department to teach both linguistics and literature at the undergraduate and graduate levels. UMCP is the flagship campus of the University of Maryland, a research university with a big student body (about 38,000 when I was there in the 70s and 80s) and a major athletic program. The English department alone had 75 full-time faculty members. Only about 20% of these were women and the tenured women numbered about six. There were an additional 50-plus graduate students who were the backbone of the extensive service arm of the department, teaching the required freshman and junior composition.

I had come from an academic environment that was nontraditional and often chaotic to one that was striving to compete for prestige in the world of public research universities nationwide. Among the junior faculty who were hired with me were several other white women, but I was the only married one. As it turned out, I was also the only untenured woman at that time to have a child pre-tenure. I followed the prescribed path, enjoying a pre-tenure sabbatical that enabled me to finish my first book, *Narration and Discourse in American Realistic Fiction*. I did not ask for maternity leave, but my chair, Shirley Strum Kenny – a mentor and role model for me, gave me a somewhat lighter load in the semester I delivered. I also took on an administrative role as Assistant Director of Graduate Studies – my first official role of this type. This work interested me, especially because most of the graduate students in the department were women, and in addition to providing guidance on graduate academic coursework, I became more involved in mentoring students on a variety of challenges, including gender discrimination, sexual harassment, and pay equity. Working with a large group of predominantly women students who were headed for academic careers and coming to grips with the challenges that they and I faced in an institution in which authority and power were vested almost entirely in white men started me on my feminist path in the academy.

In 1982 my traditional academic career ended with the decision of a university-wide tenure and promotion committee to deny my department and division's recommendation for tenure. It was a gut-wrenching experience in part because I had done all the "right" things, including significant publications, teaching across disciplines in my department, mentoring students, and accepting academic administrative service posts. I also knew that while it was not openly discrimination based on gender, had I been a white man with my academic and professional record, the outcome would likely have been different. I had not created a buffer for myself by looking for jobs elsewhere, assured that I was on the right track. By this time, I had not only a spouse but also a child and the hope for another, so the idea of uprooting my family seemed to be a nonstarter. So - what to do?

I could have joined the "revolving door" of women in academic life who are the majority of "road warriors." I did, in fact, teach in the summer of 1982 at George Mason University and contemplated putting together some part-time teaching to tide me over. I was not alone in my struggle. Between 1975 and 1985, women's participation in faculties nearly doubled, while the percentage of women in tenured and tenure track positions went up by only 2.6%. By contrast, in that same decade, the addition of women to non-tenure-track positions (over 32,000) was three times that of men. These were also ironically the years in which women accounted for two-thirds of the increase in the higher education student population. I was not ready to leave the full-time workforce, having worked so hard to find my place in it. At UMCP I had allies who pressed for reconsideration of the tenure decision to no avail. In the late summer of 1982, the Acting Chancellor of UMCP offered me a temporary full-time position as assistant to the Chancellor that became a permanent appointment when the new Chancellor took office later that fall.

Abruptly, I was catapulted from the relatively sheltered faculty rank of assistant professor of English, knowing only about three buildings on campus along with numerous parking lots, to the Chancellor's Office at the hub of the university. I also continued to teach in the English department, but now as an adjunct, not a tenured professor. My job was to write speeches, act as liaison to faculty, and coordinate with other senior administrative offices. The Chancellor has overall responsibility for the academics, finances, political and public relations, alumni relations, legal department, and athletic programs of this sprawling city-state. I became interested immediately in the governance structure and the budgetary process of the university – areas that had not loomed in my consciousness or work as a faculty member. I was also drawn to understanding the university's role within the state – its funding, its responsibility to the citizenry, and its history. The breadth and scope of the Chancellor's office portfolio provided me with a skill set that launched me as an administrator and led to my becoming a leader in higher education.

In my six years in the Chancellor's office, I learned how to write and also how to give speeches, how to prepare and manage budgets, how to deal with a variety of constituencies all with special interests, how to address the crises that arose regularly, and how to work with the external community that surrounds any higher educational institution – the public, the press, the local, state and federal government, and the list goes on. I also learned how to balance flexibility with persistence. For example, when the Women's Commission proposed an initiative to fund curricular reform to incorporate women's studies into the entire university, I went to the Chancellor for advice and support, and his recommendation was to get the highest-ranking woman in science to chair the Initiative and win support from a diverse group of faculty and staff across the disciplines and administrative areas. Ultimately, we produced the Greer Report (named for Sandra Greer, the chair of the Task Force) that resulted in new appointments, curricular changes, and a greatly enhanced women's studies department with an investment of $3m in state funding in 1988. It was groundbreaking for higher education, particularly in a research university, and was possible only because of the coalition we built between UMCP women leaders and the women's caucus of the state legislature, as well as with other women in higher education throughout the state of Maryland.

Throughout those years, I also learned how hard it is to be the only woman at the "head" table. I can remember the countless times I was mistaken for someone who should be getting coffee or copies or sitting in a different seat. I was talked over, talked down to, and ridiculed – a colleague once opined that if anyone in the administration wanted to know what women wanted, they just needed to look at the list nailed to my office door. But I learned to make alliances and find support systems, and I was fortunate that the Chancellor, John Slaughter, was the first African American leader in the UM system. In addition to his accomplishments as a "first" in many roles, he committed himself as a leader to creating a more equitable environment within the university, setting goals for increasing minority student enrollment that were long overdue and bringing clarity and resolve to issues involving diversity and social change. Over those years, I learned to speak up with a louder, more forceful voice as an administrator committed to making positive change within the academy. Chancellor Slaughter's focus on the centrality of equity to academic excellence was a guiding principle for the institution and those of us working with him.

Princeton Redux

In 1988 I left the Washington, D.C. area to return to Princeton as the Associate and later Vice Provost of the University. I was recruited to the applicant pool through my continuing contact with Princeton faculty, and I was at first skeptical about becoming involved in the search for this senior administrative position. The focus was budgetary, the shaping and managing of the operating budget through the work of a campus-wide Priorities Committee, which made annual recommendations to the Board of Trustees. I had wide-ranging administrative experience from UMCP, but my focus had never been largely on budgeting. The Princeton experience enabled me to learn first-hand how critical budget management is to leadership in all areas of academia. It is one of the critical skills that a successful presidency depends on. You can delegate budget management but unless you know how the sausage is made you can't really decipher for yourself or for others what's really in it! Budget shaping and management is also a critical link among administration, faculty, and the Board – constituencies that a president must be constantly working with and connecting.

I was the first woman and second person to occupy this position. The role had evolved to include responsibilities for the allocation of the most precious resources in any academic setting, money and space. This was also my bridge from administration in a public higher education institution to a private university – often a difficult passage for administrators to navigate. No longer is the principal constituency to cultivate the state government with its funding and regulatory powers. In the private college and university setting, the buck stops with the President and the Board of Trustees. I became one of the highest-ranking women administrators on campus (we were small in number), moving from Associate to Vice Provost and taking on a visible leadership role within the team around the President, Harold Shapiro. Given the breadth of my interests and portfolio at Maryland, I made it clear in coming to Princeton that while I intended to fulfill all responsibilities of the Vice Provost position, I would also be actively involved in developing opportunities for women at Princeton. This would not be work I would squeeze in, but rather focus on. I considered it part of my job.

In retrospect, I think I happened upon this strategy without giving it much advance thought, knowing that I would do work on behalf of women and minorities regardless of the other demands of the job. However, I think that every person in a leadership role should state from the outset of a new undertaking what values and interests will guide them. Equally important is to refine and articulate those values throughout one's work. This need for clarity and honesty is especially important in leadership roles because all the constituencies of an institution listen for that connection and direction. During my administrative time at Princeton, I acquired knowledge and skills in whole new areas of administration including fundraising, endowment management, facilities management including construction and renovation, alumni relations, faculty appointment and advancement processes, annual budgeting that involved the coordination among a myriad of administrative and academic departments, and the importance of Board engagement and cooperation – the key to a President's and an institution's success. I also co-chaired a yearlong celebration of the 20th anniversary of undergraduate co-education in an institution that was at that time almost 250 years old!

A Mills Woman

When the nominations for the Mills presidency came along, I was surprised, intrigued, and conflicted. Although I had not planned to stay at Princeton for the rest of my career, I had thought about moving after five-plus years not three, and if I had a plan, it was not for a presidency but more likely a provost position. Ultimately, I decided to accept the nomination after attending, as a guest of the Office of Women at the American Council of Education, the first summit of women presidents in Washington, D.C., in December 1990. I was inspired by the commitment and the quality of women presidents, many of whom I knew, some of whom were friends and role models. I also recognized how few women presidents there were and how many of them were operating without the benefit of strong support. I believed I could step up to these challenges if my values were aligned with the institution's and I had a sound vessel to work with. Like the move to Princeton, I wanted to take this risk. So, despite the 3000-mile cross-country move, despite the fact that I had never lived in California, even though my only association with a single-sex institution was Princeton, I was a divorced mother of two daughters, aged 8 and 12, I decided to embark on this adventure. In retrospect, maybe it was because of those improbabilities rather than in spite of them that I made the move. I was ready to take on a leadership role that would enable me to put my principles into practice, and I believed then as I do to this day that a women's college provides the best model for all of higher education.

The Mills College I encountered in 1991 was awash in contradictions. On the one hand, it had gained national and international visibility with a celebrated student and alumnae strike in 1990 that successfully secured Mills' future as a women's college at the undergraduate level. The College had just completed a major capital campaign that raised nearly $70 m for facilities and operating expenses, and it had an endowment of over $70 m. It had a strong faculty, a beautiful physical plant, a distinguished history, a strong undergraduate and graduate curriculum, and a committed alumnae body. On the other hand, it had a bare-bones administration. As a result of the turmoil surrounding the Board decision, the strike, and the Board reversal, all but the Vice President for Finance and Administration had left. The Board was burned out by the strike and the reversal of its initial decision to become coeducational. The faculty was distrustful of the Board and the interim administration as were student leaders and staff. Particularly among students, there was a strong belief that issues of racial equity had been neglected in the push to maintain Mills as a women's college. The College's reputation was damaged by the publicity surrounding the strike because one of the public explanations for the coeducational decision was a concern for long-term financial viability. That public airing of concerns was interpreted by those outside the College as an immediate financial crisis. The College had suffered physical damage in the 1989 Lomo Prieto earthquake in the Bay area and a subsequent flood that year. There were significant decisions to be made about the repair or replacement of structures, including the main building of the College, Mills Hall, that remained unoccupied. Finally, the Board had mandated that the College had a fixed period to bring the undergraduate student body to 1000 and to raise $10 m to take undergraduate co-education off the table for discussion.

Despite what at the time seemed like solid preparation for the presidency, the reality for me was not a natural progression but a high dive into deep water. I was met with tremendous expectations and urgency to deliver results to a variety of constituencies in an environment that was eager for change but low on trust. The work itself brings a whole new level of responsibility that is only elevated by the need for rebuilding and repairing relationships and confidence. Moreover, the job is much more all-encompassing than any I had previously done. As Mary Catherine Bateson astutely observes, "It is not easy, putting on a new identity as a college president, to learn to express the new role without meeting a stranger in the mirror … All the issues of identity and presentation of self are complicated by the need to provide intelligible role models, for college presidents are supposed to project not only policies but lifestyles" (Composing a Life, pp. 25–26). It took experimentation and experience to figure out how to assume this new role while staying true to myself and my personal responsibilities, especially while my family and I were adapting to a new environment.

As a president who lived on campus, I had to have help managing my household as well as managing the College. My home had to serve double duty as a center for gatherings for the College and as a personal space for family and friends. The College became central to my life and the environment in which I conducted my life, aging through my 40s and

50s, raising my family, marrying and divorcing, converting to Judaism, caring for aging parents, maintaining friendships and family relationships, and the list goes on. In hindsight, I can see that the job of a president involves a balance of opportunities and liabilities, both personal and professional. The respect and appreciation accorded a college/university president is laced with expectations that often involve tough judgments and constant scrutiny. There can be a temptation to screen out the criticism for self-protection but that in turn runs the risk of missing out on the constructive criticism that allows one to grow and change. It is hard to say what the right tenure of a president is, especially since every institution is different in its needs and expectations. I think my relatively long tenure at Mills (20 years) was productive for both me and the institution, and gave me space to grow and learn as well as giving the College time to stabilize and grow stronger.

Mills had survived a huge upheaval and I needed to attend immediately to building my administrative team, getting to know the faculty and staff, preparing for the returning students in the fall of 1991, introducing myself to alumnae and supporters as well as the community, and securing and strengthening my relationship with the Board of Trustees. My two decades of leadership at Mills were divided quite clearly into two ten-year segments. The first 10 years marked the end of the 20th century and major changes in society and higher education. My second decade at Mills kicked off with 9/11/01 and the advent of the 21st century. For Mills, the end of the 20th century was a time of rebuilding and repositioning the college; the first decade of the 21st was a time of stabilization and growth.

Over two decades, I recruited and restructured several senior teams, worked with six different Board chairs, and with that team mounted several targeted fundraising campaigns and one major capital campaign to celebrate Mills' 150th anniversary, saw new areas open within the curriculum, and grew the faculty, the student body and the staff as well as the College's financial resources. We also significantly increased the representation of people of color on the faculty and in the student body and oversaw the addition of numerous new structures and the renovation of many others. I also developed community ties within Oakland and California, work that enhanced my knowledge of the local and state community and that expanded Mills' visibility and reputation. In these leadership areas, I was always conscious of my identity as a woman and as the president of a women's college. I also took on national leadership roles in women-centered organizations, such as the Women's College Coalition and the National Council for Research on Women.

These were volunteer roles that sometimes added to my already busy schedule on behalf of Mills, but I considered it important to use my role to engage the College in high-profile activities on behalf of education and women's empowerment. The College also grew in its capacity for leadership on issues involving women in society at large through the Women's Leadership Institute which kicked off in 1994 with a National Summit on Women in Science. It was also through the Women's Leadership Institute as well as my service with the American Council on Education that I became a delegate to the United Nations Fourth World Conference on Women in Beijing in 1995. Mills took the largest contingency of any college or university in the United States to the NGO Forum that preceded the official conference – a contingency of 25 women made up of students, faculty, staff, Board members, alumnae, and my two daughters (both of whom were among the youngest attendees at the 35k gathering outside of Beijing). It was an eye-opening experience for all involved.

The work of any higher education institution involves a balance of preservation and innovation; the way that balance is managed depends vitally on the vision of the president and her/his team. It also depends on the degree of trust and confidence the president inspires in all constituencies. Both the content and the framing of the message, as well as the consistency of that message are critically important. Mills' mission from its inception as a college has been to educate and empower women. From my perspective, that mission was never designed to be exclusive – to keep men out. There had been men in graduate programs from the 1920s. However, the research based on the experience of thousands of alumnae of Mills and other women's colleges has been unequivocally clear that focusing on women means providing opportunities for women to find and use their voices in all aspects of their student experience and to be supported in their various identities – as traditional age, resuming, parenting, married, partnered, single, lesbian, straight, queer, transgendered, and the list goes on. Focusing on women in the classroom, in student organizations, in athletics, and all aspects of the College meant that remaining exclusive to women in the undergraduate admission policy was the most academically and socially sound approach. It was also the most effective way to maintain interest and support for the College without straining the College's budget to include facilities and programs for men.

The 1990s saw major shifts in public understanding and policy-making on social issues involving sexual orientation and racial justice. When I came to Mills, the question of whether to admit men as undergraduates had been closed by the Board's action, but Mills' affirmative action policy failed to include sexual orientation – a category already recognized and protected at many independent institutions at that time. The issue was a very hotly debated one at Mills because women's colleges worried about the effect on their enrollments and support were they to be perceived to be "lesbian" havens. It seemed to me and others in the administration and faculty that Mills needed to move with the times and affirm its core principles by including sexual orientation in a nondiscrimination policy and the actual life and work of the College. I was surprised by the opposition and fear that policy change caused. It took a great deal of persistence and coordinated leadership to change the minds of many members of the community from Board to prospective students. What had existed as a "secret" had to be celebrated and understood as important for strengthening Mills. Society was changing on this subject as well, and slowly but surely Mills became a model in LGBTQ policy and practice. Mills also pioneered after my tenure in becoming the first women's college to admit "women identifying" students.

Another critical issue at Mills when I arrived was diversity and racial justice – a question for many members of the community that had been left out of the battle against co-education. Mills was making some progress in recruiting undergraduate students of color, particularly African Americans, but those students remained a distinctive and sometimes stigmatized minority. Mills had made little progress in diversifying faculty to that point. It required a major initiative funded by outside sources to begin an active affirmative action campaign both to recruit faculty of color (the percentage of tenure track/tenured faculty of color moved from 3% to 25% during my tenure) and to create a more multicultural curriculum. We also made a concerted and successful effort to bring racial and gender diversity to the Board. In that period, the climate in California and nationally was becoming increasingly fraught around the subject of affirmative action with the University of California (in 1996) and the state of California (prop 207) dissolving affirmative action policies that had been effectively, if slowly, moving the dial on race and gender in employment and student admission. Mills along with many independent colleges and universities in California moved forward despite the public policy pullback and demonstrated that equity and excellence are a winning combination. The enrollment of students of color at Mills in both undergraduate and graduate programs met or exceeded 50% by the end of my tenure. Mills became nationally identified as a minority-serving institution and, more recently, as a Hispanic-serving institution as well.

In the 1990s, the question of financial viability through enrollment revenue had to be addressed head-on and immediately. Many independent colleges, even those with substantial endowments, were struggling to keep up with the competition from both state colleges and universities as well as the developing world of for-profit and distance learning. Add to that competition the issue of the rising costs of higher education and the challenges were daunting. All but the wealthiest 1% of higher education were struggling with the persistent rise in costs associated with delivering education, and the concomitant cost to students reflected in rising tuition and fees. At Mills, we worked hard to raise funds for financial aid and increase substantially the amount of financial aid offered while at the same time remaining competitive with peer institutions, but we were also facing a shrinking pool of traditional-aged students as were other independents. Many independent colleges, particularly women's colleges and HBCUs, were struggling to figure out how to adapt a liberal arts education model that was based on an idea of full-time traditional aged residential students to a population that was increasingly attending public institutions on a part-time and commuting basis and beginning to run the gamut from traditional aged to middle-aged and beyond. For many urban independent colleges, the path forward included developing more extension programs and opportunities for commuters and part-time students. Because of Mills' strong history in two areas, we took a different path and those choices contributed significantly to the strength of the College in the early 21st century.

Mills had a long history of graduate programs dating back to the 1920s when the Education graduate program was founded. Mills also had distinguished programs in Music, Art, Dance, and Creative Writing, as well as a post-baccalaureate pre-med program. By law, those programs were always co-educational and the percentage of men in the total graduate population stabilized at about 20% over the years. These programs were not only important to both undergraduate and graduate students, but they were also mechanisms for recruiting and retaining outstanding faculty. Mills also had a history of admitting and graduating "resuming" students, those who were either transferring from two-year institutions or who had interrupted their undergraduate education at some time in the past and wanted to complete it. Many of those students were able to fulfill a requirement for graduation that involved full-time enrollment in as few as three semesters, and many of those students wanted to stay on at Mills and continue with graduate work.

In the 1990s and early 2000s, with the work of faculty and outside advisors, Mills developed initiatives that were critical for the future and built on both the graduate programs and aggressive recruitment of resuming students by offering accelerated graduate degrees tied to the undergraduate experience. One initiative centered on the expansion and enhancement of graduate programs, particularly with the additions of new tracks and an Ed.D. in Education, and the addition of new graduate programs – an MBA in business and an MPP in public policy. Several of the graduate programs were designed so that they could be completed in one year after the student finished her undergraduate work, a 4 + 1, or for transfer students, a 3 + 2, model. These programs were based on research showing the importance of women having advanced degrees to attain pay equity in the workforce as well as the demonstrated desire of Mills undergraduate students to continue with graduate work at Mills. The graduate programs and their enrollment grew for Mills consistently from the late 1990s onward as did the undergraduate student body. These were just a few of the initiatives, some successful and some not, that a strong, bold senior team and a dedicated and growing faculty were able to achieve with the support of the Board. There were many contentious and uncertain moments, but through collaboration, coalition building, and strong communication, the trajectory remained positive.

Throughout my tenure as president of Mills, I learned and relearned how important fundraising is to the job. Fundraising is not just bringing in money – a common misunderstanding. It involves community building, communication, and understanding the full financial picture in the long term to determine the trade-offs as goals for both fundraising and for the institution's future are set through planning. Like all other work in higher educational leadership, fundraising requires a team and engaging administrators and staff, faculty, students, alumnae, and the wider community. At its core, fundraising also involves building trust. Donors, large and small, must believe in the mission and the strength of the institution just as students and faculty do. Folded into fundraising then are issues of tuition and financial aid, enrollment, faculty and staff size and benefits, facilities maintenance and expansion, as well as the cost of the fundraising itself. In a certain sense, I was fortunate to have some urgent projects and fundraising needs already on the books when I arrived at Mills. During those early years, I learned a great deal about the coordination of the work and the potential of Mills as well as about my abilities, both to tell the stories and outline the College's direction while building relationships with alumnae/i and donors.

Fundraising went on throughout my 20-year tenure, but we accelerated substantially in the late 1990s to take advantage of Mills' 150th anniversary in 2002. The sesquicentennial campaign begun in a quiet phase in 1998 culminated in 2005 with a total giving of $132 m (30% over the targeted goal). Funds from the campaign, provided by 1000s of donors mainly alumnae, built new LEEDS-certified structures, contributed to a significant increase in faculty and staff salaries, enhanced student financial aid, and fostered new academic initiatives. The importance of a campaign in improving any higher institution's fundraising capacity cannot be overestimated. A campaign provides the opportunity to reach new donors and to inspire past and current donors and friends by developing consensus around priorities and learning how to tell the story of the importance of those priorities.

The challenges of the first decade of the 21st century were considerable for the country as a whole and Mills was no exception. The attack on 9/11 and the subsequent developments that took the country into the Iraq war created strains within our community and concerning some key aspects of our mission and institutional health. For the most part, the community took a position opposing the war, but we had students as well as other community members and friends who were ambivalent, some having family members and friends serving in the military.

One of Mills' most distinguished alumnae, Congresswoman Barbara Lee, took a celebrated lone vote in the House of Representatives against then President Bush's request for the use of military force against terrorists, known as the AUMS act, just recently repealed. Congresswoman Lee was so vilified by some that her life was in danger, and she chose her alma mater, Mills, as the site of her first public appearance in her district after taking that infamous vote. We were honored to have her and met her with a hero's welcome. The College came under attack from many quarters and through the internet for the publicly expressed political views of faculty, staff, and students opposing the war and the Bush administration. And a few years after we celebrated the end of the sesquicentennial campaign, we – like the country and the world – experienced the shock of the economic crash of 2008. We were spared some of the worst consequences by good planning and a successful campaign, but our budget became tighter and our students were most definitely impacted.

During the decade of the early 2000s, I took on some of my most serious external leadership roles, chairing the Board of the American Council on Education, the Carnegie Foundation for the Advancement of Teaching and Learning, and joining the Board of Trustees of Princeton University, as well as several other Boards. I did so with the support of the Mills Board and a dedicated and talented senior team. I think the foundation laid in the previous decade provided this opportunity and also enhanced my capacity to serve as president.

When I retired from my presidency in 2011, I was able to say to our community that "in the past 20 years, as the State of California pulled back on its commitment to affirmative action in public higher education and on support for the public higher educational enterprise, Mills charged full speed ahead. As the country experienced unprecedented prosperity, came under attack, and went to war, Mills students, faculty, and alumnae/i invested in peace, justice, and social responsibility. As the economy experienced a roller coaster of ups and downs and the gap between rich and poor widened, Mills donors invested steadily in the future, expanding more than threefold the financial aid that we offer to our 1600 full-time students (1000 undergraduate and 600 graduate) to an astonishing $20 million a year just from our own sources, tripling our endowment, doubling our investment in faculty, and doubling our available classroom and research space, investing over $100 million in new beautiful, environmentally responsible buildings and in renovating and modernizing revered landmarks."

Transitions

During my time as president, I held the title of Susan Mills Professor, and usually taught a seminar at least one semester a year, across women's studies, English, and educational leadership. In 2011, I received tenure in the English department and planned to continue teaching after retiring from my presidency which I did until 2013. I had made lifelong friends among the faculty, particularly with administrative and Board colleagues and, with Mills as a base, the Bay Area of California had become my home.

In addition, in the years after leaving Mills, I had a strong desire to explore the one area of higher education that was unfamiliar to me – the for-profit realm that is often conflated with online education. From 2012 to 2015, I had an opportunity to do just that quite unexpectedly. A neighboring institution to Mills, Patten University serving largely the commuter local population of Oakland, asked for my help as it struggled with some serious financial challenges. At about the same time, the leadership of Patten was approached by a new entity, UniversityNow that was developing an online curriculum with an astonishing low tuition of $5200 a year that could be covered by enrolling students with employer educational benefits that were tax-free. UNOW was to be essentially free to students with these benefits and in order to keep costs low, UNOW was for-profit but did not take federal support for financial aid to students. What it needed importantly was accreditation for its online academic programs. A merger with Patten seemed like an ideal solution.

As a result of helping Patten and working with both Patten and UNOW to create this merger, I found myself once again in a presidency. This time as President of Patten University for a brief period as Patten transitioned into a partnership with UNOW. It was fascinating work, exposing me to a whole new world of educational delivery as well as bringing me closer to the heart of Oakland. Ultimately, I transitioned from Patten's campus to the headquarters of UNOW in San Francisco, serving as Senior Vice President for External Relations and serving on the Patten Board of Trustees. Once again, I found myself as one of the only women "at the table," and I learned that I needed a whole new skill set to work in the world of high-tech, online, and for-profit that included understanding even more about the state and federal requirements for higher education as well as the challenges of transitioning and educating students online. I was motivated to do this work not only to help Patten University but also by the knowledge that there are at least 50 m people in the U.S. population (a high proportion of whom are women and people of color) who started their higher education and incurred student loan debt but who have been unable to complete. UNOW/Patten seemed to me to be one very promising way to reach those non-competes. As it turned out, the concept and the approach were somewhat ahead of the times. The initial offerings have been incorporated into other operations and UNOW/Patten is no longer operating. As the organization was transitioning in 2015, I transitioned again, too, this time into a private consulting practice focusing on collaboration among higher educational institutions for greater cost-effectiveness and student engagement.

My lifelong involvement with higher education across a great diversity of institutions and in a variety of roles coupled with leadership on many governing Boards both within and outside of higher education has provided an opportunity to open doors for others and to mentor and be mentored. I became a scholar through the traditional educational avenues, but I learned to teach as a result of colleagues from my very first faculty appointment who were experienced and experimental and who freely offered help and support to those of us getting started. Similarly, learning the ropes of higher education administration in all of its complexities and within a variety of university settings was an on-the-job experience – often sink or swim with assignments and projects far outside my scholarly experience. I was fortunate to have patient and thoughtful mentors and the support of colleagues. I was also fortunate to have the support of administrative staff – the workforce infrastructure of higher education who do everything from maintaining the grounds to running the complex offices – who gave me advice, direction, and information that is invaluable to making decisions and executing in leadership roles. In turn, I had the good fortune to be able to mentor and support across the constituencies that I regularly interacted with, from those administrators in senior positions who worked with me, to Board members whom I served with or under, to students whom I continued to teach and counsel. Most important to me was finding ways to help others explore and realize their potential while also accomplishing their immediate goals. I believe every person is both capable and responsible in life for teaching and learning, and that belief has been sustaining for me in all my experiences.

Thoughts on Higher Education

It is fifty years since I entered my first classroom as an assistant professor and became part of the higher education workforce. Over those years, higher education and its role in our society has changed significantly. Doors have opened for the participation of many more people as students and in the higher educational workforce as the number and diversity of institutions have increased dramatically. Higher education has become the hub of scientific and technological advancement as well as a major driver of the economy and economic opportunity. Higher education has also expanded its role in areas ranging from the arts to athletics. However, there have been some big challenges for this diverse and multifaceted industry. While the largest growth in terms of institutions and student enrollment has been in the public sector, public financing of higher educational institutions has declined significantly in every decade since the late 20th century in every state, shifting the cost of attendance to students in both public and private institutions. Over the same period, publicly funded financial aid for students at the federal and state levels in the form of grants has stagnated or declined. The cost of delivering higher education has only risen in these decades as the principal expenditures continue to be personnel-driven in teaching, research, and institutional support. To meet these rising costs, institutions have raised the cost of attendance, but they have also significantly offset that cost increase with institutionally funded financial aid.

During my 20 years as Mills president, Mills, like other institutions with the capacity to fundraise, turned increasingly the support from donors to augment debt-free financial aid for a greater percentage of the student body both undergraduate and graduate, and, of course, that institutional endeavor added to the budget bottom line. This was also during a time when family and personal income grew much more slowly than the cost of living and, in particular, the cost of higher education. Higher educational institutions began increasingly to rely on students' ability to borrow primarily from the federal government to close the gaps in the cost of attendance. So great has this change been that we now have a national crisis in terms of a debt burden that is crippling several generations of college graduates and, even more concerning, for those who have some college education but have not been able to complete a degree. Additionally, we have a largely unregulated cost structure in higher education, and prospective consumers are faced with a daunting challenge in trying to understand the real cost of attendance at any given institution when all avenues of support and discount are explored.

In this situation, the vast diversity of institutional types and sources of funding does not serve higher education as an entity or its student populations well. I include in this spectrum all of higher education, including the for-profit and online sectors. It's one thing for prospective students to have options. It's quite another for a student to have to navigate that landscape without a map. Accreditation is required for institutions to allow their students to receive federal and state aid, but it is carried out within higher education and managed regionally without a great deal of national consistency. Every institution, regardless of type or sources of funding, competes for students with its own messaging and model. The public relies on reputation, word of mouth, proximity, and/or accessibility plus a few questionable rating systems to sort out the options. Increasingly, while the value of an undergraduate degree seems to hold in terms of lifetime earnings, the reasons for attending college are motivated by the need to get a credential not by the quality of the education and the benefits the educational community regardless of type.

Public and political discourse on the cost of higher education and the best avenues for solving the problem as the public experiences it generally misses the mark. Free college is based on the notion that someone else will pay the living expenses and all the added costs, forfeited earnings, books, transportation, fees, childcare, and the list goes on, while a student is in attendance. The students I taught at an open public university in the District of Columbia in the 70s had often to choose between enrolling for a semester and paying childcare costs or meeting a household or family emergency. Students today, even those in private institutions like Mills or Princeton, often face similar dilemmas and much more daunting financial hurdles.

If higher education is to become a universal right and a societal responsibility, then we must come up with greatly enhanced public support both for the cost of attendance and completion as well as the social safety net that enables attendance. We must also develop better systems for evaluating the wide variety of institutions and explaining the options to the student consumers. Higher education as a whole requires leadership to participate in this advocacy and reform. All too often, the higher education community takes a defensive stand on the need for greater transparency and cooperation, while maintaining individual institutional competition for donors and students.

Another set of concerns that have been central to my experience as a higher education leader centers on the role and composition of the faculty. I believe an institution's faculty is its most important asset. Faculty set the standard for the quality of education offered, for the engagement of students across disciplines and degree types, and for the preservation of knowledge and the exploration of new ideas and discoveries. A vital and well respected and supported faculty that has a real role in institutional development and governance is critical to an institution's health and to the capacity of a president to lead. Within the academy, tenure has been the system relied upon for over a century to maintain faculty quality and commitment. However, the tenure system has also presented barriers to change that are also vital to education, in particular, the achievement of true diversity of people, approaches, and ideas. As the percentage of women, women and men of color, and LGBTQ graduates of Ph.D. programs in all fields has grown significantly in the last fifty years, the representation of these constituents in tenured faculty ranks has not changed significantly. One of the explanations hinges on the hiring and promotion process that favors the replication of those already in tenured and senior ranks, still predominantly white men. Another contributing factor has been the federal law in place since the early 1990s that prohibits a mandatory retirement age for faculty. Coupled with the tenure system, this has led to a situation where many tenured faculty are aging and positions are not opening for tenure because of institutional budgetary constraints.

During this same period, higher education has seen an increase in the use of adjunct faculty on term contracts across all institutional types. This approach originated as both a cost consideration and as a result of the abundance of available Ph.D.'s particularly in core liberal arts disciplines. The higher education community has not truly evaluated the real cost of this system to institutional health and viability. We do know that the practice has generally had a demoralizing effect on those working in these conditions. Higher education leaders – administrators, boards, and faculty – are working to find alternatives to tenure that provide for the security and retention of faculty while at the same time not locking institutions into hiring and promotion practices that reinforce the status quo.

Issues around tenure also arise in the context of important intellectual and social issues that must be a part of the life of a higher educational institution. A healthy society requires an educational system that enables the free exchange of ideas and at the same time upholds the principles of valuing and respecting all members of the community. Too often, particularly since the 1980s, the issues of what is taught and how it is taught have become issues about which politicians and public pundits want to weigh in – usually against change and innovation and in favor of the so-called "canon." There is also increasingly a drumbeat for education for the workforce, however, that workforce might be defined. Boards of Trustees are sometimes inclined to weigh in with these questions about what is taught and who is teaching it. I believe the most successful presidents find a way to educate the Board and the public on policies and institutional values while working with the faculty on issues of faculty hiring, curricular and research content, and institutional priorities. Maintaining this balance is a high-wire act, requiring respect for tradition and openness to genuine concerns while recognizing that there are core educational responsibilities to the students. Ultimately, a leader must try to bring about agreement and understanding but one must also be willing to take a stand, which can sometimes mean putting one's job on the line.

Higher education in its many and varied forms has defined my life. I have become a leader, an activist, and a lifelong advocate for a system that has many flaws and presents endless challenges, but it is what we have and it is what continues to work to enhance the lives of so many in this country. As a first-generation college-educated person, I am deeply grateful for the gift of educational opportunity. As a woman who has struggled, despite my privileged status, to find my voice and to take a seat at the table, I have had the good fortune to be supported by many colleagues and to be able to open the door for women and men to follow in this work. I have also had the good fortune to have found ways within my professional life to make lifelong friendships and to benefit from the support and care of family, friends, students, and colleagues. Those of us who have had the opportunity to serve as presidents know how rewarding and how hard the work is, and it is a privilege to be part of this story as we share our experiences together.

Discussion Questions

1 Leadership involves setting a path – articulating a mission but also supporting a mission. Holmgren argues that an alignment of a president's values with an institution's mission is critically important to successful leadership. Do you agree?
2 Achieving diversity, equity, and excellence has been one of the stated goals of the majority of higher educational institutions for at least the last 25 years, yet the struggle goes on and in current times there is a growing backlash to DEIJ endeavors. Holmgren makes the point that diversity at all levels (from Board membership to students) strengthens an institution both economically and academically. Do you agree and how would you go about making this case to your community?
3 Holmgren's presidential tenure at Mills College covered twenty years. The average presidential tenure is between five and ten years. What are the advantages and disadvantages of a longer presidential tenure to an institution? What might be the advantages/disadvantages for the leader?
4 Higher educational leadership involves political, business, legal, and educational skills. Holmgren stresses the importance of attending to shared governance and engaging a variety of constituencies in institutional

decision-making, but she is firmly grounded in the centrality of faculty and academic programming as priorities. For many Boards that control presidential recruitment and retention, skills and commitment to other priorities are more critical. Is there in your view an optimal balance?

5 Holmgren was a faculty member and administrator in a wide variety of higher educational institutions before coming to a presidency. She suggests that the range of experiences from an urban, open admission predominantly African American institution to an Ivy League research institution historically all male and predominantly white/Anglo-Saxon, enhanced her ability to lead in a variety of ways, including being able to draw on colleagues from her previous institutions to help with her presidential initiatives. The path through several institutions was not one she planned but one that is more typical for minorities in leadership positions (women, women and men of color, LGBTQ people). How does turning "necessity" into "success" play out in the stories of others profiled in this volume, and how can current leaders support what still seems to be necessary risk-taking for those coming after us who are swimming against the norm?

7
AN AMERICAN INDIAN WOMAN BREAKS THROUGH BARRIERS TO REACH HIGHER EDUCATION LEADERSHIP

My Climb to the Highest Rung

Cassandra Manuelito-Kerkvliet

Abstract

Grounded in her Diné (Navajo) culture and the family legacies of endurance, resistance, and the confidence that education would ensure success, Manuelito-Kerkvliet pursued a higher education and began climbing the administrative ladder. During three years as the first woman president of Diné College, Manuelito-Kerkvliet found herself working with a male-dominated tribal government. At Diné College, besides the contradiction of patriarchal dominance in a tribe that subscribes to ancestral and matrilineal rights, low morale and low salaries, Manuelito-Kerkvliet, through determination and counseling skills in addition to administrative skills, secured funding to improve and build new facilities, established goals, and improved salaries and student enrollment. Then at Antioch University Seattle, Manuelito-Kerkvliet was chosen as the first Native American president to lead a mainstream university and served seven years. There she encountered an environment of preconceived notions about [her] ethnicity, [her] background, [her] behaviors, and belief system. Manuelito-Kerkvliet, stresses that her traditional and non-conforming ways lead her to interact with others with compassion and understanding. Of the many lessons gleaned from her journey, perhaps the most significant is how to retain one's "personal power, peace of mind, and peace in [one's] heart," while thriving and succeeding in spite of opposing cultural norms and challenges.

I am pleased to introduce myself in a way that carries more significance than just my name Cassandra Manuelito-Kerkvliet. *Shi'eiyá Kinya'áanii nishłi, Áashįį báshshíschíín; Hashlishni da shicheii, Tlogi da shináli.* I am of my mother's clan, the Towering House clan, born for my father's clan, the Salt clan, my maternal and paternal grandfathers' clans are the Mud clan and Weaver clan, respectively.

Throughout my life, I have been guided by Navajo (Diné) philosophy and traditions handed down in our creation stories and ceremonies. These have been told and retold by our ancestors for generation upon generation and were told to me by my grandparents, parents, and elders. They spoke of miraculous things happening in other times and places. Miraculous things have also occurred in my life and unfold in the following pages. I use the word Diné, which means "the People" in our language, interchangeably with the more commonly used word, Navajo.

From Humble Beginnings

I was born and raised in Laramie, Wyoming – what I describe as a small redneck western town. My family, including my grandfather, parents, aunts, and uncles were marginalized and subjected to prejudices as the sole Diné family residing there. With grit and determination, my parents left the Navajo reservation to begin anew as a young couple and find work in Laramie, Wyoming. They left the continuity and familiarity of Dinétah (Navajo Nation) to find employment. My father initially worked for the Union Pacific railroad and then as a heavy equipment operator. My mother cleaned houses of the well-to-do and then worked as a custodian at the University of Wyoming.

My parents worked very hard to provide me and my five siblings a livelihood. We attended public schools free of the physical and emotional abuses my parents had experienced while attending the Bureau of Indian Affairs boarding schools on our reservation. These boarding schools clashed with Diné culture, prohibited students from speaking the Diné language, and separated families. While we were the only Indian family in Laramie, far from the revered sacred mountains that defined Dinétah in the Southwest, my parents always kept us grounded in our Diné cultural traditions, language, and practices. They did their very best to nurture and raise me with a strong Diné foundation.

Through oral stories told by my parents and clan relatives, I was taught about my great, great grandfather *Hastiin Ch'il Haajiní*, Chief Manuelito, a great Navajo leader and spokesman. In 1864, after unsuccessfully fighting against military encroachment and western expansion, over 8000 of my ancestors were rounded up by the U.S. Army and forced marched from their homeland in the Four Corners area of the Southwest. They endured the 400-mile Long Walk to a place we called *Hwéeldi* – a place of suffering and fear, also known as Fort Sumner in eastern New Mexico Territory. They remained imprisoned for four years.

Chief Manuelito and other principal chiefs signed the Navajo Treaty of 1868. The Treaty returned my ancestors to a much-reduced area of Dinétah. Manuelito had the keen foresight to view education as a new weapon that could not be taken away from individuals. When he signed the Treaty he proclaimed, "Education is the ladder to success. Tell my grandchildren to climb the ladder." He set a personal example by sending his two eldest sons to Carlisle, Pennsylvania where the first Indian industrial school was established. Sadly, his sons soon died of diseases they had no immunity to.

My Climb to the Highest Rung

As Chief Manuelito's descendant, I adopted my grandfather's legacy that education would ensure success for his people. I was guided by his conviction to secure that education and how much the value of an education would become deeply embedded in my life's work. In my mind, there was no room for failure. To me, it was unimaginable to become a dropout statistic. I was the first in my family to graduate from high school; my brother and sisters followed and all graduated.

In high school, far too few teachers offered me hope or encouragement to attain a post-secondary education. Some seemed to assume I would fail miserably in my studies. Worthy role models who were like-minded or came from similar Native backgrounds were non-existent. But through dogged persistence and unflinching perseverance when all odds were against me, I was a high achiever, earned my diploma, and set my sights on a career of helping and giving back to my people. Upon graduation, I wanted to enroll at Navajo Community College and be among its first graduating classes. However, my parents insisted I remain closer to home to attend the University of Wyoming in Laramie. There I earned a bachelor's degree in social work and a master's degree in counseling. I began my career working in student affairs advocating for Native college students at the state universities of Wyoming, New Mexico, and Oregon. Education was the ladder to my success and my modern-day weapon to combat racial discrimination and injustices when told by many to "Go back to your reservation and collect welfare."

Briefly, tribal colleges and universities were created by federal law around the time I was in high school. Diné College, formerly named Navajo Community College, opened its doors as the first tribal college to serve Native students in 1968. Tribal colleges were established to provide self-determined control of post-secondary education by Native Americans.

They are grounded in Native cultures, languages, and philosophies for tribal members from rural, urban, and reservation backgrounds.

At Oregon State University, where I cut my teeth in mid-level management, I designed and established the Indian Education Office and was appointed as its first director. I gained tremendous knowledge and contacts by attending national higher education and leadership conferences. I invested in myself with my personal income when I was informed at times that professional development funds were unavailable. Over time and with gentle persuasion from Oregon State University President Dr. John Byrne to earn my terminal and someday become a tribal college president.

I declared my career aspiration in my introductory course when I began doctoral studies. And while it began with a declaration to myself, I carefully shared my dream with family, friends, and colleagues. I had to ride out the ambivalence I felt from professors and peers even when I was certain of what I wanted to become. Eventually, I broke through the glass ceiling when I earned a Ph.D. in education policy and management, specializing in higher education administration.

A Moccasin in the Door

My dream came true in 2000 when I was selected as the first Diné woman to lead Diné College as its president. My three years leading Diné College laid the groundwork for my second presidency in 2006 with Antioch University Seattle, where I became the first Native woman to serve as a president of an institution of higher education, outside the tribal college system.

Being the "first" was indeed an honor, but also came with added responsibilities and pressures. First, I had to represent Diné women when I worked and lobbied with an 88-member Navajo Tribal Council composed mostly of male delegates. At Diné College, I inherited an all-male executive leadership team. Working for a Diné woman president would be a "first" for my executive team. Being the "first" Native president in the White world at Antioch University Seattle also came with the added burden of representing Native people. My chancellor, governing board, faculty, staff, and students held preconceived notions about my ethnicity, my background, my behaviors, and belief system. I had to dispel stereotypes and mindsets about a Native president leading a mainstream university. Did I speak English fluently? Could I act and dress like a president should?

Stepping back, I had completed my doctoral studies and had filed my dissertation proposal when a search firm sought me out to apply for a presidential appointment at Diné College. Diné College is situated in the heart of the Navajo Nation with eight campuses spanning Arizona and

New Mexico. After a series of interviews and campus visits, I was offered the presidency by the Diné College Board of Trustees. I quickly embraced this job opportunity. I served a three-year term to lead my people in higher education and used my grandfather's legacy as my guiding light and North Star.

When I became president, Diné College was in tumult after years of a top-down presidency. I encountered low employee morale, stagnant salaries, student enrollment, and an impending reaccreditation visit from the Higher Learning Commission for our institution's reaccreditation. I experienced initial distrust for earning degrees from "those White schools" and having married a "White man" from the Dutch tribe. I was further subjected to chiding remarks that "a presidency is not a role for a woman!" This was irrespective of the fact that our tribe subscribes to the ancestral and matrilineal rights of Diné women who are positioned at the forefront.

Using my counseling skills and previous work experiences at mainstream universities, I quickly became a force to be reckoned with. With sheer determination and grit, I gained rapport and trust with my administrators, faculty, and staff. Together we strengthened Diné College and were successful in achieving reaccreditation. Student matriculation and graduation rates increased. My faculty and I established transparent checks and balances with stakeholders to meet Diné College's short and long-range goals. We lobbied for and won substantial increases in appropriations from the Navajo Nation Tribal Council. We addressed disparities for faculty and staff. We secured the largest private gift of works of art and the library collection of world-renowned Navajo artist R.C. Gorman. Each of the eight campuses outgrew its facilities and we secured the resources to build new classrooms or to renovate existing buildings.

In my three-year tenure at Diné College, I continued to attend national conferences, participate in forums, and speak on panels targeted to women and minority leadership in higher education. As a result, I established a presence and recognition among mainstream higher education leaders. With my sole, intrepid voice, I would shed light on the limited access offered to women of color to "climb the ladder" in top leadership roles. I challenged colleagues and attendees at national conferences to visit tribal colleges and to witness firsthand the remoteness and challenges faced by tribal college students, faculty, and staff. One individual took me up on my offer and came from Seattle to visit Diné College.

But without completing my terminal degree, it was unlikely that I would land a presidency beyond the tribal colleges. So, I reluctantly declined to renew my contract with Diné College and reset my goal to complete my dissertation which had been on hold for three years. I earned a Ph.D. from the University of Oregon in 2005. As luck would have it, my next presidential offer came from Antioch University Seattle and was a result of the "outside" visitor who had visited Diné College at my invitation.

Diligent research on Antioch University revealed it to be a private, non-profit, graduate school with five campuses located across the country. Historically, when Antioch College opened in 1852 in Yellow Springs, Ohio it was a forward-thinking, progressive college of its time; African Americans and women were among its first student body. Female faculty earned the same salaries as male faculty. One woman served on its governing board of trustees. Social justice was one of its core values long before the period of the Civil Rights movement as runaway slaves heading North on the Underground Railroad were provided a safe haven at the college.

Could this also become a safe haven for a Navajo woman like me? I broke the norm and expectation of landing my next presidency in a safe Native environment and sought employment back in mainstream higher education. Antioch's attention to diversity and access for all students, faculty, and administrators from all walks of life convinced me to apply for the presidency. Antioch's long-standing value in providing higher education access and inclusiveness for students of color was important to me. I wanted to continue the practice of creating a safe haven for diverse students who may have never believed they could attend a private non-profit school. In 2007, I was selected as Antioch University Seattle's fourth president.

One of the initial goals established by my chancellor and advisory board was to increase Antioch's presence in the greater Seattle area and with tribal entities in the Puget Sound region. Antioch had a special niche in the city and with further outreach to diverse communities, Antioch University Seattle was well-positioned for growth in a competitive higher education market.

At Antioch University Seattle, I and my executive team leveraged human and financial capital to strengthen academic and student affairs departments. We instituted new curricula and academic support services. We realigned institutional policies and procedures to increase student recruitment, matriculation, and graduation rates. Faculty united to create a new union to address faculty contracts and compensations. The entire Antioch governance structure was redesigned at the chancellor's level after shuttering Antioch College in Yellow Springs, Ohio. I was assigned a new advisory board of trustees who I worked with to a newly established board of governors for Antioch University. All these measures led to the successful reaccreditation from the Higher Learning Commission across Antioch University's five campuses.

Tapping Traditional Wisdom Enhanced my Distinctive Leadership Style

When I was a graduate student in Wyoming, my academic advisor admonished me with a pointed finger, asserting that I would never be successful because I was too traditional and nonconforming. That pivotal memory of being misunderstood because I guided myself with traditional teachings only strengthened my resolve to interact with people in a caring and compassionate manner. Perhaps my former training as a counselor and social worker also helped me to become a compassionate leader. I am adept at working and interacting effectively with almost everyone, particularly students. People can approach me and feel comfortable, understood, and supported. I approach my leadership as if I were weaving a Navajo rug. I work across disciplines, from the bottom up, and from the top down.

My decision-making and leadership through difficult times arise from how I nurture my personal and professional relationships – what Navajos refer to as *k'é* – a philosophical concept of relationships, not just between people, but with our natural environment and the world around us. These relational connections are an important Diné value. My father taught me to have a deep appreciation and genuine respect for people who work for and with me. I am genuinely interested in the backgrounds and interests of my faculty, staff, and students, and turned around dysfunctional and distrustful working atmospheres at both institutions by using his teachings.

The Navajo word *hózhó*, roughly translated, is a time-honored Navajo concept of living in a holistic environment of beauty, balance, harmony, and well-being. To have beauty in one's life, one has to attain balance in four realms of their lives: physical, emotional, intellectual, and spiritual. I asked my employees to envision stability and balance in all aspects of their personal and professional lives given our institutional realities. This conveyed strength in our collective efforts to embrace and create a balanced future for our graduates, ourselves, and our institution.

I took a grave risk in remaining true to my Navajo identity and roots while leading a mainstream institution. At Antioch, I introduced small Navajo rituals to my constituents. Some witnessed firsthand the prayers and chants I recited in the presence of my executive leadership team and my governing board of trustees. On rare occasions, I would assist my chancellor at decisive moments in her administration with protection prayers and rituals. I would keep a small eagle feather in my business portfolio and use it to appeal to the Holy People for leadership guidance and support. This practice kept me and my community grounded and focused on *hózhó*, to walk and work in Beauty.

Tipped off Balance

One wearisome period when I felt most overwhelmed and knocked off balance, I had a vivid dream about my deceased father who spoke to me in Navajo: *Shiyázhí, nidii'nééh, niká'iishyeed* – My baby, get up, let me help you. I felt his strong handgrip as he pulled me to my feet. When I awoke, I felt his presence and acknowledged that he would always be there in the spirit world to support me when I turn to prayers for strength to overcome difficulties and the fair share of challenges that derived from my presidential position. Whenever I navigate rough times or feel my life is out of balance, I offer traditional tobacco, or sage or cedar incense to the Holy Ones to restore *hózhó* in my life. Then I recall the Native proverb that resonates and sustains me, "A nation is not conquered until the heart of our women are on the ground. Then it is done. No matter how brave its warriors or how strong its weapons."

One major disappointment that threatened to overshadow all my accomplishments as president was two legal cases brought forth by two Native women claiming "wrongful and discriminatory" termination of employment, one at each institution. I was expressly disillusioned, to say the least, that allegations of discrimination were at the root of these two cases brought forth by two individuals who had clearly violated the terms of their contracts.

As president, I had the moral duty to protect and act on behalf of my institutions in all personnel matters. I refused to settle these disputes outside of courts and to quietly pay out large sums of money. Instead, our institution's legal representatives addressed these dismissals over the course of my presidencies and in my favor. I will never fully understand the "crab pot" mentality whereby one's own people will turn against another for personal and professional gains. I am a Navajo woman who extolls honor, decency, and respect when earned and appreciates reciprocity in return.

It Is Finished in Beauty

In 2013, I retired at the end of a seven-year contract with Antioch University Seattle. Since then, I have not known of another indigenous person who has filled my moccasins and answered the call to lead a mainstream higher education institution. Still, I have witnessed the election of two talented Native women to the U.S. Congress. And most recently, Deb Haaland, a Laguna Pueblo Indian now leads the U.S. Department of Interior as Secretary under the Biden administration. With her U.S. Senate confirmation, we are shifting the national narrative in indigenous leadership. This gives me pride and hope that Secretary Haaland will protect our Native peoples and our homelands. At the heart of it, our ancestors fought and spilled their blood and died so we could survive to this day as sovereign Indian nations.

I believe our future as Indian nations will be greater than our present one when we support the generations coming behind us. We must promote and support the inclusiveness and diversity of all peoples of color in higher education. The journey is hózhó – beautiful, but we must be still long enough to hear the voices of our ancestors. Once their ancient voices are heard, we cannot let their visions and dreams for our Indian people escape us. It is our responsibility as educational leaders to instill the importance of education in future generations of learners. They will in turn assist their communities with knowledge and expertise gained while attending school and graduating. We need to assist them to ascend their own ladders, realize their career aspirations, and full potentials.

As I reflect on my leadership at Diné College and Antioch University, it comes to this: I have been on a sacred journey while rooted and nurtured by my Diné lifeways. I came to these two institutions with a calling, a mission, and a purpose: to bring my best skills and understanding of leadership. I reached the pinnacle of my education and career when there were no financial resources or templates to follow by trusting and investing in myself. I made a clean break when I left Diné College and Antioch University Seattle. I retained my personal power, peace of mind, and peace in my heart by never attaching myself to a person, a place, an institution, an organization, or a project when I left these institutions. I accomplished a valued task and I feel gratification and pride.

Surviving challenges means living with loss, overcoming hard times, managing being different, and learning to put difficult experiences behind you. Especially important during these times were the sustenance of *k'é* – close relationships and creating a *nizhóni* (beautiful) work environment where I felt safe and protected. I have experienced difficult times and become a better, wiser person for it. As I gathered memories and reflected on my career and its vitality, tenacity sprang forth in my heart. This concludes the story of my leadership journey. I finish with phrases from a Navajo prayer in the Blessingway ceremony. This has been my private chant throughout my life:

> With beauty before me may I walk. *Shitsiji' hózhóogo naasháa doo.*
> With beauty behind me may I walk. *Shikéédéé hózhóogo naasháa doo.*
> With beauty above me may I walk. *Shik'igi hózhóogo naasháa doo.*
> With beauty below me may I walk. *Shiyaagi hózhóogo naasháa doo.*
> With beauty all around me may I walk. *T'áá altso shinaagóó hózhóogo naasháa doo.*
> It is finished in Beauty. *Hózhó náhásdlíí'.*

Discussion Questions

1 This chapter provides a narrative lens into Manuelito-Kerkvliet's leadership journey interwoven with her Diné traditions. Following her traditions, Cassandra has led with resistance, resilience, and reconciliation to be a voice for the often voiceless American Indians. In self-reflection, do you understand the "whys" of your core traditional beliefs and values? Have you reassessed any beliefs that no longer serve you or make sense to you?

2 Experiencing racism and cross-cultural misconceptions, Manuelito-Kerkvliet dared to take bold steps along her career journey. As you progress on your own career path, have you been encouraged or discouraged in achieving your goals? What effect did this have on you and how have you responded?

3 Diné values of respect, humility, and valuing relationships are critical components of Manuelito-Kerkvliet's leadership style. Have you ever been conflicted between your cultural values and that of your work expectations? How have you responded?

4 Manuelito-Kerkvliet grounds her personal and professional life in a Diné philosophy of balance called *hózhó*. She recognized the risks in being true to her Diné identity and culture. Do you understand the importance of truly integrating balance in the emotional, physical, intellectual, and spiritual aspects of your life? Do you sustain this balance, and how?

8

FROM SEGREGATION IN MISSISSIPPI TO UNIVERSITY LEADERSHIP IN CALIFORNIA

Seizing Opportunities, Making a Difference, and Paying It Forward

Horace Mitchell

Abstract

From witnessing Ku Klux Klansmen riding through his Mississippi neighborhood, to racist discouragement to seek the best, to the presidency of California State University, Bakersfield, Horace Mitchell's story is one of undaunted optimism, strategic risk-taking, determination, and the importance of networking and friendships. Mitchell is one of the first generation of Black administrators and scholars during the late 60s and early 70s, who addressed the new and often awkward diversity situations in institutions unprepared for the demographic change in students and faculty. Heavy involvement in community service, serving on the UCI cabinet, and focused but diverse experiences in higher education, led him to think about a presidency and attend the Harvard Institute for Education Management.

Mitchell's story demonstrates that during conflictive times of diversifying campuses, one can remain true to one's scholarship and teaching and forge relationships with sponsors and mentors while sponsoring and mentoring others –several of whom went on to presidencies. Accepting challenges, being innovative, taking risks strategically, and knowing the campus culture informed his approaches to student affairs, business and administrative services, and his own career progression to the presidency of CSU Bakersfield.

Prologue

I was born in a small, segregated town in Mississippi in 1944. It was a time of significant racism, social inequality, discrimination, and harassment of African Americans, with "white only" signs on water fountains, benches, doors, and many other locations. In addition, there were frequent reports of Black men being lynched across the state. On at least one occasion I witnessed hooded Ku Klux Klansmen on horseback riding through the Black section of town at night carrying burning torches and yelling racial epithets at members of my family and others in the Black community.

It was within that context that I lived until age 11 with my parents, siblings, grandparents, and other relatives. I attended the segregated Booker T. Washington Elementary School through the third grade. I had a keen awareness of the racial environment yet, somehow, I had a notion that at some point I would make a difference, that I would be an "ace" of my "race" (using letters from my first name). It was the lynching of Emmett Till, a 14-year-old Black boy visiting from Chicago in 1955, only 48 miles from where we lived, that led to my parent's decision to move the family to St. Louis for a better life.

I entered the fourth grade when we moved to St. Louis. Early on it was determined by teachers and counselors that I needed help with my speech regarding "proper English" and to "eliminate" my "southern drawl." While I was in my senior year in high school, and wanting to attend Washington University in St. Louis, I thought I was well-prepared:

- I was the president and first-ranking student in my senior class.
- I had been the student council president in my junior year and
- I was a letterman in football and wrestling.

It was known that I always expressed a desire to "help people." Because I did well in math and science, I was encouraged to think about a future career in medicine, which I did. One day the principal who happened to be White, but with whom I had a good relationship, told me that a small liberal arts college in Illinois would be inviting me to a weekend visit at the college because they were interested in enrolling more Black students. I was surprised by what he said. I said, "But you know that I want to go to Washington University." He said, "I know, and you have done very well here, but all of the students admitted to Washington University are top students and they attended high schools that are much better than this (inner city) high school. You have been a big fish in a small pond." I asked, "Are you saying I am less prepared than I thought I was?" He said, "Yes." So, I attended that weekend campus visit, but maintained my desire to attend Washington University.

Fortunately, I was admitted to Washington University with a scholarship as a pre-med student with a biology major. I was one of four Black students admitted that year (1964). Since I graduated mid-year (early), and Washington University only admitted new classes in the Fall, I started a full-time job two weeks after I graduated at McDonnell Aircraft Company. I decided to get an early start in college by taking a course during the summer. I earned a "B" in a calculus course, then decided that I would continue to work full-time when the academic year started. I was the first in my family to attend college.

With a full pre-med schedule in the Fall, I received my first set of exam scores with a poor grade in chemistry. After talking with my adviser, I understood what I was doing wrong:

- by working full-time, I was spending far less time studying than my classmates;
- I studied alone while my classmates had study groups, and
- the study groups shared copies of prior exams to which I did not have access.

It became clear to me that I could not continue to work full-time, so I changed to a part-time job. That allowed me to join study groups and to go to my professors' office hours. During my sophomore year, I took several psychology courses and enjoyed them. I concluded that a career in psychology would be another route by which I could "help people." After much thought and many things to consider, I changed my major to psychology. During the following summer (1966), I married my high school sweetheart, Barbara. As I started my senior year, Barbara and I were expecting our first child. I decided I needed to work full-time again. I returned to McDonnell Aircraft Company (then McDonnell Douglas) as a clerk-planner keeping logs of the installation of systems and components on spacecraft. I worked evenings and attended classes during the day.

Because I wanted to see what psychologists did in different settings, I arranged two independent practicum courses. The first was to serve as a volunteer at a community mental health center in inner-city St. Louis that was managed by the Association of Black Psychologists. For the second, I got permission from my supervisor at McDonnell Douglas to get off the clock for two hours during each evening shift to spend time in two departments: (1) human resources (testing and evaluation of applicants and personnel policies); and (2) human engineering. Human engineering involved research to evaluate and maximize the efficiency of man-machine systems in the Gemini spacecrafts that the company was building for NASA during that time. It was a very unique experience.

Early Introduction to Administration

One night while I was working at my desk at McDonnell Douglas, I got a phone call from Dr. John Whiteley, the chair of the master's degree program to which I had been admitted. He said the dean of the College of Arts and Sciences wanted to talk to me. My first question was, "Why?" He said the dean was in the process of recruiting for two new assistant deans, and that he had recommended me. That was a total surprise to me because it was not a possibility of which I was aware. In fact, the assistant dean with whom I had spoken on occasion was (probably) in his seventies. After an initial meeting with the dean, I completed my very comprehensive preparation for the interviews. After interviews with members of the search committee and the dean, I was selected for one of those assistant dean positions (7/1968–6/1973).

By virtue of being appointed to that position, I had an early introduction (at age 23) to university administration while I was enrolled in my master's degree program. My responsibilities included advising students on academic matters, counseling students on personal matters, coordinating the Field Study Program, coordinating the honors scholar program, and conducting research on student enrollment trends, attrition, and academic performance. I was also a resource person for other units (e.g., admissions, financial aid, counseling, and career development) regarding Black students.

My first administrative challenge occurred during the Fall of my first year. It started when a small group of Black students on campus charged that the all-white campus police were consistently harassing them. They managed to take over and sit in the campus police office. I joined the other three or four Black campus administrators in meeting with the students in an attempt to resolve the issue. I was the youngest and newest. Having graduated from the university only a few months earlier and knowing most of the students, they allowed me to stay in discussion with them even as they asked the other Black administrators to leave because they were telling the students what they should do, rather than listening to them. The sit-in was a major news story in St. Louis with all of the networks providing live coverage. At one point, a reporter asked the chancellor about the then-current status of the situation. The chancellor responded, "Things are okay; there is a Black administrator in the group."

At that point, all eyes turned to me with suspicion, wondering if I was there solely as the chancellor's agent. I told them that I wanted to understand their issues more fully and to hear their suggestions for solutions. I stayed in discussions with the group over the next day or so. Then the sit-in moved to the chancellor's office. I continued my efforts to be a facilitator between the students and the chancellor. I felt that I was in an impossible position during that time. After several more days, the students presented the chancellor with a "Black Manifesto" which called for the admission of more Black students, the recruitment of more Black faculty and staff, and the creation of a Black Studies program. The chancellor agreed to take steps toward the achievement of those goals. The sit-in ended after a few more days.

While I was still in the assistant dean role, I completed my master's degree and enrolled in the Ph.D. program in counseling psychology at Washington University. Throughout my undergraduate and graduate education at Washington University, I had many exceptional professors. As it turned out, the first African American professor I had was while I was doing the research for my dissertation. Dr. Robert L. Williams who had earned a Ph.D. in psychology at Washington University in 1961 was recruited in 1970 to be a professor of psychology and the first director of the Black Studies Program. Dr. Williams shared with many of us that while he was preparing to begin work on his doctoral dissertation, he told the chair of the psychology department that he wanted to do research on the "Black psyche." He said the chair told him that there was no such thing as a "Black psyche" and if he wanted to earn a doctorate from that department, he needed to find a different topic. He did that, then pursued his passion after he earned his Ph.D. Dr. Williams was one of the founders of the Association of Black Psychologists in 1968. I asked him to be a member of my dissertation committee. He became its most influential member. He introduced me to the new discipline of Black Psychology and the Association of Black Psychologists. He served as an invaluable mentor, and later colleague.

First Faculty Appointments

As I was nearing completion of my doctorate, I decided that I wanted to have a full-time tenure-track faculty position. I reviewed openings at several Universities. Washington University offered me what I considered to be the ideal position – Assistant Professor of Education (Counseling Psychology) & Black Studies effective Fall, 1973.

My major responsibilities included supervising the clinical training of masters and doctoral students in counseling, developing and coordinating counseling internship placements, advising masters and doctoral students, serving on dissertation committees, conducting research and writing articles, and teaching two courses each semester. Among the courses I taught were two new courses that I developed. The first was the "Seminar in Counseling Minority Groups." My preparation for that course led to my first academic publication: "Counseling Black Students: A Model in Response to the Need for Relevant Counselor Training Programs" (The Counseling Psychologist, Vol. II, No. 4). The other course was "Seminar in Black Studies for Graduate and Professional Students", which was a multidisciplinary look at several social issues that were prominent in St. Louis at that time.

For one semester, I served as acting director of the Minority Mental Health Program while the director, Dr. Williams, was on sabbatical leave. It was a grant-funded joint master's degree program in Psychology and Black Studies. The program trained mental health professionals with an emphasis on clinical services to minority clients and research on psychological issues confronting minority communities.

In Fall 1976, I was appointed as the third Director of the Black Studies Program at Washington University. Reporting to the Dean of the Faculty of Arts and Sciences, I was responsible for the administration of an academic unit that had seven full-time faculty members, two full-time staff members, and several part-time faculty and staff. The Program was multidisciplinary; offered an average of 16 courses per semester; awarded a bachelor's degree in Black Studies; and developed numerous colloquia, symposia, workshops, and a variety of other programs related to Black experience, Black culture, and student development. My responsibilities included curriculum development, academic personnel administration, and resource management.

I left Washington University at the end of the 1977–78 academic year to pursue plans that my wife and I had to relocate to California. I was a visiting assistant professor of social ecology for the summer of 1978 at UC Irvine. I had held the same position for the summer of 1977.

Middle Management

A. Special Assistant to the Vice Chancellor-Student Affairs, University of California, Irvine (6/1978-10/1980)

I served as the primary designee of the Vice Chancellor in policy development and implementation which addressed the needs of medical and graduate students; provided technical assistance to department heads; and served as a principal advisor to the Vice Chancellor in the overall operation of Student Affairs.

While I was in that position, the Vice Chancellor for Student Affairs asked me to work with the dean of the College of Medicine who was concerned about the operation of his student affairs unit. I spent several weeks examining the relevant issues and talking to relevant faculty, staff, and students. When I was done, I proposed to the dean a new organizational structure, staffing, and budget. The dean accepted my proposal and asked me to serve as interim associate dean for student affairs while he conducted a formal search. I agreed to serve in the interim position and decided that I would become a candidate for the permanent position. After the search, I was offered, and I accepted the position.

B. Associate Dean for Student and Curricular Affairs, College of Medicine, University of California, Irvine (11/1980-1/1984)

I was responsible for all administrative units and programs that were designed to support the academic mission and to facilitate the personal and professional development of medical students. The units were: Office of Admissions, Office of Financial Aid, Student Development Office, Curricular Affairs Office, Office of the Assistant Dean-Clinical, and the Health Professions Resource Center.ealth ProfessHE

In addition, I had a faculty position as assistant/associate clinical professor of psychiatry and human behavior in the Department of Psychiatry and I was a member of the department's teaching faculty for first- and second-year medical students.

I was the first person of color and first non-physician to serve in that associate dean position. I also served on the board of the Association of American Medical Colleges Western Group on Student Affairs, including serving as chair for one year.

I was appointed to several campus-wide committees. One of those was to serve as chair of the Chancellor's Advisory Committee on Minority Affairs. The role of the committee was to identify areas in which campus policies and procedures placed persons of color at a disadvantage and to make recommendations for corrective actions. The committee's members represented the broad diversity of the campus community. During a series of meetings, gay and lesbian staff and faculty made presentations on how the campus could become more respectful to them in all areas, including hiring and promotion of faculty and staff. The group asked the Advisory Committee to recommend to the Chancellor the establishment of a comparable committee to address their issues. The Advisory Committee agreed to do that, and I presented the recommendation to the Chancellor. He accepted our recommendation and established that new advisory committee.

Outside of my university responsibilities, I completed the California requirement for licensure as a psychologist. I was licensed in 1981 and I have maintained that license to date.

In 1983, Vice Chancellor Whiteley, who had recruited me, announced his intent to step down and return to the faculty. The university initiated a national search to fill that position. I thought about applying, but I hesitated because my two supervisors at the campus were the vice chancellor for student affairs, who was at odds with the executive vice chancellor, and the dean of the college of medicine, who had led an effort by College of Medicine faculty to censure the chancellor because he had withdrawn his support for the construction of a hospital on campus, supporting instead, a hospital to be built by a community group in Irvine. Therefore, the College of Medicine's hospital continued to be the former Orange County Hospital located about 13 miles away.

As I thought about the situation further, I felt that I had been loyal to both, but I did not get involved in their campus political issues. I thought of that as being "ethical loyalty," that is, not compromising my personal values as I worked hard to achieve organizational goals. At the end of the recruitment, which had a pool of 94 national candidates, the Executive Vice Chancellor called me to arrange a meeting with him for the next morning. When I met with him, his opening statement was, "I'm pleased to offer you the position of Vice Chancellor for Student Affairs." My response was, "I'm very pleased to accept it." I was the last Vice Chancellor appointed under the leadership of UCI's founding chancellor, Dr. Daniel Aldrich, and the first person of color.

Executive Appointments

A. Vice Chancellor-Student Affairs and Campus Life, University of California, Irvine (2/1984-3/1995)

I had responsibility for providing policy and managerial leadership in support of the broad educational goals of the University by providing programs, services, and facilities that were responsive to student needs and campus objectives including: bookstores; career development, counseling and health services; child care, conference, and food services; financial aid; housing; intercollegiate athletics and recreation; student activities and support services; and student and event centers, arts and lectures programs, and public ceremonies.

The first new manager I recruited (in 1985) was Dr. Thomas Parham (an African American) to serve as director of the Career Development Center. Dr. Parham is a UCI alumnus and he had been one of my students in the master's program in counseling psychology at Washington University in St. Louis. He had since completed a Ph.D. and was an assistant professor of psychology at the University of Pennsylvania. I told him during the recruitment that in addition to the role, which was open at that time, I wanted him to assist me in further enriching student development programs at UCI. He said that I had a very unusual recruitment line. I had told him to "let go of that cushy Ivy League faculty position and return home to do some real work." He talked about his desire to continue his scholarship if he took on an administrative position so that his options to return to a faculty position would still be open. I agreed and we developed a plan that would facilitate that. (Note: He was my second successor as Vice Chancellor for Student Affairs at UCI, and he is now in his third year as president of CSU Dominguez Hills.)

In the late 1980s, I appointed a special assistant to the vice chancellor for diversity. I chose Dr. Gene Awakuni who had been a pre-doctoral intern in the counseling center, and then a psychologist after he completed his doctorate at Harvard University. When the director position became available, I appointed him to fill that position. (Note: Dr. Awakuni was recruited to be an assistant vice chancellor at UC Santa Barbara. After that, he served as a vice president for student affairs at Cal Poly Pomona, and then at Columbia University before becoming the chief student affairs officer at Stanford University. He then returned home to Hawaii to become president of the University of Hawaii at West Oahu).

Among the many new programs and initiatives we started was our first Asian Awareness Conference. We developed that conference because the number of students with Asian backgrounds was increasing significantly and students and staff were uninformed about the diversity among Asian cultures. That was significant because it reduced the number of inappropriate references in addressing Asian/Asian American students and staff. In addition, we developed a First Year Experience Program in collaboration with the University of South Carolina.

Facilities initiatives we completed included new housing complexes, the Bren Events Center, new food facilities, and expansion of the Student Center to 110,000 sq. ft. As we were considering several sites for the Student Center, a decision had to be made regarding the Cross Cultural Center which was located in a trailer. The Cross Cultural Center had offices for MEChA, the Black Student Union, and Asian American student groups as well as a small classroom for cross-cultural classes, and programming. Asian American students wanted the Cross Cultural Center to be located inside the Student Center. Black and Chicano students wanted it to be on the opposite side of the campus. We decided to have a different building to house the Cross Cultural Center on the general site of the Student Center. (Note: Lori White was the director of the Cross Cultural Center during that time. In one of my mentoring sessions with her, I asked about her long-term goals. She said, "I want to have your job." I said, "When you are ready, it will be available." She decided to get a Ph.D. from Stanford University. After completing her Ph.D., Dr. White was appointed vice president for student affairs at Southern Methodist University, and then vice chancellor for student affairs at Washington University in St. Louis. She recently completed her first year as president of DePauw University in Indiana.)

In 1988, Chancellor Jack Peltason asked me to oversee the Athletics Program which had recently transitioned from NCAA Division II to NCAA Division I. As part of that assignment, he also asked me to be the campus representative at all conference CEO meetings. At first it was the Pacific Coast Athletic Association (PCAA), later renamed the Big West Conference (BWC). In 1992, I initiated a national recruitment for a new director of athletics. I selected Dan Guerrero (a Hispanic) who was at that time the Athletic Director at Cal State Dominguez Hills. He served exceptionally well for 10 years before being recruited to be the Athletic Director at his alma mater – UCLA.

Also, in 1988, Dr. Chang-Lin Tien, then vice chancellor for research at UC Berkeley, was appointed executive vice chancellor at UC Irvine. The two years he spent at UCI were the only years in his professional career that he was not at UC Berkeley. He was readily embraced by the UCI faculty and staff because of his strong academic record in teaching and research, and because of his strong support for affirmative action when there were significant voices saying you could have academic excellence or diversity, but not both. Dr. Tien strongly disagreed with those sentiments. He and I worked very well together and along with our wives; we became great friends. There was a great sense of disappointment across the campus when it was announced in 1990 that he was returning to Berkeley as its new Chancellor.

Throughout my tenure as Vice Chancellor for Student Affairs, I was heavily involved in community service as an individual and as a representative of UCI. Of the many boards on which I served, The United Way of Orange County was the most significant. I served on the board from 1990 to 1995 and I was chair of the board from 1993 until I left Orange County in 1995. In addition, as the founding vice president of the 100 Black Men of Orange County, I led a group of Black organizations in developing a strategic plan to address issues relevant to the Black community (about 2% of the population at that time).

After being a member of the UCI Chancellor's Cabinet for five years under two chancellors, I began to think more concretely about the possibility of becoming a university president or chancellor at some time in the future. My personal philosophy has always been that the best way to get one's next job is to be excellent in one's current job. I never looked around to see where the "grass was greener." So, I maintained my focus on my leadership and management responsibilities at UCI. At one of my weekly meetings with Chancellor Peltason, which included his mentoring on occasion, we discussed my thoughts about becoming a president and he committed to pay the fees for my participation in the Harvard University Institute for Educational Management (IEM). I was accepted into IEM for the summer, 1991.

It was an outstanding leadership experience with participants from institutions around the world and led by faculty from the Harvard Graduate School of Education and the School of Business. On the last day of the program, the director gave an overview of the great diversity of issues we had discussed which we were likely to experience as executive leaders in higher education. As the session was drawing to an end, I reflected on my thoughts about what qualities and attributes I considered to be fundamental for educational leaders. I shared this list with my fellow participants: "Effective leaders must: (1) care about people, (2) take pride in the things they do, (3) pay attention to what is going on around them, (4) do their homework, and (5) do the right thing." While I have elaborated on and expanded this list over the past thirty years, it continues to be the core of my personal view about essential qualities and attributes of effective leaders well beyond higher education.

About two years after I attended IEM, I became a candidate for the presidency at San José State University. I called Chancellor Tien at Berkeley and asked him if he could be a reference for me. He said "yes." He then added that he had a position at Berkeley for which I would be a very good candidate – vice chancellor for business and administrative services. I was surprised by that and said that being a psychologist, the Vice Chancellor for Student Affairs position was a natural. He said that of the 2,000 staff who would be reporting to me at Berkeley, half were in units I supervised at UCI and the other half were in units for which my units at UCI were customers. I said the other issue for me was that I wanted to go where my being there could make a difference, and Berkeley was already #1. He agreed that Berkeley was #1 academically, but he said he was worried that the campus was losing the administrative capacity to support Berkeley's academic mission. I said that if I could help in supporting Berkeley's academic mission, that would be a compelling way in which I could make a difference.

I continued in the San José State president's search process. I was one of three finalists, but another candidate was selected.

When I called Chancellor Tien to let him know the outcome of the San José State search, he said the position at Berkeley was still available. He invited me to visit the campus for a day to explore the opportunity more fully. Then he said, "And bring Barbara." We went for that campus visit which was structured as a recruitment. At the end of the day, Chancellor Tien said, "Everyone thinks you would be great." I felt that the position would be a major challenge, but it was a challenge for which I was ready. I accepted an offer of appointment several weeks later with an appointment date of April 1, 1995.

B. Vice Chancellor-Business and Administrative Services, University of California, Berkeley (4/1995-7/2004)

I was the chief business officer for the Berkeley campus, with responsibility for the administrative support of Berkeley's academic mission through campus-wide policy and managerial leadership in the areas of business services, human resources, financial controls, internal audit, facilities management, capital projects, community relations, health and counseling services, environmental health and safety, public safety and transportation, printing and mail services, intercollegiate athletics, recreational sports, and staff Ombud's. I managed a staff of more than 1,800 full-time employees and an annual operating budget of $180 million.

Of all the positions that I have held in my career, the position at Berkeley was the most challenging initially for several reasons: (a) the size and complexity of the university, (b) the size and diversity of the departments that reported to me, (c) the number of new departments which I had not supervised previously, (d) the Berkeley administrative culture, i.e., "this is Berkeley; we don't need to know what other people are doing," (e) the extent to which Berkeley was farther behind than I had understood the campus to be, e.g., a thirty-year-old financial system which was inadequate to meet campus needs, and no computerized human resources system, and (f) I was designated to be the executive sponsor for implementation of a new Berkeley financial system (BFS) and a first-ever human resources management system (HRMS). I let the Chancellor know that I did not have strong technical skills in those two areas. He said, "I understand. We have a very good technology department. I know you have skills in managing and leading complex projects. That is what we need from you in terms of the implementation of these new enterprise systems."

I was glad that my wife, Barbara, then a high school counselor in Santa Ana, and our son, then a high school sophomore in Irvine, stayed in Orange County until the end of their academic year (three and a half months) because I used virtually every waking hour getting up-to-speed at Berkeley.

I augmented the existing staff by recruiting an associate vice chancellor, changed some staff responsibilities, and moved housing and residential life to student affairs, which I considered the more appropriate division.

As we began to implement BFS using PeopleSoft software, it became clear that it was not designed for major research universities. It was only when other major research universities began to implement the software that the developer understood that significant modifications needed to be made. Unlike Berkeley's usual desire to be on the "cutting edge," I described our implementation of BFS as a situation in which Berkeley was on the "bleeding edge," implementing software that was still under development. Even after the difficult two-year implementation, another issue arose – staff resistance to being required to take the mandated training necessary to get access to the system. The campus culture was that training was voluntary. It was only after several school deans understood that the seeming inadequacies of the system (as described by their staff) were, in reality, the differences in the ability of trained versus non-trained staff to fully utilize the functionalities of the system. After additional discussions with their staff and speaking to our trainers, the Deans required their appropriate staff to get the required training. After that, it was widely understood that training was required for access to the new financial system. When implementation started for the human resources management system, it was also understood that training would be mandatory for access to that system.

As I reflected on the issues related to the implementation of the new technology systems and several other administrative issues, it became clear to me that the larger problem was one of "organizational culture." We worked tirelessly to change that organizational culture. I thought about writing an article entitled "Counter-Culture" because Berkeley had long had a reputation for being a counter-culture environment. In that case, it would have a double meaning "Counter-Culture: Countering the Administrative Organizational Culture at Berkeley." While I never wrote that article, I did make a presentation with a similar theme – "Counter-Culture: Assessing Administrative Performance and Efficiency" at the Oxford Round Table at Oxford University in England in August 2001.

From a campus-wide perspective, it was clear to me that Berkeley had long been a national stage for social activism and protests. People knew that if they had a demonstration at Berkeley, they were likely to get far more national attention than if they went to most other campuses. Since the campus police reported to me, I always wanted to make sure that their actions were appropriate whether they were dispersing crowds, making arrests, or responding to various other situations.

I attended the UC Board of Regents meeting at which they voted to end affirmative action in admissions and hiring, and in other areas. That was a major departure from the UC's long-standing support for affirmative action. Months later, California voters approved Proposition 209 (1996) which became the state law that ended affirmative action. We knew that on the morning after the election students and others would attempt to occupy campus buildings in protest. In anticipation of that, the most likely buildings were locked the night before. When I arrived on campus that morning, there was a crowd in front of the Campanile, the campus' iconic bell tower. There were students, faculty, staff, community members, news media, and police. Most were protesting the outcome of the vote. The campus police gave a briefing to Dr. Genaro Padilla, vice chancellor for student affairs, and me, stating that there were no major building occupations, but that there were protesters on the observation deck at the top of the Campanile and they refused to come down. Vice Chancellor Padilla and I decided we would go up to talk to them. When we went to the elevator, we discovered that it had been disabled. Therefore, the only way for us to get up was to take narrow stairs (about four stories). By the time we got to the top, the protestors (students from all backgrounds) had been told that we were on our way up. They had chained themselves to the iron railing. As we were engaged in dialogue with them, several of them said they knew that both of us agreed with them and that we should chain ourselves with them in solidarity. We said "yes" we agreed with their concerns, but that chaining ourselves with them was not an option. We said that we would work with Chancellor Tien and his cabinet and others to examine other strategies, recognizing that Prop 209 was now the law. We told them that they should plan to leave the Campanile by the end of the day and that they could have ongoing discussions with us and others during the remainder of the academic year. After several months, Chancellor Tien approved "The Berkeley Pledge," an admission and support program for promising low-income students.

I had thought that it would take my management team and me about five years to reach the levels of efficiency and effectiveness that we had accomplished during my tenure as the student affairs vice chancellor at UC Irvine. In reality, it took about seven years. At that point, my thought was that I would stay at Berkeley until my retirement, unless the "right" presidency was available.

In addition to my administrative duties at Berkeley, I continued to teach one course each year as an affiliated professor in African American Studies. The course was "Psychology and African American People – Current Issues." Also, in the summers of 2002 and 2003, I served as the director of the UC Berkeley/University of the West Indies Summer Session Program in Barbados. All students took two designated courses. I taught a course on "Identity Construction" and the chair of the department of sociology at the University of the West Indies-Cave Hill Campus taught a course on the "History and Culture of Barbados." Each year the program enrolled about thirty students and it was six weeks long.

One day in 2002 when former UC President Richard Atkinson was on campus, he asked me if I had heard from the NCAA. My response was, "No, what is the issue?" I was concerned because there were many national issues regarding intercollegiate athletics and athletics was one of the areas reporting to me. He didn't answer the question, saying only that I should be hearing from them soon.

While I was in Barbados, I received a phone call from an Atlanta-based search firm who said I had been nominated for the presidency of the NCAA and they were interested in talking to me regarding that position. When I said I would be in Barbados for another five weeks, the consultant said he could fly to Barbados to meet with me rather than wait until I returned to Berkeley. We had our meeting and several weeks later he informed me that I was on the NCAA Executive Committee's short list. I was then invited to visit the NCAA national office in Indianapolis for further briefings on the role and the benefits, to tour the city, and to look at housing options with my wife.

Shortly thereafter, I was identified as one of three anonymous finalists. It was well-known that the NCAA wanted to hire a university president this time, if possible, rather than a former athletics director, which had been their custom. I knew that if they found a president they wanted, who was prepared to accept their offer, then that person would be hired. The final step was a meeting with the NCAA Executive Committee (now the NCAA Board of Governors). Each of us was told that a decision would be made by the end of the three interviews on that day and that an announcement of the appointment would be made immediately thereafter. Therefore, each of us was told to have an acceptance speech prepared because one of us would be the new NCAA president. It was a very unique writing assignment. At the end of the day, the consultant called me to say, "You were very impressive, but they chose one of the other candidates who would not be identified until the press conference." The announcement was that Dr. Miles Brand, then-president of Indiana University would be the new NCAA president.

My University Presidency – CSU Bakersfield (7/2004–6/2018)

In 2003–04, I received a phone call from a consultant who was hired by the CSU Chancellor's Office. He said he was inquiring about my possible interest in the presidency of Cal State Bakersfield. I said that I had not seen that position opening, so my wife and I would have to visit the campus, do some research, and generally find out more about the campus and the community. I said I could answer his question in about two weeks after we had an opportunity to learn more. After our initial visit and research, I let the consultant know that I was interested in exploring the opportunity.

Several weeks later when I was informed that I was on the shortlist, I told Barbara, "You know, this could happen. We need to have another visit and do more research to be certain that that is something we want to do." After the second visit and more research, I moved from being "generally interested," to "I want to do this because I can see a number of ways in which I could make a difference for the university, its students, and the community." After a few more weeks, I was identified as one of three finalists.

During my official campus visit, I had meetings with faculty, staff, students, and community members as well as a campus-wide open forum. Several of those meetings confirmed my early impressions of what the campus wanted/needed: (1) a more positive self-concept, (2) stronger community engagement, (3) additional sources of funding, (4) more well-focused student academic and support services, (5) increased diversity within staff, faculty and academic programs, and (6) a decision about the NCAA status of its athletics program. In fact, I was asked in several settings, "What do you think about moving our athletics program to NCAA Division I?" Each time I responded, "That sounds like a reasonable aspiration given the great success in Division II."

After my appointment as the new president was announced and several weeks before my start date, I called then-President Arciniega. I said that I had been asked during the campus visit, "What is your vision for California State University, Bakersfield?" I told him that I had a draft of a vision, but I wanted to discuss it in a meeting with his cabinet, deans, and the chair of the academic senate to get their input so that it could be a shared vision. He agreed that I could have such a meeting. My intent was to get a sense of the tenor of the group and to demonstrate a characteristic of my leadership style – presenting my ideas about an important issue, wanting to hear the thoughts of other leaders, and modifying my position as appropriate based on their input.

We had an excellent discussion in which participants challenged each other on particular wording (e.g., "How can we become the leading campus in the CSU when we are not the largest?"). As the meeting was coming to an end, three words were changed by agreement. This vision statement was adopted by affirmation:

VISION

"By 2014–15 CSU Bakersfield will be the leading campus in the CSU system in terms of faculty and academic excellence and diversity, quality of the student experience, and community engagement. Realization of our vision will be advanced by recruitment, development and promotion of excellent and diverse staff within an organizational culture committed to excellence in all areas."

In my first academic year, 2004-05, I expanded on the vision by describing some strategies we would be implementing and by clarifying our planning assumptions. We then considered several new initiatives:

- Making additional investments in our fundraising capacity because state funding alone would not allow us to realize our vision
- Strengthening our support for faculty to write proposals for funding of contracts and grants and other sponsored programs
- Implementing the CSU Initiative to Facilitate Graduation
- Implementing a First-Year Experience Program in Fall, 2005
- Planning for the first new residence halls on campus in almost thirty years with the intent, over time, to guarantee on-campus housing for all new freshmen
- Supporting ASi (student government) in their plan to hold a student fee referendum later in the year to provide funding for a much-needed recreation and fitness center, and, if it was determined to be feasible, partial funding to move the athletics program from NCAA DII to DI

An overarching issue I observed was that many community members, and staff, had internalized a view that Bakersfield was a second-class city based on their reported regular negative comments about the city stated by Johnny Carson on his late-night TV program; and, by extension, that Cal State Bakersfield was a second-class institution. I felt that one of my early challenges would be to enhance the image of the university while also working hard to strengthen its substance. I saw that challenge as one of "identity construction" which was one area of my instructional expertise as a psychologist.

One day the then-chair of the psychology department asked me if I would continue to teach as I had done as a vice chancellor at UC Irvine and UC Berkeley. My initial response was "no" because my presidential duties were consuming all of my time. He then asked, "What about teaching a small senior seminar?" As I thought about my other role (professor of psychology), I said, "yes." So, in the Spring quarter of 2005, I taught a senior seminar on "identity construction." I chose that topic because I thought it had relevance on the individual student level as well as on the university and community levels. We discussed how individuals construct their personal identities over time based on their experiences, the meanings they give to those experiences, and the characteristics they extract from those experiences and meanings as being descriptive of who they are. One of my key "takeaways" for them was, "You (individual, institution, or community) can have an identity by default based on the perceptions of others, or you can construct your desired identity by taking proactive steps of self-definition." I said on many occasions on and off campus that at CSUB we were taking proactive steps toward self-definition.

I wanted to use my first year to get an early start on gaining greater visibility for the university and changing the perception of the university. The campus was founded as California State College, Bakersfield in 1965. It attained university status in 1988. I wanted to change the commonly used name from "Cal State" to "CSU Bakersfield", which would make more prominent the fact that the university is a campus of the statewide CSU system.

We started a campaign with the phrase "Re-introducing CSUB: It's Your University." It presented a brief history of the university, its economic impact on the region, and planned innovative projects. We used that phrase not only for alumni groups, but for current and future students, parents, and community members. We said, "In addition, for graduates of all other universities – 'CSUB is your university'", as well. That is, "it is the university that makes a difference in your community." It was an attempt to gain a greater sense of ownership and connection to the university.

A few months after my arrival as President, I was asked again, "What do you think about moving our athletics program to NCAA Division I?" I gave the same answer that I had given during my official campus visit. Then I added, "We will use this year to determine if that is feasible." Toward the end of the 2004–05 academic year it became clear that a move to Division I was feasible. In addition to other benefits, a move to NCAA Division I would also provide greater visibility for the university as well as our athletics program. I said that, unlike being in Division II, the results of our athletics contests would be reported regularly on ESPN.

In another initiative to increase the visibility of the university, we worked with Cal Trans to have signs posted on Interstate 5 near Stockdale Highway in both directions, "CSU Bakersfield," next exit. Tens of thousands of cars were passing that point annually without people knowing that CSU Bakersfield was just down the road.

I was surprised that after 34 years of existence, the university did not have an alma mater or a "fight song." We worked with the Associated Students to design a process by which proposals for each song could be submitted by students, staff, faculty, alumni, and community members. Proposed songs were reviewed by a broad-based committee in consultation with me. We chose as the alma mater, "Long Live CSUB" by alumnus

H. William Ingram. We chose as the "fight song", "CSUB Victory" by student Gwendolyn Wilcox. We decided that both songs would be debuted on the day of the 35th Anniversary Celebration – May 20, 2005.

As the campus was putting plans together to celebrate the 35th anniversary of the opening of the campus, the question arose about having a presential inauguration along with that celebration. I said that that would be a good idea. The faculty leadership's position was that having an inauguration was very important to highlight the new campus leadership. I then said that would be fine with me. As we planned for the inauguration, two additional issues arose:

1 I felt that the university seal was unclear in terms of meaning, with different people describing it in different ways. Once I heard an authoritative meaning, I gave my approval to have my medallion made. Many staff and faculty said they never liked that seal, and there were no advocates who wanted to keep it. Therefore, I decided to have a new university seal designed based on the CSU seal with information specific to CSUB. The president's medallion was made with the new seal, and the seal was first presented on the printed program.
2 There was no designated presidential robe. Previous presidents used the robe of their doctoral-granting institutions. Since the CSUB colors were blue and gold, I had a blue robe made for me with gold bars, and I adopted the UC Berkeley blue and gold doctoral hood.

In my inaugural address, I talked about our new vision and raised and answered the question, "Who is this new president?" I answered that question in terms of the construction of important aspects of my identity. I then introduced the person or persons who had the most impact on a particular aspect of my identity.

I said my identity was under construction in the early years within the context of a spiritual and loving family. Among the significant values our mother taught us was that having material possessions was less important than being a good person. She taught us to put service above self. I then introduced my mother, my sister, and my brother. I then acknowledged, as a group, all members of my family and extended family who were present.

I said another dimension of my identity emerged from the fact of my being an African-descent person growing up in America. My accomplishments over the years have not been a result of my efforts alone. I am a beneficiary of the collective and cumulative struggles and triumphs of African-descent people over time, and it is on their shoulders that I now stand. At the same time, I have taught and been taught by, mentored and been mentored by, sponsored and been sponsored by individuals from all backgrounds, and I embrace an understanding of their realities as part of my reality.

I said another aspect of my personal identity is being an educator and a psychologist. Throughout my undergraduate and graduate education at Washington University in St. Louis, I had many exceptional professors. As it turned out, the first African American professor I had was while I was doing the research for my dissertation. He introduced me to the discipline of Black Psychology and served as an invaluable mentor, and later colleague. He helped me expand the scope of my intellectual horizons to include a consideration of multiple world views. I learned from him how to become an effective academic program chair and how to become a psychologist whose knowledge of empirical methods was combined with a commitment to not just study people, but to have my research inform strategies for improving their circumstances. I then introduced Dr. Robert L. Williams, Professor of Psychology Emeritus at Washington University in St. Louis.

The person who had the most direct effect on the construction of my identity as an educational leader was the late UC Berkeley Chancellor Dr. Chang-Lien Tien. Dr. Tien was the first Asian American to head a major American research university. What I learned from Chancellor Tien was to always strive for excellence. He said, "Excellence is achieved by decisions that are made on a daily basis." He challenged his Vice Chancellors to examine our decisions – from budget allocations, to program development to faculty and staff hiring and promotion – and ask the question, "Does this decision promote excellence?"

Dr. Tien also placed a high value on diversity in all its forms. He believed in achieving both excellence and diversity. I have extended his position by taking the view that excellence within the context of an institution of higher learning requires diversity. Dr. Tien practiced what he preached at the highest levels within the university. His Chancellor's cabinet was the most diverse among institutions of higher education. Of the four vice chancellors whom he appointed, one was then in his fifth year as president of the University of Maryland – College Park and another in her third year as president of Smith College. I am the third to become a university president, and the fourth is likely to become a president within the next few years. I then said, "Please join me in honoring Dr. Tien and in welcoming our good friend, Chancellor Tien's widow, Mrs. Di-Hwa Tien."

There was one other person I introduced. He had been a sponsor for me from my first professional position. He hired me at UC Irvine, and I succeeded him as the vice chancellor for student affairs at UC Irvine in 1984. Then I introduced Dr. John M. Whiteley, professor of social ecology at UC Irvine.

The celebration of the 35th anniversary and the inauguration, which occurred a few weeks before the end of the 2004–2005 academic year, gave us the opportunity to summarize the big picture about where the campus was headed in focusing on our vision. In the summer of 2005, I appointed Dr. Soraya M. Coley, former dean of the College of Human Development and Community Service at CSU Fullerton, as our new provost and vice president for academic affairs. (Note: Dr. Coley served with great distinction for more than nine years. She was appointed President of Cal Poly Pomona by the CSU Board of Trustees. She took office in January 2015. She is their first female president).

After the first year, we were engaged in major multi-year university transformations in several areas:

1 Establishment of the university's first engineering program & agribusiness program – Enduring fiscal hardship and the absence of state funds forced us to be entrepreneurial. For example, we wanted to start academic programs that related to the two largest industries in our community – oil and agriculture. During meetings with executives in each area, I asked how we could be helpful to their respective industries.

In our discussions with the major oil companies with operations in the Bakersfield area, they said that the oil fields were managed through computer centers. An operator in a control center examines the efficiency of every single well and pinpoints any production problems that come up. That technology required computer engineers, electrical engineers, and petroleum engineers. With no state funding, we worked with our faculty in the School of Natural Sciences and Mathematics to write grants, cobbling together about $10 to $12 million. With that, we started the first engineering program, including the construction of two engineering laboratories. After the first class graduated, we sought and received accreditation from the Accreditation Board for Engineering and Technology (ABET). As a result of that success, the School of Natural Sciences and Mathematics was renamed the School of Natural Sciences, Mathematics, and Engineering.

In similar discussions with agriculture, they said that the farms in Bakersfield and its surrounding areas are not "mom-and-pop" farms. They are major agricultural companies with worldwide exports and operations. They have been growing so large that they could not keep their management talent. New hires from other communities would get one or two years of experience and then leave.

To meet that need, we initially developed a concentration in agribusiness within our bachelor of business administration degree.

The concentration expanded to a full major so that students could earn a bachelor of science in agribusiness. We established an advisory board made up of agriculture industry executives, and they recruited our students as fast as they could be produced, not only the graduates but also placing students in internships. Those companies provided significant financial support for that program.

2 Conversion of the academic calendar from quarters to semesters with curriculum transformations in 70% of our academic programs – Rather than simply converting courses that had been on the books for two or three decades, faculty members reconceptualized their curricula in anticipating future student and community needs. In addition, our academic senate worked with our faculty to totally revise our general education requirements to make sure that they were in alignment with our set of university-wide student learning outcomes.

3 Establishment of the university's first independent doctoral program, EdD in Educational Leadership – We implemented a stand-alone doctoral program in educational leadership to address an identified need for better-prepared K-12 and community college administrators. In 2011, we entered into a collaboration with Fresno State University to offer its Doctorate in Educational Leadership, on the CSUB campus. The program was geared to provide advanced education for K-12 and community college leaders, with specific goals of preparing administrators to meet the educational challenges of today and the future and improving teacher preparation.

The advantage of partnering with Fresno State University was that it allowed us to have in Bakersfield a program to meet the needs of the community ahead of the time when we could offer a program independently. The first three Bakersfield cohorts of the Fresno State program received their degrees from Fresno State. The fourth and fifth cohorts earned joint degrees from CSU Bakersfield and Fresno State. The CSUB independent doctorate in educational leadership began in 2016.

4 Securing CSU Board of Trustees approval of a new campus master plan – The plan increased the student enrollment ceiling from 12,000 FTE to 18,000 FTE. It provided conceptual approval for the construction of public-private partnership projects on vacant campus land, including a business park, a hotel and conference center, and other projects.

The plan was that those projects would benefit the university in two ways. First, there would be an annual ground lease income of several hundred thousand dollars per year. Secondly, all tenants in the office park were required to have programmatic relationships with one or

more academic units. Examples included joint research projects, student internships, and collaborative programs to serve students and the community. However, due to the continuing financial crisis, those projects were not started before I retired in June 2018.
5. Achieving certification as an engaged university – In January 2015 the Carnegie Foundation for the Advancement of Teaching classified CSU Bakersfield as an "engaged" university, after a very rigorous, evidence-based national process. That voluntary classification was a validation of our commitment to strengthening our community engagement, as stated in our vision.
6. Reaffirmation of the accreditation of the university by the Western Association of Schools and Colleges (WASC).
7. Reorganization of two schools – The intent was to increase the effectiveness of the university in its mission to serve local K-12 school districts and to achieve greater synergy among academic programs. We discontinued the standalone School of Education and combined many of its departments with social sciences departments that were in the School of Humanities and Social Sciences to form the *new* School of Social Sciences and Education. The humanities departments were combined with the arts to form the *new* School of Arts and Humanities.
8. Transitioning our athletics program from NCAA Division II to Division I and securing membership in a Division I athletics conference – After completing the NCAA's five-year transition process, and being a Division I independent for two years, we joined the Western Athletic Conference (WAC). We aspired to become a member of the Big West Conference (BWC). A multi-year strategy (mostly political) led to the Big West Conference (BWC) extending an invitation to CSUB to become a member of the conference effective July 2020. I accepted that invitation before I retired.
9. Establishment of the Alumni Hall of Fame which was initiated by the Alumni Association.
10. Construction of new academic and student services buildings – Science III, Engineering Complex, Humanities Complex, Visual Arts Center, Student Recreation Center, Student Housing Complex, and Baseball Park. As we started the University's first baseball program, an alumnus donated a million dollars and also took responsibility for the construction of the facility being that he was a developer.

In addition to the multi-year transformational processes in which we were engaged, the usual work of the university was ongoing: admitting, educating, and graduating students; hiring excellent and diverse faculty and staff; managing all areas of the university; and serving our alumni and community.

Needless to say, all of those achievements required the hard work of excellent and committed teams – the President's Cabinet, departmental leaders and staff across the campus, the faculty and Academic Senate, the Foundation Board, the Alumni Association Board, and supporters of the University.

During my tenure as President of CSU Bakersfield, I served on several higher education boards:

1 the American Council on Education (ACE)
2 the NCAA Board of Governors, Division I Board of Directors, and Division I Presidential Forum
3 the Western Association of Schools and Colleges (WASC) – commissioner and vice chair
4 the National Association of College and University Business Officers (NACUBO)
5 the Western Athletic Conference (WAC) – board chair and vice chair

Chancellor Tim White asked me to chair the Task Force on the Advancement of Ethnic Studies. He appointed to the committee faculty from ethnic studies departments/programs, academic senate faculty, four presidents, other administrators, staff, and students. We sent our final report to the chancellor in November 2017 after more than a year of deliberations, research, and dialogues. We made ten recommendations. The most significant was:

> "Recommendation 1: Ethnic Studies General Education (GE) Requirement – make Ethnic Studies a GE requirement throughout the CSU system"

The CSU Board of Trustees responded to the report by adopting a GE requirement in the area of ethnic studies and social justice. That requirement was of concern to many because it could be possible for a student to take a course in social justice to meet that requirement without ever taking a course in ethnic studies. The California Legislature adopted AB1460 which specified the requirement for a 3-unit course in one of four ethnic studies disciplines: Native American studies, African American studies, Asian American studies, and Latina/Latino studies. The Governor signed AB1460 in August 2020. The Board of Trustees amended their requirement to comply with AB1460. Assembly member Shirley Weber, a former chair of Africana Studies at San Diego State University, sponsored AB1460.

It was supported by the Legislative Black Caucus, the Asian and Pacific Islander Caucus, and the Latino Caucus.

I will end this section of the Profile with quotes from my retirement announcement at the beginning of the 2017–2018 academic year:

> "I have decided to retire at the end of the 2017–18 academic year effective June 2018."

...

> "One of my former colleagues once said, 'Being a university president is an "infinity" job and at any point in time there are always many more things to be accomplished.' I agreed with that statement. The job of being president of CSU Bakersfield will never end. However, I am now prepared to pass the torch of leadership to my immediate successor. I say, 'immediate successor' because there will be several other CSU Bakersfield presidents over the next 100 years, each of whom must lead the university during his or her time of stewardship while also positioning the university for the future beyond their tenure."

...

> "I have been president about twice as long as the average tenure of American university presidents. In addition, June 30, 2018 will mark the end of my 50-year full-time career in higher education at four great universities: Washington University in St. Louis (my alma mater), UC Irvine, UC Berkeley, and CSU Bakersfield. Most importantly, I believe we have made significant progress toward realization of our vision which is always aspirational: extending the excellence and diversity of our faculty and academic programs, enhancing the quality of the student experience, and strengthening our community engagement."

...

> "It has been my great honor and privilege to serve with you, our outstanding faculty, staff, and administrators in serving our students and community over the past thirteen years, and I have enjoyed doing so. We have been dedicated to inspiring excellence among our students and transforming their lives."

...

"That being said, I will still be here and fully engaged throughout the 2017–18 academic year. So, let's continue our important work together in serving our students and community as we address significant issues, challenges, and opportunities that lie ahead and position the university for a remarkable future."

Upon Reflection

This Presidential Profile has covered six strategic areas in which I was focused on "making a difference" at four universities based on the position (s) I held at each. As I look back over my career, having been a first-generation college student who was born in a small, segregated town in Mississippi and grew up in inner-city St. Louis, I had no idea that such a career was possible for me. That is why I inserted into the program for my inauguration the gospel song, "I Don't Feel No Ways Tired." A second gospel song that I relate to my career is "I Won't Complain." To fully understand my journey, I would encourage people to listen to these two powerful songs.

As our nation is now in a period of activism around the need to establish and demonstrate commitments to social justice, racial equality, diversity, and inclusion, we must provide opportunities for young people to explore their passions, fulfill their dreams, and use their gifts to help others in ways they might not have been aware. Every child should be exposed to role models, mentors, advocates, and sponsors as they continue to grow. In addition to their educational and degree programs, there is an important role that higher education institutions can play in this area, working with other organizations to achieve these goals.

While I have retired from my career in higher education, I continue to place a high priority on mentoring, sponsoring, and supporting higher education leaders who have aspirations of becoming college and university presidents/chancellors. One of the ways in which I work to achieve that is by being a member of the UC Berkeley Executive Leadership Academy (ELA) Advisory Board and by being an ELA faculty member.

"A luta continua!"

Discussion Questions

1 What opportunities have you "seized" to make a difference in advancing your institution's social justice agenda?
2 What have been your most important efforts to "make a difference" in the culture of your institution? How would you measure the effectiveness of those efforts?
3 In what ways have you "paid it forward" by mentoring students and/or faculty and staff to increase their ability to be effective advocates for your institution's diversity, equity, and inclusion efforts?

9

DIVINELY ORDERED STEPS TO LEADERSHIP

Positioned for Purpose

Shirley Pippins

Abstract

Shirley Pippins' relating of her years before her professional life could serve as a guidepost for underrepresented students to embrace race, class, and gender differences, discrimination, and struggles with faith, courage, self-empowerment, and optimism. A "Colored" girl from East Chicago buoyed by her family's middle-class values and civil rights advocacy, she took advantage of opportunities to learn and lead wherever they occurred – from Church, where she learned to present publicly at events and teach in Sunday School to vice president of her high school student government where she decided "never to be vice president of anything [she] could lead" when the Dean of Girls told her after the election that she could have been president. Among the many lessons she gleaned from her experiences is that "I learned that I could compete and excel in any environment: I didn't have to be comfortable to do it." Faith, family empowerment, and the desire to make a difference in the lives of others led her to draw on her professional experiences as a coach and senior consultant for searches.

Who knew that a Colored girl who grew up next to a liquor store, behind her father's store, in a small steel mill town in Northwest Indiana would grow up to become the president of three colleges and a Senior Vice President of the American Council on Education? My earliest goals were simple: I wanted to be a math teacher, live in a nice neighborhood, and have a nice car. I had never seen a college president and certainly had never conceived of becoming one. On paper, I was more likely to become a statistic.

Yet, in retrospect, it is clear that being a statistic was never the plan for my life. I truly believe my steps were ordered by God and that God positioned me for purpose. That is why when people ask me what prepared me to become a college president, I tell them this: Everything I ever experienced prepared me; every step I unknowingly took led me to what I now see as my purpose.

Here, I wish to share with you that journey and the path on which God guided me.

Family Background and Early Influences

In some ways, my path began before I was even born. According to family lore, my ancestors' time in America began with the separation of twin African brothers. The brother from whose lineage I came was a slave on the plantation of a man who kept written documents about his slaves. My grandmother, who married one of this twin's descendants, was an educated woman and ensured her children were also educated. When I trace my ancestry, I find a son named King in one family in each generation. Although he did not initially share the meaning of his initials (K.T.), my father's actual name was King Theodore Robinson.

My mother's father was a carpenter. All her siblings were educated, and she and my father were both teachers in the South. That those two people should meet and produce my sister and me was, in my mind, one of the first steps on a pathway to achievement and purpose.

My parents were change agents and examples of empowered people who empowered others. I did not realize it at the time, but they would form a foundation for my future. Originally teaching in the South, and unable to do so in the North because of discrimination, they used their talents to fight the racism and opposition that surrounded them. They were working-class people with middle-class, Christian values. Although I lived next to a liquor store and behind a family store, my father owned that family store and was a respected businessman and community leader. I did not know we lived in what others considered a ghetto until I was much older and ventured outside my little piece of the world.

My father was a civil rights leader. He led protests and boycotts that resulted in the hiring of the first Black policemen, firemen, sales clerks, and bank clerks in our area. Regardless of how others may have labeled us, my sister and I did not feel small. We did not feel disadvantaged or under-represented. We were special and significant in our own little world. From a social perspective, my father and his status had a huge impact on our lived experiences.

As an adult, I see even more the powerful impact that my mother had on my life. She seemed to live quietly in the background, always working hard, always making a way. She exposed us to important experiences. My mother played the piano, and she insisted that my sister and I take lessons. We were always dressed nicely and had the necessary supplies for school and extracurricular activities even when resources were sparse. Some of our peers did not. My mother was the class act in the family. Although later in life she had limited funds, she kept a singular sense of pride and faith. I believe we acquired this mindset from her.

Members of my extended family also served as role models and change agents. My favorite uncle was a highly respected minister locally and was active on the state and national stage. One of my favorite older cousins was a dynamic speaker and a nurse. Without knowing it, I absorbed these influences and felt special and privileged. I began to set my own goals very early in life.

One of my earliest childhood memories was attending a reading circle in the first grade. The previous weekend, my father had taken me to the local library. I still remember the Black librarian's name, Mrs. Williams. I must have read a book containing the then-new word, "umbrella." That Monday morning at school, the teacher asked who knew it and I raised my hand and identified the word. The teacher was impressed and shared her admiration, and the rest is, in many ways, history: I was hooked on praise. I did not realize it then, but even this incentive was God working to push me to achieve and strive for bigger things. More core operating principles and values came from that reading circle, far more powerful than the new vocabulary word. I was beginning to experience how knowledge could create opportunities. I now ask myself, why did we go to the library that weekend? Why did I select a book containing the word "umbrella?" I now believe God's guiding hand was at work.

Church was the epicenter of my youth in many ways and was a critical place in which God positioned me for purpose. I was given crucial opportunities to grow in faith as well as excel. I performed in the Easter celebrations, for example, (a major event in the Black Christian Church). While as a youth I enjoyed having a beautiful new Easter outfit on an aesthetic level, I was unconsciously learning lessons in professionalism and presentation. Soon I would regularly have the longest Easter speech and the lead part in the Easter play. These skills would later serve me well as a president and keynote speaker.

I also was fortunate to serve as the secretary of the Sunday School in my uncle's church. He had many nieces. What did he see in me? Could it have been those long Easter speeches? He not only made me secretary of the Sunday School, but I also was teaching a class by the time I was in my early teens. As a Sunday School teacher, I prepared my lessons and organized the report from my class. I tracked the attendance and income every Sunday. I did not recognize it at the time, but these experiences gave me skills I would need to perform well in other leadership contexts. When I return home for community events, I am amazed when people remind me that I was their Sunday School teacher. As a teen, I did not give much thought to the impact I was having in that spiritual and educational role. As an adult, while serving as president of Victory University, one of my greatest joys was being part of a team of Christian ladies who taught the New Members Class at my church. It was truly a full circle moment, one that I could appreciate much more at that phase of life.

My favorite uncle also took me to meals in restaurants and at the YMCA. I can only assume that he and my Home Economics teacher were responsible for my etiquette skills and comfort in formal dinner circles. Can you imagine the first time my family ate together at a restaurant was when I graduated from college?

Another major influence was one of my favorite older cousins, Edna. My parents took me to many afternoon and evening programs at church, and my cousin Edna served as mistress of ceremonies. She was responsible for pulling the pieces of the program seamlessly together. There was no script, so she had to be good on her feet. I can still see Edna in her elegant suits and hats as she led those programs. I remember one special evening, many years later. I had just successfully presided over a church dinner. As I was walking back to my car and reflecting, it suddenly occurred to me I had been my cousin Edna that night. I felt so proud to have emulated her. I called Edna and together we celebrated that moment. I later wrote a speech entitled, "You Never Know Who's Watching." As a young woman, I had been watching and admiring her, and unconsciously absorbing key skills.

I would learn another crucial principle early in life: I could change situations, and I could obtain the things I wanted. After my parents decided there was no need to buy me toys as gifts for Christmas, I determined that I could secure the gifts I wanted myself. If I had a plan, if I worked hard, I could make it happen. One holiday season, I asked my father if I could work in the store and earn 50 cents an hour to save for a Tom Thumb typewriter for Christmas. As I reflect back, it did not bother me that I had earned the money for that typewriter. I was exercising control and building a sense of agency. I could hardly sleep the night before I had the opportunity to open the present I earned.

I built upon this work ethic in other areas of my life. Using the piano skills passed down by my mother, I played for a local church while I was in high school and earned the funds for the clothing I wanted as a young woman. While at the time, my focus was on concerns such as outfits for out-of-town athletic events and the Sadie Hawkins dance, I was learning about financial stewardship. I even remember opening my first lay-away plan at the local Goldblatt's store. Who knew one could be positioned for purpose even through teenage wardrobe aspirations and acquisitions?

This is also the period where I began to develop another critical mindset, a view I have come to call my Indiana Jones perspective on life: Never give up, do not waste time panicking, and always believe that you have the power to change things for the better. In those potentially last moments during a life-threatening situation, when most people prepare for death, Indiana Jones believes he will escape. He continues to focus on survival – and he survives! I was encouraged to adapt that same perspective, to not give up, and to work for the things I wanted. This view would ultimately combine with my growing faith and a sound belief my parents shared with me: "God does not close one door without opening another door more widely." These two beliefs have carried me through some incredibly difficult moments.

High school in Indiana held other important lessons for me. During my junior year, I decided to run for vice president of the student government. "Decided" is perhaps the wrong word. I do not think I even considered running for class president. A Colored person had never been president of the student body at my school. I still remember Miss Winters, the Dean of Girls at the high school, saying after the election, "You know you could have been president?" I promised myself I would never be vice president of anything I could lead as president. Even more, the next year I strongly supported a young man who would become the first Black person to serve as student government president in the history of my high school.

Since that moment, I have always gone for the highest position I thought I could achieve or obtain. My initial desire simply to avoid positions in which I lacked agency expanded to include the belief that I was worthy and prepared to perform at the highest levels. I had the skills, the abilities, and a vision for what was possible. As I advanced in my career, in each new position I established high standards, brought quality and credibility to the initiative, and, above all, aimed to help others achieve independence and agency. I sought to use my positions to make a difference.

My extracurricular activities became another area in which to grow and excel. In high school, I took a Home Economics class. It was a good thing, because as a teenager, I could not even fry an egg. My mother, I realize in retrospect, encouraged academic achievement, and was not overly concerned with my domestic skills. I remember practicing cracking and frying an egg over and over so I could ace that course. My parents probably thought I was crazy, but they did not complain. They just ate the eggs. By the end of my high school years, I went from an egg destroyer to the president of the high school chapter of the Future Homemakers of America. In this role, I had the privilege to speak before the annual dinner. My mother, along with other parents, would sit proudly in the audience. My drive to succeed in all areas enabled me to be well-rounded and opened new avenues for me.

My position with the Future Homemakers of America provided my first opportunity to travel to the more rural parts of Indiana (home of the KKK) as The Only. Over the years, I got increasingly comfortable with being The Only. It is important to note, however, that "increasingly comfortable" is different from being truly comfortable. But I learned how to do it, how to be an excellent, articulate example of my race. Hence, when I would later attend a small Wisconsin college, I was – as we say during interviews – "uniquely prepared to handle" being one of only three or four people of color.

During my high school years, I also was a member of the American Beauty Rosebuds, a youth organization of the Federation of Women's Clubs. These women were tremendous role models. I still remember their motto: "Step by Step We Reach the Heights, Lifting as We Climb." Participation in this group gave me additional exposure and opportunities to travel. I recall sleeping on the floor of the home of one of the members during a weekend trip with the club. This experience would set me apart from many of my peers who would go away to college never having traveled and never having stayed in a non-family member's home.

In another stroke of fate, I gained an unexpected leadership experience through the Girl Scouts for a period. My scout leader became ill and in our small community, there was no one to replace her. This was another seemingly small way in which God was positioning me as a future leader. I still remember walking to the White part of town to participate along with young White girls to earn a badge during a summer program. I was getting practice negotiating in the spaces where I would later have to lead and live.

My time at Girls State was similarly impactful. I traveled with a mixed group of Black and White students. On the trip down through southern Indiana, I had my first experience being seated in the back of a restaurant. I had not eaten in many restaurants, but I understood the significance of being escorted past other tables to the back for a seat. It was also at Girls State that I had an important introduction to class issues even within the Black community. My roommate at Girls State was another Negro girl. I still remember her name: Sharron.[1] Sharron and I were great friends throughout the program. Her parents picked us up from the location and offered me a ride home. During the trip, we passed through a neighborhood similar to the one in which I lived. I will never forget Sharron's words: "I would be so embarrassed if I lived in a neighborhood like this." I was terrified all the way home. Silence fell over the car as they entered my neighborhood. Three years later, Sharron and I were in the same cotillion. She was there because her father was a doctor and a member of the organization sponsoring the event. I was there because I was the highest-ranking Negro in my high school graduating class. My parents bought the right clothes from the most expensive store in town. My father even learned the waltz. (I still wonder who taught him). Yet I never felt like I belonged. Sharron's words were still in my ear. This experience would lay the foundation for my understanding of the intersections of race, class, and gender.

Graduating as the highest-ranking Negro in my class resulted in several life-altering experiences. The head of the Federation of Women's Clubs came to my church to present a scholarship to me. My uncle proudly shared that I was not the first in my family to graduate from college. I had not really thought about the implications of his educational background nor those of my parents. I remember my dad sharing a striking exchange with my assistant principal. At first, the principal told my father, "You have a daughter that any Negro could be proud of." Then the principal amended, "You have a daughter that any *person* could be proud of."

Young Adult Years and Early Work

I graduated in 1965, the first year of the National Achievement Scholarship for Outstanding Negro Students, and was a semifinalist. (In retrospect, this was quite an accomplishment since we were told you could not study for the test and the best and only preparation was a good night's sleep.) Why did the National Merit Scholarship Program begin the year I graduated from high school? I was in the right place at the right time with the right skills. What a difference that opportunity made. It gave me options. I did not realize it until that moment, but my parents did not have the funds to send me to college. We had never talked about it. I had just assumed I would go. Behind the scenes, God was orchestrating the way for me to go.

This honor opened many doors, doors of which I did not fully know how to take advantage. I received scholarship offers to schools I had never even heard of at the time, like the University of Chicago. My math teacher and my high school principal decided I should attend a small liberal arts college in Ashland, Wisconsin by the name of Northland College. I can still see myself standing there with them as they made that choice. Northland was eight hours north of Chicago; and, at the time, it felt like it was also eight hours north from any other Black people. As I look back, I wonder why my high school principal and my math teacher chose Northland over the University of Chicago. I had been offered full scholarships to both schools. I now believe my steps were ordered.

Northland taught me crucial life lessons. For one, I learned that I could compete and excel in any environment; I didn't have to be comfortable to do it. I attended Northland in the 1960s, so it was not unusual for talented Blacks to find themselves integrating into an institution. But life as a symbol 24/7, even in a friendly campus environment, took its toll. I needed to call on all my previous experiences with being "increasingly comfortable." Although the town was not outwardly hostile to Blacks, the area had little experience with Black people. Cars would slow down as we walked to various destinations. I still remember entering the local Baptist church and having the service literally stop in reaction to us. I remember eyes watching me as I showered to see what would happen to my hair. I remember thinking long and hard about the formation of a question before I asked it. I even had a White roommate, so there was nowhere I could go and just be me, be Black, and not have to think about grammar and representation. I felt the pressure to be articulate and represent every Negro in America. I find myself doing this unconsciously at times even now.

Those years of isolation, of again being one of only a few, of excelling despite the challenges and functioning in the spotlight, would prepare me to be "increasingly comfortable" leading predominantly White institutions and operating in a predominantly White world. Deciding to leave Northland and the positive results of that decision were also significant steps in my development as a leader. I had to go to Northland to decide to leave Northland. I had to learn to exercise the courage muscles I would need for the future.

I survived two years at Northland – and "survived" is the right word. I knew I needed another type of environment to thrive emotionally and intellectually. I felt an inner drive that gave me the desire for something better, fuller, and more supportive. I often ask myself where I found the courage to defy my parents and leave the security of a full scholarship. Shirley, the ever-obedient child, had to defy her parents to make this decision. This was no small step. I believe it was the same spirit that propelled me to develop a strategy to secure the Tom Thumb typewriter that helped me get on a bus and travel countless hours to secure a scholarship to the University of Illinois in 1967. I still remember the admissions counselor saying to me, "You know you will never do as well here as you did at Northland?" His comments did not faze me. (I would graduate Phi Beta Kappa – and a semester early.)

If Northland was a small world, the University of Illinois Urbana-Champaign was an enormous one. There were 34,000 students and two hundred Blacks. Two hundred may feel like a small number in the context of 34,000 students. But two hundred was enough to establish a real Black community with sororities and fraternities and homecomings. It was a much more supportive environment. My experiences at Northland helped me understand the importance of a critical mass of students for emotional health. We needed a place to feel comfortable and recharge before going back into a world filled with people who did not look like us. I already knew how to operate in a White world. But I now had places for restoration. I thrived at the University of Illinois. These lessons in the role of community in holistic health and success would remain with me.

While finishing my time at the University of Illinois, I was also beginning a career as a Project Manager for a National Head Start and Follow Through model. I had taken a graduate class taught by the creator of one of the models and he hired me. Why did I take the specific course that exposed me to the leaders of that national model? What did they see in me? Had I not had the courage and that Tom Thumb muscle, I would have never left Northland, and never have transferred to the University of Illinois. I would have never had the opportunity to begin my professional career as a Project Manager.

The transition period from my undergraduate years to balancing my work with Head Start and graduate school at the University of Illinois was another critical crossroads. At that time, B.F. Skinner was still teaching at the University. This was also the height of the 1960s revolution and the University admitted several African American graduate students to its Ph.D. program in Psychology. At that time, the University housed the number one program in the country. The African American graduate students in the program were the top performers of their institutions. This was not good enough for the faculty. One of the faculty members shared with me that there was no way there could be so many African Americans qualified to be in the program. I shared with him that I had graduated Phi Beta Kappa from the undergraduate program at the University of Illinois. He responded, "Then you belong here." I was the first to leave, in 1970 – by choice, not due to lack of talent. I was ready for a different life. I was born and positioned for work on the ground with people, not with mice in a lab. With any reasonable level of advising I would have been counseled into a Ph.D. program more consistent with my interests. But then, perhaps I would not have made the choices that led me to my future career.

In my role working with Head Start and Follow Through, I would find more meaning and make a bigger difference. I traveled around the country and managed seven projects ranging from the poorest county in South Carolina to the Gold Coast of Chicago. I believed in the Head Start model I represented. I saw the impact it made in the academic lives of young children. As a leader, I was called upon to make speeches and presentations. Those Sunday School, church, and extracurricular skills were definitely useful.

I discerned important principles through the contrasts in the projects on which I worked. I began to understand empowerment and the language of possibilities. Since the project was a national model, the curriculum was standardized. Yet while the curriculum was the same at all the sites, the process of teaching was different. In South Carolina, the teachers had specific agendas. At a predetermined time, reading was taught; at another predetermined time, math was taught, and so on. On the Gold Coast of Chicago, students made choices and teachers taught a variety of concepts with the same materials. I saw the process of empowerment in action. In South Carolina, students were taught to be followers (building unknowingly upon the legacy of slavery). On the Gold Coast, students were taught to be leaders; they were taught they had choices. I never forgot this principle: Process is at least as important as content. Even further, from a development perspective, process can be *more* important than content. Rote learning creates rote thinkers. Later, in my time as a consultant and project manager, I began to question even the content of the curriculum. Why not create material specific to the African American context? Why not teach the students about their history as the children learn to read?

Career Beginnings

With my personal life, vision, and vocation clearer, I moved to New York in 1973 to pursue a career in education. I had no idea at the time what challenges and victories awaited me. I took a job as Educational Director at a Head Start Program in Harlem. The Center had locations in two parts of Harlem. One Center served a largely Black population and the other served a largely Latino population. I saw myself working with my people and making a difference. There were still some difficulties, however. Many of the employees saw me as an upper-middle-class woman who happened to be Black coming into their area to work. I was not immediately accepted. It was a growth experience for me, and it forced me to further develop my spiritual faith and courage.

My first major position in New York State was as a Child Development Specialist for the County of Westchester. I served on the County Executive's staff and coordinated his response to childcare. In this position, I could create and fund ideas such as training for family daycare.

Notably, this was my official introduction to politics. The skills I learned there would serve me well in my future presidential roles. I saw the importance of setting a stage for the success of a political leader; creating an amazing event where the politician would be honored and recognized for all your hard work. This was difficult, but I also discerned that you could secure power by making someone else look good. People – and perhaps especially politicians – do not forget who made them look good or who made them look bad.

I next secured a leadership position as Director of the Employment and Training Programs for the County of Westchester; and, ultimately, in 1980, a commissioner-level appointment over the Office of Employment and Training with 125 employees and a major budget. This was politics on a big stage. I jokingly shared with my friends that it was my job to keep me and my boss out of jail. The challenge was finding a way to bring quality to projects and funds that were often assigned to individuals or entities for political reasons. We instituted group screening programs for participants and implemented evaluation criteria for projects. It worked. In a short period (one year) we moved from a significant number of findings to receiving the highest performance rating given by the Department of Labor. I saw my role as bringing quality to job training programs that, by definition, had political implications. I improved the program from one with performance issues to a program with model status. My work ethic – built over decades – paid off in this position. I remember carrying home boxes of work late at night. Perhaps the dream of being a college president was beginning to form within me.

During my tenure, a new governor was elected, and our County Executive became Lt. governor overnight. The County Executive was replaced by a leader from the opposing party and – also overnight – I lost my position. I had amassed too much political power for them to fire me, so in 1984 they sent me to the Community College where they thought I would simply fade quietly away. I would not fade away. But, in the initial aftermath, when I lost my status in Westchester County, it felt as if my world had come to an end. It was one of the most painful experiences of my life. But this hardship laid the foundation for a motto I would later adopt: "If you wound me, you better kill me."

I remember singing gospel songs over and over again. I would repeat the inspirational lyrics and hope and pray they were true. I not only survived at Westchester Community College, I thrived. It was yet another example of how God can prosper you in unlikely situations. I ascended from the title of Director of Corporate Education to associate dean to dean (while on maternity leave!). Ultimately, I became Vice President of Adult and Continuing Education after securing my doctorate and working full-time. If I had not lost my former position, I would have never had the opportunity to work at Westchester Community College. I probably never would have gone back to get my doctorate. I would likely have never had the privilege of being a college president. The closing of the Westchester County government door allowed another door to open wider. God truly had not brought me this far to leave me. I would reflect on this moment many times. No situation was quite so scary after that experience.

When the path opened to a doctoral program in 1988, I had three children, one of them an infant. I often joke that when I decided to pursue the degree, I must have temporarily lost my mind; and by the time I recovered, it would have been crazier not to complete the program. It was in graduate school at Columbia that I reconnected with the theme of empowerment. I studied the life-transforming work of Palo Freire and came to understand the theoretical underpinnings of oppression and taking on the beliefs and behaviors of the oppressor. From Freire, I came to appreciate the importance of liberated teachers in the lives of students. One of my core "Freirean" beliefs is that a teacher who is not liberated, not free (mentally), cannot liberate or empower others. His work made the legacy of slavery so much clearer as well as helped give clarity to my own experiences.

Earning my doctorate was pivotal in several ways. The educational experiences would ground my future ideologies. It also opened paths to broader opportunities. Further, it introduced me to a new colleague and friend, Dr. Joan Wilson, who provided me with the opportunity to visit Africa in 1991. I traveled there as part of an effort to introduce the community college system to a multi-racial group of leaders. Going to Africa for the first time felt like going home after being away for college. It also allowed me to put another face to the philosophies and dynamics I had been studying. I remember marveling at how so few people could keep so many Black South Africans enslaved. It was in South Africa that the language of possibilities was on display, live and in living color. My decisions as a junior in high school fit perfectly into that paradigm, for instance. I did not think more was possible and therefore limited myself by running for vice president.

There was one saying I repeatedly encountered during my travels in South Africa that further epitomized the language of possibilities: "I cried because I had no shoes until I met a man who had no feet." I wanted to scream out that a person should have shoes and should also cry for the man who has no feet. People have a right to be sad when they have no shoes. I remember feeling overwhelmed with anger in response to the sense of hopelessness there. I still recall one of the children sitting at the back of a room of about a hundred students saying, "When are you coming back for us?" Can you imagine being taught in a classroom with so many children that if you were not tall enough you could not even see your teacher?

The vastness of the poverty was stunning. I remember saying in my remarks to the group supporting my trip, "as far as the eyes of God could see, poverty covered everything." I shuddered at classrooms with nothing on the walls. When I asked why this was, I was told that the teachers had given up, because everything they put up one day was gone by the next morning. I thought about the powerlessness of the teachers and reflected on how even more powerless the children must have felt. If the teachers could not do anything about the situation, what could the children envision they could do? Thus, the language of powerlessness instead of the language of possibilities was passed down. Another important belief became a central part of my operating premises: Teachers who are not empowered cannot empower students.

In a moment I will never forget, I saw the language of possibilities in play in a wonderful way in South Africa. My colleague and traveling companion, Dr. Joan Wilson, was also a trained opera singer. One day, she shared her beautiful voice with the children and sang to us. At the end of the song, there is an incredible high note. As we were going back to our car, we heard one of the South African young women, seemingly out of the blue, hit that same note. Something new was now possible. Their world had been forever changed. The experience is still part of me.

Back in White Plains, there were also issues of power and privilege to address. During the time my son was in high school, I was persuaded to serve on the board of education in our school district. This was an amazing opportunity to make a difference and give back. It was also amazingly time-consuming and challenging. In this role, I saw first-hand inequity and fought hard to make sure that all the schools in the city were resourced fairly. I did this work not just for my children but for all the children, especially the children whose parents felt powerless. It was not easy. It also brought back memories of other outsider experiences. We lived in the nicest area of White Plains. Our neighborhood school was barely integrated, especially in the classrooms where children appeared to be tracked from the very beginning. I remember feeling uncomfortable entering the school, even with my position and status at that point. I sat with that feeling and vowed to somehow find ways for parents with less influence than me to feel welcomed when entering their children's schools.

College Presidency and Beyond

The decision to apply for a college presidency at Thomas Nelson Community College was another turning point. The school, named after a not-well-known signer of the Declaration of Independence, was a major player in the Hampton Roads portion of southern Virginia. I had to flex every Tom Thumb, Indiana Jones, and faith muscle I possessed to make that choice. On a personal level, I was in my second act of parenting and was suddenly a single mother. I had two young girls, one just exiting the special education track in White Plains, and the oldest a thirteen-year-old who, in the despair of leaving, cried, "Your frivolous decision has ruined our lives." At the time, part of me worried she could be right.

On a professional level, I had much fear to overcome when I became president in 1995. There was no special training academy to which I could be sent. It was truly on-the-job training. I received two important pieces of advice in advance from friends: (1) "This is not a job for people who need to be liked"; and (2) "Fake it until you make it." In a moment I could only laugh about years later, I remember attending the goodbye event for the interim president at Thomas Nelson Community College. It was the night before my presidency officially began and I do not think I had ever seen a person happier than he had been at the party. I remember thinking, "What does he know that I don't know?" I had trouble sleeping that night!

In retrospect, I realize that my steps had been ordered and, without my realizing it, I was prepared "for such a time as this" (Esther 4:14). I was blessed to serve my first presidency in a military town. The military teaches its members to respect position. This made it easier for me in some ways. When I entered the room, my cabinet members did not sit until I sat. When your position is given that level of respect, you almost absorb some of the power.

Yet it did still require some "faking it until you make it," even after I had technically already made it. I remember the honor of being invited by Judith Sturnick and Donna Shavlik to make presentations at their ACE programs for aspiring leaders, for example. I would make my presentation and stay and listen to all the other presidents share their knowledge. I recall sitting in the audience as a new president and watching Dr. Yolanda Moses in action and feeling a sense of awe in her ability to make such an amazing speech. I wondered what they had seen in me to invite me there.

A year later, I was on the Commission for Women at the American Council on Education (another door opened through Judith). Two years later, I was chair of the Commission for Women at ACE. I still remember sitting at the head of that big table at ACE for the first time. The little girl from the small steel mill town in Indiana came with me. She was nervous and not quite convinced that she belonged at the head of the table. It took more than a minute to get comfortable. The experiences of that girl, however, had prepared me for this moment.

Similarly, being raised under Baptist ministers had given me experience living in a proverbial glass house. Growing up, everyone knew K.T. Robinson's daughters. There were always visitors in the house and privacy seemed nonexistent. So, I was somewhat ready for the moment when my hair was being colored at a local salon, and a woman called out, "There is the new president of Thomas Nelson!" It was no longer just my hairdresser who knew what my real hair color was.

People would stop me on the street and introduce me to their children. It was a big deal what church I attended and what local organizations with which I was affiliated. My life was clearly no longer my own. As was also the case at Northland College, I felt as if I represented my entire race. Even some of the challenges of childrearing took on a larger weight as I chased after that mythical work-life balance. While I was fortunate enough to be in a position where I could continue to make participating in my children's lives a priority (working odd and long hours to be able to attend extracurricular events), it was not easy. And, of course, there was the drama of raising adolescent daughters, monitoring their social lives and attitude adjustments. I remember attending more disciplinary school meetings than I would like to admit. Or who could forget when my youngest daughter decided to almost get herself kicked out of an after-school program? The children of the first Black president of a college live in a fishbowl and it is not always fun. Some adults held what they saw as the child of a leader's privilege against the children, and I had to intercede and call people and organizations out at times.

Fortunately, there were major support systems to aid me. The church – that constant safehouse – its activities, and its leaders provided crucial aid. I owe a debt forever to Macedonia Baptist church for my children's and, indeed, my own spiritual development. I will also never forget those wonderful sports parents who helped me through various challenges. Parents, especially single parents, live with stress around the hard choices they must make and sometimes have guilt after they make those choices. With the benefit of 20/20 hindsight, my children felt loved, and the models I provided were lasting. The child whose life I ruined with my frivolous decision, for instance, became homecoming queen and class president. This would have been a major accomplishment anywhere. In the South, it was almost miraculous. Today she is a successful partner at a prestigious law firm.

Professionally, it was not long after my tenure began at TNCC that I encountered my first major political challenge. Hampton is in southern Virginia. And southern Virginia is, indeed, in the South. When I arrived, there was a flag that was essentially equivalent to the Confederate flag flying proudly over the campus. The local NAACP chapter soon visited me and asked me to take down the flag. This was an issue that required my past experiences negotiating political and intercultural dynamics. Did I like coming to work at an institution over which the Confederate flag was flying? No! I saw it every morning as I walked from the parking lot to my car. Theoretically, as president, I had the power to just take that awful flag down. Yet my prior political training had taught me to use my power shrewdly. I asked for and received grace and patience while I systematically brought all the major constituencies on board with changing our logo. All the flags came down in the dead of night and were replaced by the flags of our international sister cities. No one seemed to notice. I did. Crisis averted and moral victory systematically achieved.

Many other challenges would follow. Yet, all along the way, God strengthened and sustained me. During my tenure, I led a successful major gifts campaign (the first supporter was a female corporate leader who had become a friend). I started a literary circle, proudly put the "prayer" back in a prayer breakfast at a local church, and oversaw the naming of the Mary Christian Performing Arts Center.

I secured $7.9 million in funding from the Virginia legislature and all six localities in the College's service area to build the Peninsula Workforce Development Center. The Center and its programs were recognized by the U.S. Department of Labor as a national model for workforce development. A major highlight of my time at Thomas Nelson Community College was the opportunity to participate in the Department of Defense-sponsored Joint Civilian Orientation Conference. This intensive orientation program provided a unique opportunity for me as a civilian to understand and experience elements of the five branches of the United States military services.

I saw God use me in powerful ways and answer so many prayers. While I had been a Christian almost my entire life, it was in Hampton that my relationship with God ascended to a new level. As I often tell others, before I went to Hampton, I thought I knew God, but after Hampton, I *knew* that I knew him. I knew Him in a greater way.

After serving joyfully and faithfully at Thomas Nelson, I took a position as president at Suffolk County Community College on Long Island, New York in 2002. As often happens in life, I had so much more perspective the second time around. I was able to truly perceive the significance, and I cherished my inauguration ceremony at Suffolk. Indeed, one of the major highlights of my life centered around the presence of two of my favorite cousins, Edna and Irene, at the ceremony. I can still see the pride on their faces and the tears in their eyes as they watched White women robe me – that Colored girl from East Chicago. My cousins had faced such discrimination. They had shared with me the pain they felt when other children laughed at them because of their clothing. Having my cousins with me on that special day healed the pain I carried and felt for them. (Until the pain was gone, I had not consciously realized it was there). We shared a collective pride. Not only my family was proud, but it felt like the entire African American community was proud. Even the chancellor was impressed. As he put the medallion around my neck, he whispered, "Don't mess this up."

By God's grace, I did not.

Suffolk presented new obstacles. My home was literally on the last exit of the Long Island Expressway, and it could get so dark driving home at night that I sometimes jokingly wondered if I had missed an area evacuation. Hardships could make the long ride seem even longer, the dark nights even darker. It could have been easy to feel incredibly isolated without the support of another wonderful church community, Faith Baptist Church. Can you sense a theme?

One of the greatest trials was being covered by an overcritical and overzealous local reporter. I would ultimately shut down any slander, but it did not make the process any less difficult. I remember I would start listening to TV sermons from the moment I woke up to the moment I left the door, and on the way to work. My faith and past experiences sustained me.

Once again, I thrived. It was during my tenure that Suffolk became the largest community college in the SUNY system. I facilitated the renovation and opening of a new culinary arts center and instilled greater campus unity by holding a joint graduation ceremony. I was also blessed to receive a five-million-dollar anonymous gift to the college.

My accomplishments would have been unfathomable to that little girl from East Chicago. And yet, God was not done positioning me for a greater purpose. After my tenure at Suffolk ended in 2011, some of my happiest and most challenging years were spent at ACE. I loved being Sr. Vice President of Programs and Services. As my youngest daughter would remind me in my most challenging moments, no one can take that tremendous honor away from me. I had been affiliated with ACE for years and I loved the work of the organization. That version of myself who had sat nervously at ACE conferences years ago, probably could not have conceived that she ever would have the honor of serving in such a role. It was wonderful having the platform to represent and share a national perspective on issues.

Even more, it was through my work with ACE that I made my return trip to South Africa. This second trip was after the liberation of Nelson Mandela. I traveled in the more rural areas and worked with comrades to effect change. Power had shifted, but the lived experiences of so many were still painful. On my original trip, I remember reflecting on the possibilities for disappointment because the task was so large. Once again, I observed that "as far as the eyes of God could see, there was poverty." As I had anticipated during my initial visit, it would take significant time to tackle a problem so large and so internalized. The lack of change for the masses led to a question that was echoed by those who could not feel the difference in their lived experiences: "It could not have been for this just so a few could have more." During my second visit, however, the young people were already fighting for greater change, calling for another revolution. A new era of greater empowerment awaited.

After fulfilling my dream of working at ACE, I took a position as president of Victory University in Memphis, Tennessee. I accepted the position despite its for-profit status. In my eyes, I viewed it more as a small Christian liberal arts institution that also happened to be for-profit. I wish there had been some mythical bootcamp I could have gone to in preparation for my tenure. Yet, once again, there are some things for which there can be no full preparation. You must simply go through them. I had so many wonderful experiences and relationships at Victory. I also had many frightening moments and many sleepless nights. Ultimately, the greatest and hardest lesson I learned there was how to lead an organization through its darkest moments.

Overall, I enjoyed presiding over a Christian institution. I often began my remarks at conferences and public events by proudly informing the audience that I was the daughter of as well as a niece of Baptist ministers. It gave me a certain license (Baptist ministers are known for taking a text and then talking about anything they choose). It also provided a context for my thinking and the organization of my remarks. It was wonderful to pray with students and teachers in the halls, to see believers at their high and low points, and yet still dedicated and serious about their spiritual lives. At Victory, I witnessed the power of content and belief in action. Regardless of the topic, Christian principles were taught through every aspect of the content. Classes began with prayers for those who arrived for an evening class, tired and worn from a long day's work. There was even a master's degree offered in Christian Counseling. Victory's educational model was the Gold Coast preschool theory put into practice at the higher education level.

It was also an honor to decide to give scholarships to Hispanic students who were top of their class and could not afford to attend school in other institutions because of state laws regarding their status. However, financial aid came with many challenges as well. Perhaps some of the most frightening moments of my life were spent worrying about getting funds to students and fully coming to understand how students accrue mounds of debt – not just for their education, but to pay bills with their financial aid awards. I still remember a man explaining to me why he desperately needed his financial aid check, saying "How can I be head of my household if I don't have these funds to pay my bills?" I remember student athletes who waited urgently for their financial aid checks because their mothers needed money to pay rent. It bought shoes and clothing for the kids for school. One major problem was, of course, that if you did not complete your education, you could not pay off your financial aid obligations.

In the end, it was an incredibly painful experience having to shut down the institution. The financial investors lost confidence in the business proposition. Providing quality education in an environment where a significant number of students are economically and financially challenged is expensive and doesn't yield financial dividends in the short run. In 2014, the institution closed its doors. For many students, especially the very talented immigrant students to whom we gave full scholarships, this was a dream denied.

Every moment during those last weeks at Victory was stressful and fear-inducing. The responsibility I felt for the students, faculty, and the community was enormous. And, although investors played a large role in the ultimate decision to close the institution, the closure was a very public failure. My prior experience in Westchester at the end of my time as lead of the Office of Employment and Training, and my belief that there would be a path forward eased the pain and kept me hopeful. I had learned early that there is life after failure. That was a powerful lesson, yet no easier to experience. Even this hardship had a purpose in my spiritual life, however. My faith had to grow to sustain me. As one pastor described, there are three levels of faith: I think, I believe, and I know. By, the end of my time in Memphis, I truly knew the power of God.

Current Work and Reflections

Amazingly, even after my time at Victory, God has continued to open doors for me and to position me for a purpose. I have been incredibly blessed to work as a senior consultant and coach for Academic Search. It has been so fulfilling to assist institutions in finding strong leaders as well as to help those leaders develop their skills so that they can make a difference in the lives of others. What joy I have felt at those moments when a historic first was hired by an institution. I knew what a difference that leader would make firsthand – not just in that institution, but perhaps more importantly, in that community. That leader's very presence would confirm the language of possibilities.

This opportunity has also granted me a fascinating new perspective on campus leadership. Through coaching, I can experience the dynamics of being on campus with the benefit of 20/20 hindsight and without the 24/7 stress. (In some ways, it is analogous to the difference between being a parent and a grandparent). I begin to see the institution as my institution. I feel the challenges the president faces and find great joy when each obstacle is conquered. It feels good. I am making a difference. I am using old skills and developing new skills along the way.

As I struggled with a conclusion, I realized a conclusion would be inappropriate. The same hands that have always positioned me for purpose have plans that I can probably only imagine. Did I imagine that I would be president of three colleges? Or a Senior Vice President at ACE? Did I ever imagine all the ordered steps along the way? The best and most appropriate end to this chapter, then, would be "To Be Continued."

Discussion Questions

1. Reflect on the following:
   What were the key decision points in Shirley Pippins' life?
   What factors or life experiences informed those decisions?
   How did these key decisions and life experiences inform her leadership journey?
   What have been the key decision points in your life and leadership journey?
   What key decisions and life experiences informed your journey?
2. Dr. Pippins overcame a number of potentially significant obstacles. How does overcoming obstacles strengthen a leader?
3. Do you believe in divinely ordered steps? What forces do you believe have impacted the steps in your leadership journey?
4. How did each choice impact the range of the next set of choices on Dr. Pippins' journey? Reflect on your leadership journey. Do you see similar patterns?
5. How did Dr. Pippins' belief in a divine presence evolve over time and impact her future decision-making? How has your personal belief system informed your decision-making?

Note

1. Her name has been changed for anonymity.

10

THE LEADERSHIP JOURNEY OF THE BLACK, LATINA, AND NATIVE AMERICAN COLLEGE PRESIDENT

From Poverty to the Presidency

Elñora Tena Webb

Abstract

Over thirty-eight years in the UC and CSU systems, a private university, and the California Community College system, Elñora Tena Webb focused on her "grand vision – students' access to quality higher education and student excellence." Her undergraduate education led her to connect her previously necessary survivalist mode to the larger context of diverse knowledge and people with similar goals while she earned her Ph.D. and continued to develop her servant leadership as Dean of Humanities, Language Arts, and Social Sciences; Vice President of Instruction/Academic Affairs; College President; and Executive Vice Chancellor for Strategic Planning, Partnership, and Advancement. Moving through foster care, she learned the important lesson that she was not her circumstances, that she could "safeguard [her] spirit from harm" and ultimately "design her life."

Her story gives us a complete picture of the teamwork and partnerships that can result in student growth and excellence. Careful planning and inclusive and strategic leadership can result in not only positive student outcomes but also the inspiration for greater achievement. Her story also demonstrates that servant leadership is not easy, and at times is challenged by the very successes it engenders. Her chapter is a cathartic guide for engaging the struggles in one's early life as well as those in seeking excellence for all in higher education.

For over fifty years, I've heard individuals describe the magnificence of their honeymoon plans. Each time, their stories caused me to smile big and feel excited for the married couple. Frequently, I'd learn some of the details of their honeymoons and, usually, those sets of details entailed much more than the couples could have imagined. Most dreamed big and set their sights on particular experiences and outcomes as the basis of building their relationships. Yet, they would later characterize their experiences as rollercoaster rides. In all instances, they learned much about their partners, the nature of marriage, and themselves. Many have remained married, several for at least 50 years. They attribute the longevity of their relationships to intentional learning, communicating openly and honestly, honoring the partner AND self, and taking full responsibility for their choices. Foremost, they learned to more fully experience the present and plan for wonderful journeys while releasing any demand for perfection. Their growth mindset enabled them to be open to possibilities, welcome uncertainties, and embrace one another.

Akin to an extended honeymoon of rollercoaster rides, my 38-year professional career in higher education had many twists and turns yet my dreams were more than fulfilled. I asked and I received. I made decisions, believed, executed plans, and manifested my vision. Fortunes abound throughout my journey. I provided direct service to nine distinct colleges and universities, and five different systems of higher education, including all four in California – the University of California system, the California State University system, a private university, and the California Community College system – while influencing many others.

Part 1: The Big Dream

Higher education equipped me with tools that enabled me to see my worth and great capacity, breaking me out of survival mode. It instilled grit and profound courage, as well, it cemented my vision *to inspire and help an ever-expanding base of people, families, communities, and the society at large* and to do so as an educational ambassador. While I did not initially imagine working or leading in higher education – i.e., being a college president, an executive vice chancellor, and a member of state, regional, and national boards influencing policies that affected millions of lives – my dream was big enough to welcome these accomplishments and much more.

My Vision was and remains to transform lives through minds and hearts. Learning that anyone can design her|his|their life was a crucial insight for me. I needed others to understand that they, too, could choose to thrive; the growth I experienced due to higher education energized me to facilitate experiences that would inspire within others the desire to leverage higher education to grow and prosper, ensuring their overall well-being while each contributed to cultivating within us all more humane conditions and rewards.

Altruistic by nature, my career is a testament to my *selfish* concern for the well-being of students, colleagues, teams of partners, including direct reports, and the many great communities for (and in) which I was fortunate to work. My passion for serving others could sting anyone within my reach. Initially, while at the University of California Riverside and Sonoma State University, I was determined to expose as many K-12 youth in California (and beyond) to essential as well as practical aspects of higher education. I felt consistent urges to develop new pitches and enhance collateral marketing materials to educate and otherwise compel high school youth and community college students to secure bachelor's, master's, and terminal degrees. They needed to know what I had learned – that they could do much more than survive, they could leverage colleges and universities to learn how to design their lives as they saw fit. According to high school counselors, principals, students' parents, and many of the students, my enthusiasm inspired growing numbers of individuals to pursue studies in higher education.

My devotion to students – their engagement, learning, and growth – had no time limits; I was accessible to students 24/7/365. I recall an after-midnight call during the early 1980s from several of my newly admitted students whom I had recruited from high schools in East Los Angeles. They called me because their vehicle had broken down on the interstate 5 Hwy en route to Sonoma State University. Without hesitation, I quickly dressed to drive the 3.5–4 hours to pick up these young people. It turned out, not one of them had a place to shelter. Because I had ample space, they stayed with me and at the residence of another university colleague. These students, and, over time, thousands of others, knew they could count on a team of us to expedite their readiness to engage and succeed. We advised, mentored, and coached to facilitate students' engagement, learning, achievements, graduation, and contributions to society in diverse ways.

As an undergrad at the University of California Riverside (UCR), I discovered that I truly had wings. The steps to my discovery and continuous transformations are numerous. Here are a few tip-of-the-iceberg influential factors:

- As a sophomore enrolled in a class filled with upperclassmen, I was charged to present on behalf of teammates in a Psychology course. This would be my first time doing so, and not only was I in shock by the requirement, I was terrified. You see, their grade would be based on my performance, and I believed I was a complete imposter in this class,

wondering how I got in and was able to remain. Well, the time came – *standing in front of the class of a lot of folks as the youngest in the class* (18 or 19 years old while the average age seemed over 35 and with some in their 60s). I was standing in a state of shock, and I could hear others' breathing due to the silence awaiting my presentation. After what felt like an eternity, likely about 90 seconds later, the professor directed me to sit down because I "clearly did not know the content." Out of anger and distress, I opened my mouth, and words flowed with pertinent content conveyed for all to hear. It was followed by applause. Our team aced the assignment. To this day, I can not say with clarity how I did it!
- Another professor summoned me into her office. Surprised because I was certain that by sitting in the back of a 200-person room, she would not see me. Fearful that my "imposter" status was confirmed for sure, I made it to her office early and kept my head down. Taking notes and collecting as many of her words as possible, my thinking seemed on hold. It wasn't until I left her office and later reviewed my notes did I understood why she targeted me. Using herself as a model, she described how she planned for and then wrote articles, books, and other documents. She emphasized writing as a process with peer reviews, strategic edits, and subsequent reviews before submitting a final draft. Yet all I could hear was that I was an incompetent writer and would likely fail her class. But, this was not her intent. She sought to guide me, instructing me on how to write effectively. I began that journey thanks to her!
- By my senior year, I had taken a diverse set of courses in the humanities, social sciences, mathematics, biological and natural sciences, fine and performing arts, etc. while observing and working in several business environments on campus (outreach and tutoring centers, natural sciences departments) and in the local community (county health department and corporate environments). My mind had collected so much information, new and life-changing connections were being made in my brain, with professionals, with peers, and with institutions. The interconnections among people and with systems were strong and replaced many old views. No longer was I an isolate, functioning just to protect myself or to survive. Now, my context had expanded, I *felt* like a member of a worldwide community, connected to all that was and could be.

The Decision to Inspire Others to Leverage Higher Education

By year five at UC Riverside (or after approximately 40,000 hours of education), I'd found *my place* in higher education – it felt like home where my mission of service grew as well as my commitment to continuous learning.

I'd welcomed into my consciousness new ideas, read and wrote about concepts and findings from studies, and observed and listened to folks from countries throughout the world. Frequently, I sat side-by-side with individuals, in the community, with folks I was supposed to be afraid of. Initially, it felt just right – even given the awkward moments – many resulting from ignorance about the cultures and intents of others. Yet the context of higher education was ripe for leaning in and learning from such experiences, and I welcomed many more of those experiences. Ultimately, I understood a powerful and critical aspect of higher education – *to facilitate understanding of others and self – to navigate life effectively!* Yes, earning degrees that signal one's readiness for professions is essential. Indeed, research is invaluable for progress in particular fields of study and commercial industries, and, more broadly, to elevate humanity. Yet when I began to triangulate the interconnections among the disciplines that I'd studied, constantly seeing how one can not fully understand one field of study without sufficient knowledge of many other fields of study i.e., sociology, psychology, biology, ecology, history, philosophy, ethnic studies, the arts – all related. More to the point, I developed language and learned analytical tools to access more of me, including the ability to better assess my nature to inform my development. All feedback received – whether from a professor, a peer, or an administrator supervising my work – helped me to place myself into a considerably larger context.

Higher education had awakened me to how I would be in service to others, which initially entailed being a university tutor, staff support to departments and special programs, then outreach officer and quickly assuming more responsible roles within student affairs coordinating support services i.e., financial aid reviews, student advising, intercultural center with seminars, an art gallery, a professional mentor program, faculty affairs, part-time teaching, and much more. I began in student affairs at Riverside City College in 1978 and the University of California Riverside and, by 1981, advanced to Sonoma State University during 1982–1988, ensuring thousands of students attended the institution because of the promise to enhance their lot in life. Determined to be impactful, my priority for learning led me to earn a Master's degree in Educational Administration with an emphasis on educational technology from San Francisco State University in 1988. This experience prompted me to expand my professional responsibilities. From 1989–1992, I assumed more administrative and managerial responsibilities in human resources while also receiving leadership training, which prepared me for even greater responsibilities.

By the time I'd arrived at Stanford University, several people had suggested that I needed to find a "real job." In fact, during the early 1990s, while in doctoral studies and engaged in research at UC Berkeley, one of my brothers asked, "When will you *leave* the embryo?" My humble reaction also reflected my confusion, thus my response, "what do you mean – embryo, uterus, unborn child?" As it turns out, he was asking me when I would grow up and find a real job. From his perspective as a technician|engineer in a well-known for-profit corporation, and the viewpoint of many others who knew me, I was stuck in an education funnel. What they did not know was that I'd found my voice via my early higher education experiences and, as a result, I decided to become an educational ambassador ensuring that countless others with limited exposure to quality education would discover that they, too, could understand their capabilities, dream big, and use their voices, intellectual capabilities, and other core competencies to lead as they chose to design the lives of their dreams.

Opting to guard against more questioning, I sheltered myself, honing in on my grand vision – students' access to quality higher education and student excellence. I did not feel the need to answer his or any other person's questions that could undermine the pursuit of my dream; instead, while on my journey, I remained steadfast, engaging in research, earning my Ph.D., and advancing within higher education as a Dean of Humanities, Language Arts, and Social Sciences, Vice President of Instruction/Academic Affairs, College President, then Executive Vice Chancellor for Strategic Planning, Partnership, and Advancement, and doing so much more.

The Achievements of Former Students

I cherish all of the successes of former students as well as clients and mentees among colleagues. It has been a wonderful experience to learn about the accomplishments of former students. Many are now parents while serving in key roles across our greater society, and those roles include chief executive officers, chief operating officers, university presidents, vice presidents, college deans, corporate leaders, physicians, nurses, agents, accountants, engineers, community leaders, artists, educators, counselors, police officers, judges, analysts, musicians, elected officials. So many are paying forward the support they received resulting in many more beneficiaries from our deeds.

Many former students sought me out long after they graduated, entered professions, created families, established other commitments, and otherwise added to the foundation of their lives. LinkedIn and Facebook are among the social media methods they use to share their appreciation for what they've received from me. Some called, emailed, or wrote letters while some showed up, and visited me in different locations, including Stanford, Cal Berkeley, Laney, and executive offices to say "thank you," and to learn how to advance careers, policy-making, or entrepreneurship. One former student shared his respect for the way I honored him when he sought a mentor to help him with his career pursuit and guidance on how to understand himself via ancestral cultural roots because he deemed these matters essential to his success, especially since his parents discounted such information and discouraged him from learning about his diverse European ancestry and just accept being financially wealthy. Another former student who was highlighted as having become a remarkable law enforcement officer, later wrote to me from prison seeking guidance before his release. As with all others, I took care in responding to his request and, according to him, he was pleasantly surprised for he assumed I'd either never receive his letter or ignore it because of his shame. A Latino couple remembered mentorship that inspired them to persist in leading in their respective industries when they previously had no examples to follow. A multi-ethnic woman who proudly identified as Black expressed gratitude for the listening ear that she attributes to her being an effective legal representative within the judicial system. Several men from historically distressed as well as economically advantaged communities assumed vice presidential roles because of what they witnessed as modeled by me when they were undergraduate and graduate students.

My Trajectory from Childhood to Adulthood

During my childhood, as early as I can recall, consciously, I imagined being housed in healthy conditions, living my life with ease, being a positive example to others, and facilitating greatness within others. I imprinted these images at the subconscious level and often awoke to remember dreams where I flew at will wherever I sought to go. Unconsciously, I was preparing for the life I would lead.

Our Power to Choose to Promote Success

By the age of 12, long before I understood what a chief executive officer was, my mental and physical activities centered me on being the CEO of my life – making strategic decisions and choosing to follow my vision.

Who Am I and Why?

I'm very fortunate to be alive due to the grace of a thirteen-year-old who had been abused for most of her life. Because of her gift to me – giving me birth, I've always felt the responsibility to be authentic with a deep responsibility to life itself. As an example, unconscious of my actions, as a very introverted 10 or 11-year-old, I stood up in a church – that the then foster parents, Mrs. Odessa and Mr. Oliver Carr, sent my brothers and me to – and proclaimed that I would tell the world that "God is, Jesus is," and that I would pay forward the life I was granted by serving all life honorably. Wow! Immediately, I sat down and wondered what had occurred, feeling my mind racing to understand, to be, and to do more than simply survive – as if I felt that I was on a fast track to something remarkable.

Foster Care – From a Focus on Survival to Designing My Life

As young as seven, I knew that I was not my circumstances and that I would survive the challenging circumstances I faced daily. Seemingly, my wiring was to quietly question everything and to ponder "why?" My thirst for information captivated much of my attention. These perennial states were characterized by me asking myself, why was I with strangers? I wanted to know why my birth mother left me with strangers at three years old. Why were foster care parents abusive or otherwise negating or simply uninterested in my fate? Why were some of my siblings and I deemed throw-away children? Why was I responsible for my safety at 7, 10, or even 13 years of age? Fortunately for me, my intuition was accurate, and unbeknownst to me, I was astute. Just as I knew my power to safeguard my spirit from harm, I also knew that I was not my circumstances; thus, I deduced that the physical and psychological abuse would only be temporary, whereas how I chose to deal with my circumstances would be permanent. **So I decided to deal … and to dream big!**

Without a clear understanding, I wanted more than being diagnosed as mentally retarded as a child, dismissed from being adopted, or deemed unworthy of being hugged or unconditionally cared for. I wanted freedom, thus, I leaned in and experienced most of my life as a *race* to the finish line – a line that continued to be moved with each major achievement – survival, designing my life, living my passion, expanding my reach, and, now, more fully actualizing my grand purpose; this is freedom and it feels powerful.

Survival

Why I went to College? Driven by a desire to avoid homelessness again, I sought out college and then attended the University of California at Riverside. Throughout my childhood, I'd experienced uncertainty, traumas, and concern about how best to protect myself in the future too, especially as a 16-year-old who would soon be aging out of the foster care system. When I overheard a fellow high school student discuss college and housing at colleges, I decided to pursue a bachelor's degree as it would assure me housing – or so I had deduced.

Inspired to Design My Life

The outcome of attending the University of California at Riverside was life-transforming. Akin to my high school years, I acted and engaged in ways to render myself invisible – I sat in the back of classes – that is unless I couldn't read what was written on the board (or any other pertinent visual in the front of the class), then I sat in the front of the class; I hid in plain sight behind books, student activities, and embedded myself in public activities so that one could say they knew me – and never would they seek to "know me" really, especially in terms of my birth origins, current living situations/conditions i.e., being a ward of the State of California in foster care, moving from one household to another (at least six) and, foremost, opting to go to college only because someone said there was housing for students.

Living My Passion

A burning desire to impact lives positively was all-encompassing. Thus, I was always expanding my reach to actualize my purpose. I dared to make a difference in ways that would enable the person on the receiving end to be illuminated. My moves were always leveraging the aid of countless others – many of whom were unaware of my actions. Through what proved to be an awesome journey, I learned that life itself is the goal – to live with passion – and less about a contrived human-constructed model of completion or achievement.

My Higher Education Journey

University of California, Riverside

Entering the higher education system through the University of California's educational opportunity program (EOP) summer bridge session, my housing situation would be set. I got to witness diverse men and women, mostly young people who were experiencing their first home-away stay with folks from many countries, who were sharing their customs and traditions, in very tight quarters of dormitories. It was interesting, exciting, and weird with mostly unfamiliar experiences. Observing primarily, my captivation with hundreds, then thousands of people kept me alert and mindful. As classes began, I efficiently sought ways to be anonymous, yet that would not occur in this environment with fewer Black, Latina, and Native American students. We found one another within established organizations; I was encouraged to join some of them, including a drama club, modern dance group, student government, and study teams. Later, I would join Alpha Kappa Alpha Sorority Inc. to welcome other women as I tutored and mentored young girls from the local community of Rubidoux, California. Interestingly, and seemingly overnight, we were taking these young girls from economically disadvantaged environments to elite circles, including fine and performing arts events and meeting entertainers and dignitaries in choice Los Angeles (L.A.) locations. In part, as a result, I recall picking up a nationally famed poet, Gwendolyn Brooks, from her humble abode to speak with hundreds of university scholars. That trip from and back to L.A. was a trip. She informed me of her journey and armed me with her truths about my worth and the worth of all girls and women. By the time of my graduation, I was honored by the then Chancellor, Tomás Rivera, with The Chancellor's Award for remarkable service as a student leader. Chancellor Rivera was the first university CEO with whom I was invited to meet. During our one-on-one meeting, he left me spellbound by his exceptional stories that revealed his youth, powerful mindset, and leadership advocacy.

Even though my primary reason for higher education was to achieve housing security, my undergraduate experiences helped me understand that I was much more than that child or young sentient being seeking to survive – I was filled with untapped leadership potential. During this time, I read The Bhagavad Gita, and a statement struck me and it still resonates with me, "A gift is pure when it is given from the heart to the right person at the right time and at the right place, and when we expect nothing in return."

Sonoma State University

I chose to be in service so that every student knew that s/he/they were valued unconditionally. Holding positions within Student Affairs i.e., outreach officer, advisor, coordinator, facilitator, mentor, trainer, and more, I facilitated the success of students with university educators, K-12 and 2-year college representatives, as well as hundreds of professionals in the career fields of interest to my diverse students – from professional roles as engineering to judgeships to veterinarians to medicine. Because my energy seemed to have no bounds, I would begin work before 6 AM and end after 8 PM. It was a joyful, meaningful, and remarkable experience. In the Educational Opportunity Program, Student Affirmative Action, Career and Academic Advising Center, Ethnic Studies and Sociology departments, and the Inter-Cultural Center, I got to live to give. My rewards were most personal – my heart was filled with joy almost daily watching diverse individuals who might not otherwise consider a university experience, learn how to succeed and many exceeded their expectations. Asians, Blacks, Latinos, Pacific Islanders, Native Americans, Whites, foreign and native-born learning, pushing forward, falling/failing forward, getting up continuously, and being supported to meet challenges, plan, execute, and progress.

> *I recall a woman in her late 60s who joined her son – a recent high school graduate with an exceptional GPA and manner – who had just been admitted to the university. The joy and admiration on her face was infectious. In honor of her and her son, I asked her if she had gone to college. Before continuing to share that she too could join her son if that were her wish depending on her level of education, her face quickly transformed – she was angry at me, then stated, "Clearly, I'm poor White trash, why would you ask me that? …", then she stormed out of my office. In shock, her son and I briefly stared at one another, me curious, him commencing to apologize for his mom's behavior. After apologizing for inadvertently inciting his mom's reaction, I shared what I had observed – her loving disposition, clear intelligence, and high value for him, then explained the purpose of my statement to her. While there is so much more to this classic and not unusual account for me, the short story is that within the week, she called and we both apologized and during his first year, she joined her son as a university student. Fast forward, she graduated with her son and with honors, then began her first professional role at Hewlett Packard, quickly advancing to leading teams.*

Stanford University

Inspired to expand my reach to impact the lives of more individuals, I pursued the roles of director and manager within Human Resources at Stanford University. Beginning this successful journey in 1988, I chose to interview leaders who would be in a position to influence my effectiveness in those roles. Those thirty individuals included local executives, elected officials, and other community leaders. Most introduced me to others with whom I spoke. For example, after a rich and compelling meeting with the honorable Rev. Dr. John Wesley Rice, Jr. in an East Palo Alto community center, he referred me to his daughter, then Associate Professor Condoleezza Rice.

With the same grace and openness as her father – who honored his deep roots championing excellence, civil rights, and equity – Dr. Rice "Conde" welcomed me into her inner office, posed questions to me, and shared information with me. It was like her father had stated, I felt like I was with my sister – although a more educated and accomplished professional – my humble disposition towards her became more exacting later when I learned more about her achievements at such a young age. The key takeaways from both Dr. John Rice and later U.S. Secretary of State Condoleezza Rice were (1) our choices determine our fate – choose wisely, (2) chief among our responsibilities is the creation of conditions that elevate the well-being of ourselves, our families, our communities, and society-at-large, and (3) leverage and share resources.

After assuming my new role as Manager and Director of the Stanford Employment Experience and the Youth Opportunity Program in January of 1989, I adapted, built connections, sought details from long-timers (tenured professors, administrators, staff), and quickly began learning to understand how to complement this new higher education environment.

My tour of duty at Stanford was exceptional, I served (a) hundreds of youth from low-income communities, (b) hundreds of adults from economically disadvantaged backgrounds using training programs and services for their advancements, and (c) while also leading executive searches to place senior-level professionals in essential roles throughout the university, including the Medical Center. I was tapped for leadership and management training programs, interacting and learning from some of the brightest minds in higher education and Silicon Valley. My team and I were able to partner with corporate leaders to enhance operations and human resources. And yet, by my last year, my focus was less on service to the internal and external communities of the institution, and more on addressing fiscal retrenchment-related matters, which necessitated the first set of layoffs in the University's history following nationally elected officials questioning and penalizing the institution for its indirect fund-related practices. The unintended negative consequences were many, including widespread fears of job loss and units closing, heightened uncertainty, jockeying for positions, sabotaging to outperform another, and loss of trust in the institution among many long-timers. While continuing to serve and studying to help neutralize some of the negative consequences, I experienced a great shift in my perspective – my conditions no longer fit me, and cognitive dissonance had set in, even though my grand vision remained. My reflections and self-questioning shifted to "how," which led me to imagine doctoral studies in higher education.

What I had learned from my higher education experiences to this point were to (1) take nothing for granted, (2) be clear about my vision, (3) live my passion, (4) ensure that I value the role(s) I assume, and (5) give all I have to ensure that my teams and I actualize the institution's mission while holding to core values and experiencing excellence. As I assumed whatever role this institution required to address the ever-changing conditions (i.e., assignments such as developing the layoff transition program, no benchmarks, and constrained resources), I continued to assess my professional well-being and progress in relationship to my vision. *It was time to lead with distinction.* Up until this point, I was singularly focused on others – youth, adults, professionals, and the great communities we served. This major institutional hiccup shook me at my core. Now, I had to learn more while ensuring "congruence" among my vision, thoughts, attitudes, actions, and status. I saw myself growing significantly and leading professionals to enhance the conditions of communities. Yet I was in a role that had quickly (and seemingly organically) shifted to a completely different paradigm, where I was a part of a network of systems – a node for sure – yet one that was being neutralized *from* doing good, being a servant leader, providing practical tools to help others understand their capacity, live their greatness, and contributing in massive ways to society.

By re-focusing my efforts, I set a new pace for myself – akin to moving from playing checkers to learning to play chess. Previously naive about institutional systems, professions, and even opportunities, I quickly leveraged the training and mentoring at Stanford and from Silicon Valley leaders, deciding to move forward differently. Just as many messages were shared when I told confidantes about my decision to pursue working at Stanford University, many cautioned me from leaving, indicating that I had a good gig and not to "blow it" by pursuing entry into one of the top public higher education institutions in the United States. Fortunately, I did the same thing I had done when transitioning into roles at Stanford, I told folks after I was accepted into the University of California at Berkeley. After they'd made their thoughts known, they learned of my status, and without fail, all switched quickly to sharing that they knew I'd be successful because of who I am.

University of California Berkeley

My actions and subsequent successes were greatly informed by my doctoral studies in the Graduate Schools of Education Higher Education Administration and Policy program and, subsequently, the Haas School of Business Organizational Behavior and Industrial (Labor) Relations program. During this period, I served as a researcher, interviewed and observed hundreds of educators, studied higher education institutions and concentrated on community colleges, and helped co-author Honored But Invisible, An Inside Look at Teaching In Community Colleges, while being mentored by distinguished higher education researchers and leaders, including K. Patricia Cross, Warner Norton Grubb III, Glenn R. Carroll, and Robert "Bob" McCabe. The complexities of leadership, organizational systems, structures, and networks along with historical precedences that inform current conditions deepened my respect for the roles and responsibilities of higher education institutions. Many nuanced decisions, experiences, and difficulties led me to destinations and subsequent strategies that positioned me for more learning and leadership responsibilities. Professor Cross' mentorship revealed the power of qualitative research, using my voice, and leveraging resources to help adult learners, institutions, and myself. Professor Grubb's investments in me illuminated the importance of compassion even as he seemed to want everyone to believe he possessed an unwavering stance and was unreasonably demanding. He valued quantitative research and revealed the promise and facts about vocational, career, and technical education. Professor Carroll's guidance was swift and steady as he exposed me to research on the behaviors of organizations in addition to labor relations. He parsimoniously dripped gems, golden nuggets sufficient to cause me to think deeper and integrate my Ph.D. studies. All led their Ph.D. programs – Cross and Grubb in Higher Education at Cal Berkeley and Carroll at the Haas School of Business, then the Graduate School of Business at Stanford. These three professors were brilliant; in unique ways, they demonstrated genius. Honored I was and am to have had their influence during such a pivotal period in my professional life.

Miami-Dade Community College System

Being mentored as an administrative intern to President/CEO Robert "Bob" McCabe was another exceptional experience. Viewing leadership up close from administrative/bureaucratic, symbolic, human resource, and political frames enabled me to better understand the nature and capacity of chief executives. Among higher education leaders, Bob was one of the early innovators of community colleges. He is credited for transforming a very small college campus into the nation's largest and most impactful community college with campuses across Southern Florida. (His success had been informed and illuminated by one of my mentors, Former Cornell University Dean and UC Berkeley Emerita Professor Higher Education K. Patricia Cross.) Here, I witnessed more of the political realities of leadership among presidents and chancellors as they worked locally, regionally, statewide, and with national leaders. These mostly confidential spaces compelled me to do more and think more deeply about my professional experiences, doctoral studies, and expansive readings about leadership. These and my subsequent experiences would humble me much more. I recall being on a Miami yacht with over 60 of Florida's college and university presidents and chancellors expressing how they held Bob in high esteem. Several commenters also shared how fortunate I was to be able to develop professionally under his tutelage and given his political acumen.

Contra Costa Community College District (CCCCD), leveraging Bob's insights and the direct learnings from hundreds of faculty and staff, my support to the CCCC District Vice Chancellor of Educational Services and Chancellor enabled me to once again expand my reach and deepen my knowledge. In this District Office, my fortunes included drafting successful grant proposals, developing regional meetings with stakeholders, and negotiating partnerships and plans as part of my administrative support and strategic planning roles. Here I deepened my understanding of how to leverage resources, work across more constituencies at the County and State levels, and the importance of brevity. In doing so, it was essential to understand the values and needs of special interest groups that were internal and external to the institution.

Corporate Consultancy

I parlayed my professional and educational experiences by providing human resources consultancy to secure and maintain talent for non-profit and for-profit organizations, including firms in Silicon Valley, California. Here my work with executives exposed me to more belief systems, including why particular cultural, educational, and value-laden nuances were deemed essential to hiring and maintaining individuals for particular roles. Perceptions and strong biases were explicit. For example, key executives were prescriptive about the type of degree-granting institutions from where their new hires would come. More specifically, these largely technical giants wanted particular roles filled by individuals with a clear "employee mindset," or folks who could be managed. On the other hand, they only wanted prospects for hire into the top-level posts who were alums of select tier-one research institutions with "business-mindset" or "growth mindset curricula," where alums were educated to think critically as a leader to "direct" professional endeavors.

Peralta Community College District

While here from 2002 to 2017, I was fortunate to inspire confidence in this Distrct while helping to build the integrity, image, and capacity of Laney College, the City of Oakland, and beyond. During this period, I served on nine boards and held other memberships with local, regional, and national groups, informed state and national policies, led accreditation and planning efforts, fundraised, and added to the number of key governance bodies I joined to advance HEI strategic agendas. Together with more than

1,000 professionals and leaders, we partnered to share resources and enhance offerings.

Part 2: Collective Capacity and Impact

In writing this chapter, I'm reflecting on the numerous actions I took in partnership with so many to stabilize, innovate, and transform conditions in diverse settings where teams of professionals and I were fortunate to serve. At each of those institutions, student access, excellence, and success were the ends on which we focused. Before and during my tenure in the Peralta Community College District, I used my strengths in the area of planning – strategic, master, and educational, consistently leaning in to help units, divisions, and entire institutions build capacity, especially securing human, technology, fiscal, and facilities resources. I did whatever it took as long as it was moral, ethical, and legal to ensure the achievement of mission-oriented goals. In discrete, cross-functional, and collaborative teams, we carried out policy work, led strategic initiatives, and so much more while assessing the efficacy of administrative and educational offerings, enhancing curricula, programs, and services, drafting a myriad of grant and partnership proposals, screening thousands of candidates, readying facilities for teaching and learning, providing student intake, fostering rituals to celebrate achievements, and even hand delivering thank you notes. Macro and micro functions were important. Key to progress and consistent successes were the partnerships fostered with professionals, institutions, and diverse stakeholders from within the college and district as well as across diverse communities.

All of the efforts described above were among the highlights of my presidency at Laney College thanks largely to my team of administrators, faculty, and staff. We were deliberate in:

- Hiring, evaluating, and promoting hundreds of educators and staff with excellence, integrity, equity, and diversity as guiding parameters;
- Leading institution-wide upgrades of the technology infrastructure and over $60M in improvements to classrooms, science/high tech career and technical labs, and administrative buildings affecting 21,000 students;
- Doubling the college's budget to meet instructional, laboratory, services, and administrative demands while supporting the operational needs of other Peralta colleges;
- Producing a billion-dollar facilities master plan; and
- Revitalizing and building over 300 public-private partnerships.

As I assumed greater responsibilities, my team and I sharpened our talents for engaging stakeholders. Targeting key networks and community leaders led to more and stronger partnerships that could ensure greater positive impacts in support of Bay Area communities. As a result, more in-kind services were provided along with donations from businesses such as the California Energy Commission, the University of California, California State Universities, national labs, PG&E, Bay Area Rapid Transit District, and local governmental agencies, including county offices. We worked on:

- Local, State, and Federal level legislation;
- Public-private partnerships with organizations across the United States and in other countries;
- Regional innovations to address the demand for a skilled workforce and leaders in competitive industries i.e., educational hub for Manufacturing Education i.e., industrial, bio- and advanced manufacturing, the construction trades, architecture and engineering, energy efficiency, advanced electronics, culinary arts, and much more;
- Regional, national, and international conventions;
- International presentations and special tours by world leaders;
- Programmatic enhancements in undergraduate education, career and technical education, transfer education, and graduate education; and
- Million-dollar campaigns and billion-dollar infrastructure projects.

Strategic Partnerships

Key to all of my successes was my disposition to design alliances and build relationships that would develop into partnerships with fellow professionals, leaders in the community, and institutions. I believed that alone I had limitations, yet in partnership with key others, there could be no barrier to achieving a mission that served the greatest good. Likely, it was that little girl in me who witnessed just how adults leveraged to get what they required or provided leverage to ensure that others obtained what they needed. More likely, it resulted from the countless memories, feelings, and other subconscious emotional matters that reinforced my predisposition to embrace all – even the detractor, sometimes especially the detractor – to accomplish something of value that contributes to the greater good.

Professional Partnerships

Focused on student learning and student success, my teams and I demonstrated our value for collaboration among professionals, which led to innovations and higher quality education and all-time high enrollment levels at several institutions, including Laney College with significant increases in student achievement far beyond the established benchmarks imposed on the college. Constantly, I welcomed new understandings that led to more achievements.

My collaborations resulted in creating, designing, implementing, and advancing a host of systems, programs, and support mechanisms to ensure people could have access to learn and use key resources to break through mental, emotional, and even physical constraints to transform as desired and in ways that exceeded expectations. Together, teams of folks and I:

- Designed and delivered an advanced Professional Mentor Program – over 100 professionals annually worked one-on-one with students to ensure meaningful experiences to prepare all to successfully pursue their selected careers. The professionals matched students in gender, ethnicity, and career/professional areas being pursued (SSU)
- Built networks among staff, professors, and administrators (multiple institutions)
- Reaffirmed institutions' accreditation (multiple institutions)
- Provided quality educational programs and services even when institutions experienced harmful fiscal exigencies, including a 25% reduction in funding to Laney College due to State-level financial retrenchment (multiple institutions)
- Researched community colleges across the United States – observing, interviewing, and studying, documenting the findings on 32 institutions (UC Berkeley)
- Secured grants and developed partnerships with federal and state-level governmental and non-governmental bodies to ensure the students' success (multiple institutions)
- Built reflective inquiry communities among professionals leveraging the Carnegie Foundation for the Advancement of Teaching at Stanford University (at Laney College while Academic Dean)
- Applied research practices in assessing and providing performance feedback in support of faculty (multiple institutions)
- Partnered with hundreds of business and industry partners to build career and technical programs, run seminars, conferences, and workshops, and enhance conventions
- Overhauled curricula – approximately 100 programs and hundreds of courses (Laney College) and revitalized the educational environment with enhanced strategic and transparent communications, rituals, and symbols that honored learning, the use of the college's facilities by the community stakeholders, and all educators and all employees with a primary focus on the hopes, aspirations of students and preparation to meet the respective needs of each student. Established Laney College as the heart of the Oakland community with annual events, and celebrations

such as EcoFest Sustainability, Peace Corps Event, Faculty Appreciation Day, Classified Appreciation Day, Annual Breakfast for Faculty and Staff to highlight and present awards and gifts to retirees, service milestones, and more; White House Summit on Education Excellence, Annual Student Awards Banquets in addition to the Graduation to honor and celebrate student achievements with meals, gifts, and other forms of recognition.

Institutional and Community Partnerships

The institutional and community partnerships that we promoted were numerous and they influenced all aspects of the organizations. At Laney College, in particular, members of my team shared the value of institutional and community partnerships – via service on boards, in advisory groups, think tanks, policy forums, and much more. My time on the national, regional, and state-level committees and boards i.e., the Statewide Community College League CEO Board exposed me to more effective practices in many formal and informal settings. As a result, we transformed the institution from the inside and outside. The external forces enabled us to:

- Enhance the level of federal and state resources for financial aid, grants, alliances, and public/private partnerships;
- Strengthen educational programs and services to align/match industry demands and 4-year HEI requirements;
- Prompt innovations, enhance resources, and build collaboration for student success to internationalizing Laney College – visits by educators, governmental officials, and business executives from a host of countries, including Singapore, Mexico, China, Nigeria, and Japan – leading to partnerships that enhance the number of students to enroll at, student, and become scholars, scientists, and engineers;
- Influence policies that affected hundreds of institutions within California, the United States, and in other countries in the continent of Asia, Africa, Europe, and South America;
- Significantly enhance student access, engagement, equity, and success – addressing barriers to access and success;
- Become among the top 10 community colleges in the State to transfer students to UC Berkeley

How were these feats accomplished? Importantly, professionals among the teaching faculty, researchers, staff, and administrators were (and are) essential to building the educational context that enables individuals to self-actualize and thrive. Additionally, innovation in services, core curricula, technical devices, and facilities that promote engagement and learning are all very important. However, these things work for many when – and frequently only when – care, respect, due consideration for individuals, and other key values highlighted in the next section are apparent and preferably ubiquitous.

I was determined to help and succeeded in helping numerous colleagues and students consciously choose to enhance their realities by understanding the powerful influence of mindset, mental models, learning, and personal experiences. My decision to become an educational ambassador, largely due to the undeniable impact of my undergraduate studies, helped me to grow and allowed me to guide countless others to leverage colleges and universities so that they too could better understand (and live more of) their innate capacity (intellectually), physically, spiritually and otherwise.

I got what I asked for, yet it was like riding roller coasters in student affairs, academic affairs, human resources, and administrative and executive leadership. Always, I honored my commitment to helping people, learning systems, influencing institutional systems, expanding my reach, and marshaling teams of individuals to exceed our expectations for the greater good.

I reasoned that I must model what I envisioned of students and members of our teams; it worked. At several institutions, my teams and I exceeded benchmarks in strategic areas, including enrollment, student outcomes, curricula innovations, human resources, institutional advancement, faculty development, etc.

While president of Laney College, a role I served in from 2010 – 2016, an outsider's misrepresentation of institutional outcomes led me to gather facts from State and district sources only to learn that the college had far exceeded the required goals. Already, I had received direct messages from university chancellors and provosts, and other key institutional leaders of the receiving transfer institutions that our entering transfers outperformed students who qualified for entry as freshmen who were themselves also juniors (like the transfers). Curious still, many of these accomplishments were initially considered by team members to be unreasonable and unrealistic expectations fostered by me – their college president. They could only imagine marginal improvements in particular areas. I set the bar high, incentivized the entire team of 800 employees, communicated the expectations college-wide and regularly, ensured widespread posting of the priorities of the institution in all classrooms, offices, and meeting centers i.e., library, student centers – then highlighted the progress being made, and championed the faculty, staff, and student leaders who demonstrated leadership to ensure success. Engaging such actions was intentional to welcome all students and staff as well as faculty and administrators into the discussion about how to (1) achieve manifestation of the vision, mission, and values published; (2) keep everyone, especially me as the college president accountable for achieving the published goals; (3) engage in strategic discourse that may be uncomfortable, yet essential to making necessary changes, including securing additional resources; and (4) honor the progress and everyone engaged in efforts to strengthen the institution for students.

During five years, faculty led the overhauling of the curriculum, the staff made service area improvements, administrators provided needed support including enhancements to procedures while informing policies, and student leaders answered the call to provide input to usher in substantive means to strengthen the institution to ensure student success. In the end, student achievement had ratcheted up in ways inconceivable by many because of the externally imposed fiscal retrenchment, marked reduction in faculty and staff, and other constraints.

Our capacity is much greater than what many of us currently imagine. Since we rise to the level of belief, why not believe big – dream big – codify that dream into a vision, operationalize it further into a goal(s) that can be measured, and then map out a plan that is open to experts and key others to inform the "how" then take action. And VOILA! Before we know it, we're at our planned (desired) destination.

My behavior modeled the belief that since we can dream big – and we get what we ask and work for, let's choose to lead with distinction – dream big, and be unwavering in our pursuit of that dream no matter the distance it takes us!

Part 3: Illuminating Greatness

While institutional excellence entailed many accreditation-related requirements and standards, community perceptions, and investments, **Student Outcomes** were always the ends we highlighted even as colleagues/partners discussed those other priorities. The impact my colleagues and I have had on over 100,000 students is far beyond what I'd hoped as I started my professional journey. I took advantage of an awesome opportunity to inspire others to understand themselves and aspire to greatness, distinguishing the new self significantly from a previous self, and distinguishing others' actions from the status quo to facilitate eminence. I'm fortunate to have witnessed thousands of people opt for such pursuits, and to work side-by-side with the teams of staff, faculty, professors, administrators, and other professionals who provided in-kind support such as coaching, mentoring, and professional role shadowing in and out of formal educational environments. Importantly, our students were distinctly brilliant in ways to inspire a library of books, yet below is just a sample:

- In a classroom – I recall the major milestone achieved by an 80-year-old student and his excellent performance in a math class – inspired by a part-time instructor and his younger student peers. During my interview with him, he shared his early beginnings in the "deep south" of the United States and years of torment having been chastised as a child by his teachers and his guardians as incapable of learning mathematics or any other subject, which he attributed to his being a Black male
- In a workplace – I reflect on a child of Mexican immigrants and a first-generation college student from a highly segregated urban community leading within one of the country's Federal Reserve Banks
- Among scholars – I think about the young woman graduate, now Rhodes Scholar from her humble origins on a farm, child of immigrant parents for whom she interprets
- In an industry – I look back on the expert way the seasoned CPA led a certified public accounting firm and a professional network after her early struggles to find her path to college
- Among scientists – I smile as I think of a self-described nerdy kid with dreads dancing his way to winning choice scholarships from prestigious institutions and highly selective internships with national laboratories, now informing top-secret innovations that may influence all of humanity
- In a community center – I remember the professional who guides a nonprofit team after being awarded academic honors from a distinguished university. She achieved such after learning how to neutralize the negative effects of learning disabilities and while rearing an autistic child who is now an adult earning a doctorate from another valued accredited university
- Among educational leaders – I think about one who initially desired only to be a staff member, this mother of three who earned her doctorate and witnessed her children receive their bachelor's degrees is now a college vice president. She supports and guides teams of educators
- In the national political arena – I witnessed how a once shy and unassuming young teenager who had lost his mom before he turned 10 years old, chose to become the first in his family to obtain AA degrees on the same day he graduated high school, then advance to secure a BA, a MA, and a doctorate while influencing policy at the national level
- In professional sports – I return to the young man who was inspired by his philosophy professor and head coach (and supported by the family

atmosphere within the college), to go against long odds, and after not being recruited to a Division 1 university – to scoring the winning play in Super Bowl 50

- Among national athletes – I contemplate just how this woman who was raised by her grandmother, and with anger control issues, went from what she described as "... a statistic" from Richmond, CA who "wasn't supposed to go this far" to the Olympic trials and the NCAA Track and Field

Each of the individuals highlighted above is remarkable – and so are countless others. Like the athletes, they benefitted from someone seeing their inherent talents rather than assuming that they were limited. The national athlete stated that she "made a liar out of everyone who told me that I was either going to be in jail or dead." What a way to live – knowing that others have such low expectations of you. She went on to state that "It feels great" to have proven everyone a liar. She and so many other successful alumni reveal the importance of widening paths to opportunities as a precondition to building more powerful and positive legacies.

Part 4: Learnings, Gratitude, and Reminders

Indeed fortunate for sure, I have lived the words, *we become what we think about*. I maintained an insatiable thirst for knowledge, was fixated on providing quality service, and was focused on helping folks actualize more of who they could be. These aspects of me drove my 15–20 hour work-days (sometimes I'd work multiple days with few hours of sleep – so much to do, time had to be leveraged), which reflected my assuming greater responsibilities independent of expectations or professional gains e.g., promotion, compensation. At times, I'd have multiple full-time roles that I'd carry out as though I had a substantial staff – when I might have none or one, as when I was an academic dean from 2002 to 2005. Absolutely and completely, I loved my vocation. I felt indistinguishable from my work. Continuously, I increased my capacity – i.e., returned to school to learn more to be of service, especially in response to the ever-changing demographics of students, colleagues, and systems within which I worked and would lead. Importantly, I was always mindful that I did not know what I did not know while envisioning my expansion. And I got what I had asked for and much more.

Leadership Lessons Learned in Multicultural Context

My 38 years of work inspiring, educating, and otherwise facilitating thousands of individuals to exceed their expectations by learning to understand their genius and how to achieve greatness has been very instructive. I've gained immensely in terms of intrinsic rewards and an enhanced understanding of a myriad of matters that I now apply routinely. And, independent of the financial backgrounds of these students, they, too, benefited from the richly diverse Asian, Black, Latina/o, Pacific Islander, Native American, White, and other USA and foreign-born individuals of all genders and diverse interests, needs, and capabilities. All of the colleges and universities provided contexts for growth that have fostered leaders who appreciate the multicultural nature of our lived realities. In so doing, they have prepared us all for a better future where more of us are:

- Equipped to use our critical mental faculties to reason, thinking at our highest levels to originate thoughts to formulate logical ideas;
- Imagining how to form new creations from fantasy, and theories, to facts;
- Leveraging our intuitions, our instinctive, innate capacity;
- Perceivingmatters using a growth mindset as part of imagining possibilities; and
- Exercising the will to focus and concentrate to master and succeed at what one chooses.

When strengthening the mental faculties of reason, imagination, intuition, perception, will, and memory – using them in concerted ways – and *in partnership with other people who are different from ourselves* – to advance a more humane, civil society globally, which is within reach. Intentionally, I encouraged the adoption of shared values e.g., "we're all one" to connect mind and heart through collaborative experiences where listening to understand was foremost.

As an important exercise, I would encourage all to take time to imagine everyone successful, experiencing their inherent genius, and living authentically with integrity. Now, I ask you, What would this world feel like, look like, and be with such an outcome? Let's imagine the awesome possibilities – then take action to operationalize those feelings and imaginings. This is what the greats have done and do. We credit them for the results of great passions, imaginings, thinking, and execution – their remarkable architecture, seminal paintings, pure mathematical concepts, philosophical ideas, scientific breakthroughs, technological creations, and practical solutions i.e., ingenuity in medical devices, cooking tools, computing machines, other technologies, distribution systems, gadgets, and so much more.

Let's remember the statement attributed to Henry David Thoreau (and written on his desk): "In the long run men hit only what they aim at. Therefore, though they should fail immediately, they had better aim at something high." In other words, we all profit from aiming high because we're going to hit something anyway. And should we fail, we'll have the opportunity to join all the other greats we call geniuses, who learned from their failures, by *failing forward*. We recall the achievements of geniuses but are often not aware of (or we forget) the many failures they experienced to learn what was essential to get to greatness.

While passionate about being an educational ambassador, I found it essential to pursue peace. I retired after thirty-eight years of professional service within higher education even though I assumed that I would serve continuously. As an educational ambassador, I've been able to inspire an ever-expanding base of people, families, communities, and society at large leveraging higher education to enhance the state of humanity. Whenever I'm asked, "How are you?," typically I respond "fortunate, blessed, and well." The gifts that I received throughout my career in higher education far surpassed what I had imagined at the beginning of my career. Notably, however, akin to honeymoons, my *rollercoaster* career was replete with experiences that I would have cautioned others to avoid. Aware of the massive support that had been built over the years for me by colleagues external and internal to my professional environment, I still appreciated that I had become exhausted and even transfixed by what had been an onslaught of political attacks. When faced with any attack, my wiring had been to lean in to seek to understand, obtain insights to identify, then test solutions, and with intelligence gathered (or developed), forge an action plan to resolve the matter, seeking wins for all parties, with peace and resolution always being the goal. As a formula, this seemed to work consistently even with a few adaptations. However, left out of this equation typically were the costs to me. How long could I sustain attacks before exhaustion or even bewilderment set in?

Exhausted

My life reflected a 24/7/365 commitment to the HEI's vision without regard to any personal desires. I did not know "joy" for the sake of personal happiness unless it was to honor or celebrate others – loved ones, countless students and professional colleagues, and the great communities in which I was honored to work and lead. Unwavering commitment to whatever another needed without consideration for self came with a desired benefit – effective service – yet at a cost that kept increasing.

Bewildered

I could not imagine that my predisposition to serve would be the very thing that incentivized others to attack me professionally – an oversight for which I had to forgive myself. Insiders later informed me that it was jealousy, fear, desire to see me fail miserably, or some other reported self-interests. Whatever the reason(s), my disposition to self-analyze to improve my own performance did not allow me to accept any of those views initially. Such self-criticism delayed my recovery.

Transfixed

Recovery, I did, for sure. Really because of the physical manifestations that ensued, medical attention was essential and had to be exacting – traditional and nontraditional. Foremost, the recovery required unceasing meditative prayers and leveraging a trained psychologist who would help facilitate me on my journey of inner discovery. While very painful, this journey catapulted me out of the deep end of a sea of troubled water; for someone who had yet to learn to swim (but could float), that was an essential feat!

It is true that the different universities and colleges where I was fortunate to contribute, learn, and experience remarkable growth, also exposed me to controlling and unhealthy people who opted to live out their pathologies of fear, biases, racism, and other malicious, unscrupulous, and dishonorable behaviors; the list of those experiences would be too much for this chapter. Independent of the details of the challenges that ensued, due largely to negative politicking, each experience presented me with the opportunity to learn and then leverage that learning. *With enhanced hindsight, each of the political experiences helped me grow and build a more solid foundation for leading with distinction.* Also, importantly, in every instance, my subsequent actions remained focused on my big dream – the vision. In general, my professional experiences further solidified my belief that *life* is the biggest learning ground and that everything happens for a reason even if the *players* in this important game called life are unaware of the roles they are playing.

Above all, in reflecting on some of the detractors and their political gaming of the systems in which we all worked, my attention is drawn to hundreds of colleagues who also led as college and university presidents, chancellors, superintendents, provosts, vice presidents, and deans. While we had distinct environments, we all had challenges. Yet for those of us who had clarity and conviction in the following areas, we were able to sustain our leadership commitments:

1 Using a grand vision that we were passionate about and that was big enough to include the visions or priorities of others with whom we were working;

2 Maintaining our values and living with integrity 24/7;
3 Assuring synergy of our heart-mind – valuing self, engendering trust, and demonstrating it via rewards to grow, refresh, recharge, and rejuvenate;
4 Fostering leaders among colleagues who demonstrate growth mindsets, ensuring that succession planning is embedded within the culture of organizations; and
5 Leveraging coaches and mentors for guidance to actualize our visions.

Know that a leader's mindset is the "mental lens that dictates what information [to] take in and use to make sense of and navigate the situations ... encounter[ed]." Growth mindsets predispose each one of us to see situations as opportunities to learn. Whereas fixed mindsets lead us to view those same situations as threats. More is achieved by leaders with growth mindsets, including welcoming enhancements to systems, developing leaders among all people, and welcoming creativity, strategic risks, and innovations.

Brilliant leaders abound among students, educators, researchers, staff, administrators, and executives in our colleges and universities. They have visions, make decisions (tough and otherwise), inspire and are self-motivated, self-initiate forward-moving actions, model sound behaviors, own the outcomes of their actions, exercise accountability, and are communicative and massively grateful.

Gratitude and Reminders

Writing this chapter has been intellectually and emotionally cathartic, prompting an abundance of memories. I've been so blessed to have discovered my voice via higher education and used it to promote the entitlement of everyone to her/his/their inherent significance in service to the greatest good.

Gratitude to you for reading this book. We aim to inspire you to lead and to do so with distinction. All 5,000 plus accredited colleges and universities throughout the United States (and the over 25,000 throughout the world), now and into the future, demand exceptional leadership characterized by their resiliency, agility, partnerships, and ability to unlock expertise within and across teams of individuals while accelerating collaborative learning. And at the core of their needs are leaders who choose carefully their core values. Oftentimes, we adopt the values of the persons to whom we have devoted time, especially during our childhood. The proper study of those values might result in a necessary upgrade. This becomes apparent when evaluating how one's values *square* with those of their students, the learning environment, and the greater community being served.

One with values that are congruent with self-image, and vision, and support those for whom we care and serve as well as with whom we work elevates us all. Intentionally, I choose core values of excellence (quality), accountability, altruism, collaboration, inclusion, equity, diversity, integrity, and with the fundamental belief in the oneness of all life. Recently, I've been more mindful of elevating my values for my faith, family, fitness, finance, and fun – enabling me to experience pure freedom. Doing so enables me to daily give birth to my dreams.

Discussion Questions

1 Professional partnerships and collaborations among staff, faculty, and administrators, like several discussed within this chapter, all have an important impact on student success and the overall quality of education. Reflect on your own leadership experiences within higher education and identify specific examples of a collaboration that you were involved in that led to positive outcomes for students, the institution, and the broader community the institution serves. What were the key factors that contributed to the success of these collaborations and partnerships? What key lessons and takeaways can be drawn from this example?
2 Overcoming challenges such as fiscal exigencies and other limited resources while also providing high-quality academic programs is an important issue as discussed within this chapter. Draw from your background in higher education administration and describe a situation where you or your institution faced significant financial constraints. How did you navigate these challenges while still prioritizing student learning and success? What innovative strategies, partnerships, or changes in approach were employed to meet the needs of both supporting high-quality academic programs as well as supporting student achievement during such difficult times? In retrospect, what advice would you have given yourself or your institution to manage these difficulties?
3 This chapter emphasizes the role of values, mindset, and interpersonal dynamics in achieving institutional success. Reflecting on your leadership in higher education, how has your work (or your institution) fostered a values-driven environment that promotes collaboration and accountability in strategic planning? What are some best practices that were used to create a culture where faculty, staff, administrators, and students collectively worked towards exceeding institutional goals? How

can these lessons be applied to other higher education contexts to promote student achievement and institutional growth?
4 Adapting to changing environments, values, roles, and even different institutions is a key skill for effective leaders within higher education as this chapter demonstrates. Drawing from your professional journey, identify pivotal moments when you needed to reevaluate your vision and approach due to unexpected shifts or challenges. How did you manage the tension between your initial aspirations and the evolving circumstances? What strategies did you employ to better align your personal vision, the institutional goals, and the well-being of the larger community you were serving? How do these experiences inform your current leadership style and philosophy?
5 The conclusion of this chapter discusses a framework for leadership commitment and five key aspects of a "leader's mindset." Reflect on your current position within your institution and consider the following: How do these aspects intersect with and apply to your leadership style? How would you define a "leader's mindset"? What are some institution-specific or position-specific elements that you think would be helpful to add to this framework?

AFTERWORD

Climbing the Rough Side of the Mountain

Career Journeys imparts crucial lessons of self-reflection, planning, and strong conviction for diversity and equity, as "firsts" multicultural servant leaders relate stories of reaching the top of the mountain while laying the foundation for diverse leadership in higher education. The African American gospel song, "Climbing the Rough Side of the Mountain," speaks to them as well as to those who seek diversity and equity in our flawed democracy.

Ghosh, Indian woman professor of Quantum Physics, the only international contributor to *Career Journeys,* finds a wellspring for creativity crossing the silos in liberal education. From physics, she learned the importance of structure; from music and literature, "the sense of logic, the essence of rhythm and the value of life." Embracing an educational experiment with creativity at Shiv Nadar University, she focused uncompromisingly on quality, addressing structural problems of inequality and poverty. Ghosh's leadership model, based on the pursuit of excellence, intellectual diversity, and social justice, is grounded in integrating education, technology, human potential, and human lives. Her acronym, VUCA (volatile, uncertain, complex, and ambiguous), encapsulates the context of higher education for the past 50 years and now, whether domestic or international. That she is "a product of a generation where some of us have 'made it' *in spite* of the system and *not because* of the system" holds for all contributors, as does her determination to "change this for my next generation."

Baltodano early on determined never to be left behind and developed her "ability to pay attention to detail while at the same time seeing the big picture." Building on lessons from her Hispanic family and community-minded parents, Baltodano strategically combined her visionary passion for social justice, philanthropy, community service, and networking opportunities to enhance her legal studies and fundraising abilities, leading to success at various institutions. She realized her goal of a college presidency, but more importantly, used her networking, fundraising, organizational, and leadership skills to found and lead the Executive Leadership Academy at Berkeley (2011 to present), a profound legacy of her early determination to succeed, her leadership and coaching abilities, and of her caring for others. A distinctly multicultural leadership academy, ELA presently has 16 presidents/chancellors; 37 provosts/VPs; and 20 deans, associate and assistant deans among the 574 ELA alums to date. All contributors to *Career Journeys* have served as ELA faculty.

Astrophysicist Blumenthal seized opportunities for scientific research and graduate school involvement beyond science, providing a foundation for later engagement with the complexities of and possible synergies among institutions, faculty governance, and administrative leadership – a lesson especially for first-generation graduate students and faculty aspirants to higher education leadership. As a faculty member and later administrator working with Santa Cruz's legendary provost, Herman Blake, in building Oakes College, the multicultural community at UCSC, Blumenthal developed his understanding of the relationships among higher education, fundraising, diversity, and inclusion. Among numerous lessons leading to his chancellorship, he advises addressing thorny issues at various levels of leadership by understanding institutions, expecting the realistic best of others, embracing compromise to overcome resistance, and knowing who you are and your potential amid institutional growth and change.

Most, like Ghosh, credit liberal education for shaping their expansive worldviews and bringing their whole selves to their leadership quests. Currie, a Chinese American immigrant from Taiwan, lived briefly in Francophone Africa in her teens, coming to Dayton, Ohio to complete high school. At a Midwest college she "discovered the world of humanity through the liberal arts curriculum … … . and began to search for and understand who [she] was as a person with multiple identities" in contrast to being identified as an "Alien with an assigned number … and outsider trying to figure out if there was room on the inside for [her]." She elaborates on three leadership lessons from her journey to the chancellorship of the Coast Community College District in California: 1) Keep your soul intact with authenticity and spiritual anchors; 2) Leaders are not born, they are made; and 3) Understand the importance of power and exercise it with balance. Currie's poem, "I am at the crossroads, must I choose?" serves as a primer for all who must navigate their differences and those of others, as she melds the value of personal and sociocultural diversity with the necessity of community colleges in our educational landscape.

Gonzalez and Mitchell emphasize personal and academic grounding in one's identity as the basis of success. The son of Mexican immigrants, for Gonzalez ethnicity and diversity were always factors, positive or negative. As a Latino "first" in higher education during the Civil Rights and Chicano movements, he argues that it will take many years to achieve parity between students and leadership resembling them, questioning whether there will be minority leaders to fill leadership positions. Being *"bien educados"* from the East L.A. barrio during the 1950s and '60s became the "crucible that forged [his] identity and career in higher education." Gonzalez learned to "balance notions of morality with strict adherence to societal norms" as he explored his interests from the Air Force to Law School to psychology research, taking risks that fit his sense of direction. Searching for his academic "fit" led him to an observation that those who strive to bring about equitable change must manage: that "faculty life is often a solitary experience, but also that this individualistic approach to success is what is rewarded. Being cooperative and working for the good of the whole is, in many ways, contrary to the basic motivational structure of the university."

From witnessing Ku Klux Klansmen riding through his Mississippi neighborhood to racist discouragement to seek the best, Mitchell explored academic interests and facilitated, during his first university position, student demands for Black faculty and programs with the Chancellor. A Black Studies scholar, he demonstrates that one can remain true to one's scholarship and teaching, no matter how marginalized the field. Exploring opportunities means not only accepting positions that come your way, as Mitchell demonstrates, but also being innovative and willing to make proposals to improve policy, staffing, budget, and organizational structure. Using opportunities to learn how institutions functioned, he built on his experiences and skills to succeed in areas new to him. The advice of his most influential mentor, UC Berkeley Chancellor Dr. Chang-Lin Tien, sums up the lessons of Mitchell's experiences: "Excellence is achieved by decisions made on a daily basis." Examine your decisions asking, "Does this decision promote excellence?"

Holmgren and Pippins exemplify how the intersectionality of race and gender is an integral part of life and institutional structure. A first-generation college graduate, supported by her parents' unwavering commitment to the value of education, Holmgren became engaged during her college years in the late 1960s in the work of creating greater equity in society and educational opportunity for women and people of color "despite clear evidence of how hard those changes would be." She became acutely aware of "embedded gender discrimination" that gave her "minority" and "outsider" status as a graduate student at Princeton University. Her professional experiences across three higher education institutions as an administrator and faculty member – the University of District Columbia, the University of Maryland at College Park, and Princeton University--led her eventually to a twenty-year presidency at a distinguished women's college, Mills College, in California, where she was most able to match her values to her work for diversity, equity, and academic excellence. Lessons emerge from her story such as the importance of family support; balancing flexibility with persistence; working with communities surrounding an institution; making alliances; balancing preservation with innovation; finding support systems to fulfill personal responsibilities as mother, daughter, and sister; and learning from a mentor who likely does not share your background.

Pippins's years before her professional life could serve as a model for underrepresented students and leaders to overcome not belonging. Growing up in the world of Jim Crow, family support guided her through struggles with faith, courage, self-empowerment, and optimism. Most importantly, she learned that she "could compete and excel in any environment: 'I didn't have to be comfortable to do it.'" With a strong desire to make a difference in the lives of others and self-reflection, Pippins developed the skills and confidence for successful leadership of two community colleges, one that became the largest in the SUNY system during her tenure. Leaning on her strong belief that there is always a path forward, she weathered disappointment when, as president, she had to close a small, for-profit Christian college. Of the many lessons her journey reveals, one stands out as a principle she never forgot: Process is at least as important as content.

Grounded in her Diné (Navajo) culture and family legacies of endurance, resistance, and the confidence that education would ensure success, Manuelito-Kerkvliet earned her doctorate intending to be a college president "despite the ambivalence [she] felt from professors and peers ...." A lesson permeating her journey is to accept and nurture mentoring wherever its origin as long as it is genuine. As a "first" woman leader at Diné College in a patriarchal environment contradicting the tribe's culture of ancestral and matrilineal rights, she demonstrates another lesson: transfer your skills, in this case, her counseling skills as well as administrative skills, while remaining focused on addressing key issues affecting the lives of students, staff, and faculty. Her traditional and nonconforming ways led Manuelito-Kerkvliet to act with compassion and understanding, making decisions through embracing relationships among people, the environment, and the world around us, seeking balance. Perhaps the most significant lesson gleaned from her journey is how, by grounding in the traditions of family and culture, one can retain "personal power, peace of mind, and peace in [one's] heart," while surviving and succeeding regardless of opposing cultural norms and challenges.

Not blessed with guiding family traditions, Webb moved through foster care, learning she could "safeguard [her] spirit from harm" and "design her life," ultimately growing through her Black, Latina, and Native American background. Among her many lessons are that mentoring can come from both casual acquaintances and seasoned colleagues; inspiration from diverse knowledge bases and students' achievements as well as teamwork and partnerships; and success from "actualiz(ing) the institution's mission while holding to core values and experiencing excellence." Careful planning, inclusive and strategic leadership can result in both positive student outcomes and inspiration for greater achievement. Her story also demonstrates that servant leadership is difficult, sometimes challenged by the very successes it engenders. The key, however, to personal fulfillment is gleaning self-knowledge from early life struggles as well as consistent growth through self and organizational assessment, while seeking excellence and living with passion rather than "a contrived human constructed model of completion or achievement."

Liberal education, social justice, self-awareness, and reflection led these chancellors/presidents to share their experiences both as ELA faculty and as contributors to this volume at this vexed time in higher education and in our democracy. Arguably, the side of the mountain has gotten rougher but the joy of success and of lifting others as they climbed should inspire current and future leaders to continue the journey with fortitude and perseverance.

Johnnella E. Butler
Professor Emerita and Former Provost, Spelman College;
Founding Fellow and Faculty Member, Executive Leadership Academy;
Affiliated Faculty, Center for Studies in Higher Education, University of California, Berkeley

INDEX

AAHHE *see* American Association of Hispanics in Higher Education, Inc. (AAHHE)
AAPI *see* Asian American and Pacific Islander (AAPI)
ABET *see* Accreditation Board for Engineering and Technology (ABET)
Accreditation Board for Engineering and Technology (ABET) 171
ACE *see* American Council on Education (ACE)
ACE Women's Network 36–37
American Association of Community Colleges 50, 61
American Association of Hispanics in Higher Education, Inc. (AAHHE) x, 40
American Association of Universities 14
American Association of University Professors 11
American Beauty Rosebuds 183
American Council on Education (ACE) x, 126, 129, 174, 191, 194, 195; *American College President Study 2017* 60, 92, 93
Antioch College 146
Antioch University Seattle 146, 148; Higher Learning Commission 146

Asian American and Pacific Islander (AAPI) 107
Association of Black Psychologists 154, 156
Association of Community College Trustees 61
Atal Incubation Center (AIC) 84
Atkinson, R. 165
authentic leadership style 52–54
Awakuni, G. 159

Bahá'í Faith 51, 65
Baltodano, J. C. x–xxi, 25, 89, 227–228; 1980–1998 developing programs at UC Berkeley 34–35; advice and practical tips 41–42; early life of 28–31; education background 31–34; lessons and learning from mentors 35–36; serving at ACE Women's Network 36–37; serving at Alliant International University 36; serving at John F. Kennedy University 36; serving at Marian University 37–40; Transformative Development Program at UC Berkeley, establishing 40–41
Barnes, B. 59
Bateson, M. C. 127
Bay Area Rapid Transit District 214

Berkeley financial system (BFS) 162, 163
"Berkeley Pledge, The" 164
BFS *see* Berkeley financial system (BFS)
Biestman, K. xx
Big West Conference (BWC) 160, 173
Black Manifesto 155
Black psyche 156
Blake, J. H. 1, 6
Blumenthal, G. xxi, 89, 228; as academic senate 8–13; afterlife of chancellorship 24–26; Chancellor of UC Santa Cruz 1, 13–24; faculty years 4–8; as first-generation astrophysics student 2–4; regental service 8–13
Board of the American Council on Education 133
Board of Trustees of Princeton University 133
Boggs, G. 60–61
Brand, M. 165
Brossel, K. 75
buddy system 96
BWC *see* Big West Conference (BWC)
Byrne, J. 144

California Association for Research in Astronomy 25
California Community College: advancing equity and opportunity through 50–51
California Energy Commission 214
California Institute for Regenerative Medicine 25
California Master Plan 111, 112
California State Universities 214
Carnegie Foundation for the Advancement of Teaching and Learning 133
Carroll, C. 57
Carroll, G. R. 210
Castro, J. xxii
CCCCD *see* Contra Costa Community College District (CCCCD)
Center for Studies in Higher Education (CSHE),: University of California-Berkeley 25
Center for the Social Organization of Schools, Johns Hopkins University, Baltimore 99
Cepeda, R. 60

Chatterjee, P. xxi
Chirikov, I. xxii
Civil Rights Movement 97, 146
Claremont Colleges: Chicano Studies program 97
Coastline College 66
Coastline Community College 60
Cohen-Tannoudji, C. 75
Coley, S. M. 171
community partners 63
Confucius 50
congruency 51–52
consumerism 80
Contra Costa Community College District (CCCCD) 212
Coonerty, R. 16
corporate consultancy 212
Council of Chancellors 14
COVID-19 pandemic xx, 85, 86
creative leadership, in institution building 70–90
critical conscientiousness 66
Cross, K. P. 210, 211
Croughan, M. 25
CSHE *see* Center for Studies in Higher Education (CSHE), University of California-Berkeley
CSU Board of Trustees 106
Currie, D.-J. H. 228–229; advancing equity and opportunity through California's Community Colleges 50–51; as Asian women president 44–68; bravery 46; diversity in Africa, experiencing 46–47; falling in love in California 49; intact with authenticity and spiritual anchors 51–56; leading with wholeness 65–68; as outsider in America 47–49; on power 61–65

DEI (diversity, equity, and inclusion) 113
Denton, D. 13–14
Department of Energy, US 12
Department of Labor, US 193
Desjardins, C. 56
Destination 2010 105
Diné College 141, 143–146, 230; Board of Trustees 145
diversity xx, 20–22, 46–47, 61, 67–68, 91–113
Doffoney, N. 55

Dolan, T. M. 42
Drake, M. 15
Dynes, B. 14

EdD in Educational Leadership 172
EIR *see* Environmental Impact Report (EIR)
ELA *see* Executive Leadership Academy (ELA)
Environmental Impact Report (EIR) 16
equity 51, 59–60
ethnicity 91–113
Executive Leadership Academy (ELA) 25, 26, 28, 41, 88, 228; Advisory Board xxii; history of x–xxiii

Faber, S. 5
Faculty Code of Conduct, UC 9–11
family leave 87
Federal City College 121
Federation of Indian Chambers of Commerce and Industry (FICCI) 83
FICCI *see* Federation of Indian Chambers of Commerce and Industry (FICCI)
Field Study Program 154
Freire, P. 189
Fresno State 91, 98–100, 102
Friedan, B. 34
From Good to Great 38

Galloway, A. 23
Gender Committee 83
Gender Sensitization Committee against Sexual Harassment (GSCASH) 75; Rules and Procedures 76
George Mason University 123
Ghosh, R. xxi, 70–90, 227; on culture 85–87; early days 71–72; education 72–74; leadership 75–78; new inning 78–85; professional life 74–75
Gifted Student Scholarship 84
Gilligan, C. 56–57
Glasser, C. E. 36
Goldman School of Public Policy (GSPP) x, 28
Gonzalez, A. 91–113, 229; academic ladder 100–103; achievements 107–108; experience 93–94; lessons learned 108–110; path to academe 94–100; presidency 103–106; Presidency in Higher Education 92–93
Good Fellows, The 29
Gorman, R. C. 145
Gould, B. 3
Graduate Record Exam 3
Greenler, R. 2–3
Greenwood, M. R. C. 8
Grubb III, W. N. 210, 211
GSCASH *see* Gender Sensitization Committee against Sexual Harassment (GSCASH)
GSPP *see* Goldman School of Public Policy (GSPP)
Guerrero, D. 160

Haak, H. 102
Harvard Graduate School of Education 161
Harvard Institute for Education Management 152
Harvard Law School 98
Harvard School of Business 161
Head Start 186
Heyman, M. 34
Hispanic Serving Institution (HSI) 14, 21, 22, 107
Holmgren, J. L. 114–140, 229–230; as Assistant Director of Graduate Studies 122; education 116–117; family 116–117; higher education 118–119; *Narration and Discourse in American Realistic Fiction* 122; presidency at Mills College 114–116, 126–134; as Princeton woman 119–122; return to Princeton 125–126; serving at University of Maryland College Park 122–124; thoughts on higher education 135–139; transitions 134–135
HSI *see* Hispanic Serving Institution (HSI)
humanity 88

"I Am Going to College" program 63
ICC *see* Internal Complaints Committee (ICC)
IEM *see* Institute for Educational Management (IEM), Harvard University

IFCPAR/CEFIPRA *see* Indo-French Centre for the Promotion of Advanced Research (IFCPAR/CEFIPRA)
ikigai 89
inclusivity xx, 20–22, 40
Indo-French Centre for the Promotion of Advanced Research (IFCPAR/CEFIPRA) 75
Industry 4.0 80
Industry 5.0 81
Ingram, H. W. 169
inner lioness 56–57
inner peace 68
Institute for Educational Management (IEM), Harvard University 161
institutional and community partnerships 216–218
integrity 55–56
Internal Complaints Committee (ICC) 83
Institution of Eminence (IoE) 85
ISO 14001:2015 for Environment Management System 83
ISO 45001:2018 for Occupational Health & Safety Management System 83

justice 59–60

King, J. C. x
Kishore Vaigyanik Protsahan Yojana (KVPY) 77
Kliger, D. 13
KQED 35
KVPY *see* Kishore Vaigyanik Protsahan Yojana (KVPY)

Laney College 213–216; Professional Mentor Program 215
Lapp, K. 18
Lee, B. 133
Lee, H. 20
Livermore Laboratory 12
Los Alamos National Laboratory 12

Manuelito-Kerkvliet, C. xx, 141–150, 230–231; disappointment 148; early life of 142–143; highest ranking of 143–144; leadership style 147; serving at Diné College 144–146

Mary Christian Performing Arts Center 193
Maternity Benefit Act, 1961 87
maternity leave 87
McCabe, R. "Bob" 211
McDonnell Aircraft Company (McDonnell Douglas) 153, 155
Merit-cum-Means Scholarship 84
Miami-Dade Community College System 211–212
Mills College 114–116, 126–134; Boards of Trustees 138
Milwaukee Public Library system 2
mistakes 62
Mitchell, H. xx, 152–177, 229; early introduction to administration 154–155; executive appointments 158–165; first faculty appointments 156–157; middle management 157–159; presidency at CSU Bakersfield 165–176; Presidential Profile 176; prologue 151–153
Moses, Y. 191
Murphy, D. 23

NAACP 192
NACUBO *see* National Association of College and University Business Officers (NACUBO)
Napolitano, J. 24
National Achievement Scholarship for Outstanding Negro Students 184
National Assessment and Accreditation Council 84
National Association of College and University Business Officers (NACUBO) 174
National Council for Research on Women 128
National Council of Educational Research and Training (NCERT) 77
National Institute for Leadership Development (NILD) 56, 57
National Institutional Ranking Framework 83
National Merit Scholarship Program 184
National Science Foundation graduate fellowship 3
Navajo Community College *see* Diné College

Navajo Nation Tribal Council 145
NCAA 160; Board of Governors 165; Executive Committee 165
NCERT *see* National Council of Educational Research and Training (NCERT)
Newsom, G. 25
NILD *see* National Institute for Leadership Development (NILD)
Niti Aayog: AIM (Atal Incubation Mission) program 83
Northland College 192
Norton, W. W. 6

Office of Women for the American Council on Education *see* ACE Women's Network
Olivas, L. x
Oliver Johnson Award 13
Olmos, J. 96
O'Neil, B. 56
OPM *see* other people's money (OPM)
Oregon State University 144
other people's money (OPM) 63
OUR ("Opportunities for Undergraduate Research") program 82

Pacific Coast Athletic Association (PCAA) *see* Big West Conference (BWC)
Padilla, G. 164
Parham, T. 158–159
participatory management 76
Patten University 134–135; Board of Trustees 134
PCAA *see* Pacific Coast Athletic Association (PCAA)
Peltason, J. 160
Peninsula Workforce Development Center 193
Peralta Community College District 212–213
Pippins, S. 178–197, 229, 230; career beginnings 187–190; college presidency 191–197; current work 196–197; early influences of 179–184; early work of 184–187; family background of 179–184; "You Never Know Who's Watching" 181; young adult years 184–187

Pitts, L. 12
Pitzer College 98
Pomona College 97, 98
power: garnering 61–62; nucleus of 63–64; sustaining 61–62
professional partnerships 214–215

quality leadership 57–58

race 91–113
Ramirez, M. 98, 99
Refugee Assistance Program, Long Beach City College 49
resource generation 63
Rice, C. 208, 209
Rice, J. W., Jr. 208, 209
Right to Freedom 76
Rio Hondo College 49, 57, 63
Robert's Rules of Order 10
Robinson, K. T. 191
role models 58–59
Rotary Club 42
Rubin, V. 5
Rural Scholarship 84
Rushing, S. A. xx, xxii

Saddleback College: *Psychology of Prejudice* and *Ethnic Cultures of the United States* 66
Sahni, A. 21
School of Physical Sciences 74
Scott-Heron, G. 121
sexual harassment 76
sexual orientation 129
Shapiro, H. 125
Sharma, R. xxi
Shiv Nadar Foundation 79, 81
Shiv Nadar University xxi, 41, 79, 84; Center for Environmental Sciences & Engineering 80
Simic, K. 34
Skinner, B. F. 186
social justice 34
Sonoma State University 207–208
Sports Scholarship 84
Stand and Deliver 96
Stanford University 208–210
"STEAM" curriculum 81
strategic partnerships 214–218
Suffolk County Community College 193, 194

Index **237**

SUNY system 194

Tai Chi 64–65
Thomas Nelson Community College (TNCC) 190, 192, 193
Thoreau, H. D. 221
Tien, C.-L. 160–164, 170, 229
Till, E. 152
TNCC *see* Thomas Nelson Community College (TNCC)
21st Century Astronomy 6

UC Academic Senate Manual, The 8
UC Berkeley 210–211; 1980–1998 developing programs 34–35; Center for Studies in Higher Education (CSHE) x, 28; Educational Opportunity Program 33; Equal Educational Opportunity Program/ Affirmative Action Coordinator (EOP/AA) 34; Giving Tuesday Campaign xx; "Keeping the Promise" campaign 35; Transformative Development Program 40–41
UC Office of the President (UCOP) 11, 13, 14, 17–19
UCOP *see* UC Office of the President (UCOP)
UCPT *see* University Committee on Privilege and Tenure (UCPT)
UC Santa Cruz (UCSC) 1–26; Academic Assembly 11, 12; Academic Council 12; Black Experience Team 21; Board of Regents 11, 16; Chancellor's Diversity Advisory Committee 20, 21; Coastal Commission 17; Community Advisory Group 17; comprehensive fundraising campaign 22–24; diversity 20–22; Diversity Advisory Council 21; Diversity Certificate program 21; Fly Communications 24; Founders Day 22, 23; growth and town-gown relations 15–18; Hate/Bias Response program 21; inclusion 20–22; Long Range Development Plan (LRDP) 15–17, 24; "Original Authority on Questioning Authority, The" 24; People of Color Sustainability Collective 21; rebenching 18–20; Senate Executive Committee 15
UGC *see* University Grants Commission (UGC)
UMCP *see* University of Maryland College Park (UMCP)
Understanding Our Universe 6
UNESCO 87
unity 67
University Budget Advisory Committee 106
University Committee on Privilege and Tenure (UCPT) 9
University Grants Commission (UGC) 76, 83
University of California, Riverside 206–207, 214; educational opportunity program (EOP) 206
University of Maryland College Park (UMCP) 122–124; Board of Trustees 125; Priorities Committee 125
University of Wyoming 143
University's Office of General Counsel 9

Vega, B. 58, 60
VUCA (volatile, uncertain, complex, and ambiguous) 85, 227

WAC *see* Western Athletic Conference (WAC)
WASC *see* Western Association of Schools and Colleges (WASC)
Washington University 152
Webb, E. T. 198–226, 231; on achievements of former students 203–204; adulthood 204–206; childhood 204–206; collective capacity 213–218; decision to inspire others to leverage higher education 201–203; dream of 199–213; gratitude 224–225; greatness 218–220; higher education 206–213; leadership lessons learned in multicultural context 220–224; reminders 224–225; transformations 200–201; vision of 199–200
Weisberg, K. 4
Western Association of Schools and Colleges (WASC) 173, 174
Western Athletic Conference (WAC) 173, 174

White, T. 174
Williams, R. L. 156
Wilson, J. 189, 190
win-win-win partnerships 66
Wisconsin State Educational System 31
Women's College Coalition 128

Women's Movement 97
Wong, E. 58, 59

Yudof, M. 19

Zapata, E. 59